CHILD OF
MORNING STAR

CHILD OF MORNING STAR

*Embers of an
Ancient Dawn*

ANTOINE MOUNTAIN

Foreword: Bonnie Devine

Scan for
Antoine
Mountain's
gallery and
extras at
Durvile.com

DURVILE &
UpRoute Books

Calgary, Alberta, Canada

DURVILE.COM

DURVILE
UpRoute Books

UpRoute Imprint of Durvile Publications Ltd.
Calgary, Alberta, Canada
www.durvile.com

Copyright © 2022 Antoine Mountain

Library and Archives Cataloguing in Publications Data

CHILD OF MORNING STAR
EMBERS OF AN ANCIENT DAWN

Mountain, Antoine; Author
Devine, Bonnie; Foreword
Metcalf, Mary, Editor

1. Dene | 2. First Nations | 3. Indigenous | 4. Northwest Territories
5. Art | 6. Poetry | 7. History

Child of
Morning Star at
Durvile.com

The UpRoute Spirit of Nature Series
and the Durvile Reflections Series
Series Editors, Raymond Yakeleya and Lorene Shyba

Issued in print and electronic formats
ISBN: 978-1-990735-10-3 (pbk); 978-1-990735-23-3 (e-pub)
978-1-990735-22-6 (audiobook)

Front cover design, Austin Andrews
Front cover photograph, Banff Centre Archives
Book design, Lorene Shyba

Durvile Publications recognizes the land upon which our studios are located.
We extend gratitude to the Indigenous Peoples of Southern Alberta, which include the
Siksika, Piikani, and Kainai of the Blackfoot Confederacy; the Dene Tsuut'ina;
and the Chiniki, Bearspaw, and Wesley Stoney Nakoda First Nations;
and the Region 3 Métis Nation of Alberta.

Durvile Publications gratefully acknowledges the financial support of
the Government of Canada through Canadian Heritage Canada Book Fund
and the Government of Alberta, Alberta Media Fund.
Antoine Mountain would like to thank the NWT Arts Council.

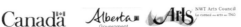

Dedication

To the *LAST* of *Us,* to Board that
FREEDOM Train!

and

To the 87-year-old
American WWII veteran soldier,
when confronted by French customs,
fumbling for his passport,
fired back at an especially rude and harsh agent, :
"To be honest, the last time I was in France
on D-Day in 1944 there wasn't a
Frenchman in sight to show my passport to."

"Brethren"

CONTENTS

f, Caravaggio's Bacchus

Foreword

Bonnie Devine

I'M NOT SURPRISED that this is Antoine Mountain's second book. From the time I first met him at OCAD University where he was my student in the Indigenous Visual Culture program, Antoine has been a prodigious storyteller. In addition to keeping up with a demanding academic schedule and producing drawings and paintings for class assignments and for sale, Antoine was the author of a regular newspaper column called *A Mountain View* in the Yellowknife *News North*. His visual art and published articles were then, and still are, remarkable for their extensive references to a multitude of influences, ideas, and international cultures. Yet his writing has always remained rooted in his personal, well-travelled experience.

Written from the heart by a residential school survivor, *Child of Morning Star, Embers of an Ancient Dawn*, is more than a memoir and more than a collection of interrelated stories. In a creative work that combines poetry and prose, painting and philosophy, Antoine Mountain has developed an entirely individual written format—part dream, part revelation, part elegiac remembrance and part creation story. The resulting book offers a slowly coalescing depiction of contemporary Indigenous thought.

While it contains many references to his experiences at the residential schools he attended as a child, *Child of Morning Star, Embers of an Ancient Dawn* moves on from his first book, *From Bear Rock Mountain: The Life and Times of a Dene Residential School Survivor*, to examine the continuing education of the child, tracing in a non-linear, non-chronological style his time as a young art student at *Arts' Sake*, a radical experiment in art education in Toronto, and his later studies in Florence under the auspices of the painting department at the Ontario College of Art and Design. He describes encounters with artists and waiters, medicine people and teachers in a variety of international settings. He discusses politics and religion, history, and aesthetics, horror and comedy, and the occasional enigmatic message from a non-human intermediary.

Indigenous survivors of the holocaust of colonialism are often described as resilient. But to say that Antoine's voice is resilient and wise does not adequately describe the unique sensation this book evokes. We are told of personages and incidents in an apparently non-sequential order that gradually illuminates Antoine's deeply layered observation of modern life and reveals fragments of historic and cultural content that are rare and precious indeed.

Antoine's book is a modern creation story written with both irony and warmth. It is a harbinger of dawn and an awakening into recognition.

—Bonnie Devine,
Founding Chair of OCAD University's Indigenous
Visual Culture Program, Toronto, 2022

"Tadidiin (Corn Pollen) Hour"

Introduction

The near-total dark always felt a stranger but one withholding a familiar blanket. When all of Creation Holds its Breath.

Long before Sun, there is the suspended time, of earliest morn, 'round about four, when night meets its new mistress, Morning Star, at times in company of Moon.

After checking to see the woodstove is still warming the traditional home, Hogan, an old man, emerges from the chilly high desert Arizona gloom to stand before the opened heavens, where countless doorway stars themselves fall to sleep.

Nearby Navajo Reservation dogs take up a call, to him a kind of reverie, answered from distance-dotted places by coyotes. A weathered hand reaches out from under thinly wrapped, Pendleton-blanketed shoulders

1

into a worn leather pouch, coming forth with a pinch of corn pollen, tradition, to mouth and top of snow-covered head.

Four motions
To Newer Tymes...
Softly mumbled prayers glistened off
Iridescent sage...

In this near dream, he imagined himself as nameless of generation:

...a Life-sized, Statue of glowing coals
On embers of Space,
Addressing an underground
Flaming log,

'Areyoneh Segot'ineh, All My Relations'...

These cave walls engraved,
With Talking Gods,
Dispelling future myths,
Fronted by Dolphin Queen,
To one ear and ashes of birds,
Aloft within.

After a number of years living with *From Bear Rock Mountain: the Life and Times of a Dene Residential School Survivor*, my first book, I thought to follow up that time of death and resurrection with another, dedicated to these, when our world manages to pause just long enough to have a look around, to see what we still have to call a future. Dwelling on the essentials of an evil time, now past, can only serve to, like the best of Dutch painter Van Gogh's genius, suck you right into another strange but deadly paradise.

Coming from humble beginnings, I always think that individual people, the human *self* speaketh in volumes most poignant. The hardest part of the first, of course, was having to revisit the grim ghosts of my abusive, traumatic past at the hands of the Canadian Government, the club of these residential schools wielded by zealous priests and nuns of the Roman Catholic Church.

Coming from a traditional Dene background, one sure way of simply getting my story to page involved shutting down somewhat emotionally, much the same as I did when only 12, at one of these horrible places, writing from rote, much the same as when we prayed at the altar of colonialism. I found the starting chapters to be the hardest, a child's faltering steps into the unknowable.

There were many ways to go, but the lack of practice made for a slower exchange, a writer with a message, a single canoe in the path of some gigantic colonial ship. On the one hand, church and government knew exactly what they were doing, wresting culture from the Indians. On the other, we innocent children had no idea what was expected of us.

> We were always on edge,
> Never being able to finish anything,
> Made to run from one to another,
>
> Prayer by rote, forcing down foreign food,
> Trying to sleep through tears,
> Always on edge.

The funniest, strangest part is that you really, physically have to go through carrying all of that accumulated weight, whomsoever it actually belongs to, to get to the clean, fresh air of a revival of your human spirit.

> Now unburdened of much of this psychic burden, this newer,
> Child of Morning Star
> promises to rise to a new awakening.
> Whether or not it does, in the end,
> Means what you intended,
> Matters not so much,
> As in the doing, Leaving your mark.

The part intentionally gutted from our Dene selves—our culture, the substance of it, then—is what this work is about. What remains, of course, beating at the very heart of our Indigeneity, thousands of years of simple survival . . .

> The mystery of the Realm, Intact.

As with the first book, I went to a developmental editor, Mary Metcalfe, to help map out possible ways to give continued voice to a multi-dimensional life too resilient to have been silenced by tragedy and trauma. Among the many and varied reactions from readers of my initial, pain-filled memoir, was a request for more poetry. Its inclusion was a direct result of a wounded soul eventually somehow agleam from a distant gloaming wreckage of a sad chapter in Canadian history, a direct but failed attempt at cultural genocide.

When you allow this closer look, you begin to realize, that yes, this is you. The moment before, you were just another of some 150,000 survivors of the Indian residential schools, now you've become a recognizable soul, a living breathing human being with yet another, more individual, and unique story to tell—along with the thought to at least honour these requests with an added structure of story and artistic pictorials.

One apparent result was the move, among others, to include *From Bear Rock Mountain* as poetic text for an Aurora College course in Yellowknife. A constant, too, throughout, publisher and scholar Taryn Boyd took no pains to let me know that, as a writer, I need not stray from this creative non-fiction approach. Her words were to the effect that my life is already so fictional I have no problem holding the reader's attention.

In this vein, the aim here is less to follow a linear, European-influenced rendering but more in line of a very close and personal friend, dreamily recalling their life along certain familiar themes, coming as an inner voice. The chronological has more to do with memory and maybe prophesy. This approach is either faulty at best or downright self-serving, as history often is.

Indigenous Ways of Knowing are so much more holistic, say, to the point of expanded, subconscious rendering than direct recollection, or even reference. Given the move away from things colonial today, even scientists have begun to think the way we Indians always have: everything is alive, even the stones we light to make our marks on and with.

It is no surprise, then,
That we are more Spirit than Man,
Closer to Mother Earth than Father Time.

The beginning thus underlies a traditional Indigenous Medicine Wheel format, drawn from an oral historical approach. Some direct historical references then follow. With the idea of how the Arts reflect the health of any society, I wanted to delve into how this is easier yet more difficult, a more land-based Northern setting, given our collective intergenerational residential school trauma.

Finally, some spiritual direction must come from it all…

Beyond all of these set plans underlies the real, more personal, human tones, always just within the needs of the old Navajo Dineh man's Morning Star pleadings…. Too, this divine expression of humanity can go to gauge how all of the Arts also come to define and sustain the health of Community. An added feature of Indigeneity, too, allows for a sense of mystery to any of the possibilities. More than any other, we of the First Nations dwell in this world of an extended, parallel universe.

Of course, any intended dream doesn't come out full-blown, just for the wanting. Italian philosopher Dante Alighieri managed to somehow offer up an entirely new written format, well over two exiled decades in the works, in the 1300s, without the use of computers and sweetgrass. Why not at least an attempt by a simple Dene writer to give our tired human words newer expression?

After all, any attempt
Is better than none at all.
… Meanwhile …

Whilst the old man's proffered white corn pollen hangs in the chill air, his heart, too, longs to hear just this sound…

…Heaven-sent heartbeat
of the Holy People…

He always felt of his absolute, yet unfathomed personal need to do this, certainly beyond the call to tradition…

…and from this Spark,
Guardian Kingfisher
Looks furtive, askance, both south and north,
Whence once injury led.

Past lands vast, of empty talk,
To this relative
Before Arizona sage,

O'er many scores through wintry deep,
Fought I unreckoned chasms,
Entombed in deeded shame.

Now saving grace
With arms
Of Mooned altar
Within the ripples
In Mother Waterbird's Tail

…Feeling sprinkled Songs
Taking root

…With such self-willed amnesia, yes, bold restives, invoke all abandon and pray, board these silent yearnings, casting off idling slumber…. Learn to lazily drift aloft.

On wings
of the now-creative pollen offering,
Child of Morning Star

—Antoine Mountain, 2022

PART ONE

ASTRAL ECHOES

BEFORE THE DRUM

An Astral Key

"Another world is not only possible, she is on her way.
On a quiet day I can hear her breathing."
—Arundhati Roy

"Every one of us is like a man who sees things in a dream
and thinks that he knows them perfectly and then
wakes up to find that he knows nothing."
—Plato, Statesman

MEANWHILE, the ceremonial Hogan swirls in dense *Nat'oh*, smoke.... An elevated, separate, but yet very real connection is set aside just for these occasions.

Noon on a Navajo Nation Christmas Day passed as ordinarily as any other, at least in the traditional eight-sided building and away from the sounds of merriment just outside.

The Vietnam Vet, turned *Hatathlie*, Medicine Man/Singer, patiently listened as an elderly woman explained her slowed life, now sitting frail in a comfortable armchair. Her wheelchair waited by the blanket door, on the other side of a daughter who helped fill in where memory and ear failed. The matter at hand for the medicine man was to help the old rancher lady carry on her work, even in a truck or 4x4, if necessary. As

I sat by my adopted 'twin' Dene brother Lawrence, it gradually dawned that I, too, could ask a favour of the medicine man for my schooling, which I was now on a holiday break from.

At his duties, the former Vietnam soldier imperceptibly switched into the higher, ceremonial form of Navajo Dineh, to better suit this special event. As Elder he also heard, noted my request, and acknowledged assent. We both wore our hair in braids and were fond of cowboy hats. We only differed in one noticeable way—when Lawrence brewed his extra-vital Max J. Brandenstein (MJB) coffee in the morning and the horses took to neighing, with the goats butting heads in consternation!

Secretly, the Navajo cowboy in him even confessed to a past of being noted for his skills in boot-scoot-n-boogie over many a sawdust floor. After his elderly patient was wheeled out to her truck, I was directed to take her spot on the west side of the building still under alterations, gyprock sheets leaned against the north wall.

When given the go-ahead, I explained that all was going well with this my second year of PhD studies, with an A- average, all but for the theory-based academic writing part, the academic format being new to my Indigenous mind. I'd been coming to visit amongst these southern relatives for over a quarter a century now, convinced both of their ceremonial modern-day use and now how it all might relate to my world of study and research.

As the Singer's assistant, my brother brought over a small load of coals from the battered homemade stove. A small mound of it now took on a handful of cedar, filling the air with its distinct smudging scent. After a long, extended pause, Spirit Helper began, each time using the impersonal and traditional 'they' to refer to spirit messengers his prayers had called forth. In its way, it always reminded me of how we of the natural world already see our place as simple visitors here on Mother Earth, knowing our place.

"They say you will need her protection. Your part is already done, and they know you as one of their own, with the Spirits. But others want to know what you are doing, so you must be careful with how you use this." There was a lot of other talk about the life at my school, which all served to remind me of how all of it was at the command of those called forth through the crystals before the Elder.

In the pause before the big Smoke, brother Lawrence filled in the

Scan to see paintings and photos in the book in colour.

Sacred Mountains are gathering places, storing energy from the stars.

gaps in essentially what was all foreign to me, even as a Dene relative from the Far North.

> These crystals he uses come from the four sacred mountains, which are like gathering places, communicating and storing the energy and information from the stars. The Singer's prayers are all in Navajo. They have certain words and phrases which awaken Spirit Helpers for what you are talking about. That *Nat'oh,* tobacco you will smoke, also comes from those mountains. After you go ahead and use it, we will add some water, which you will sprinkle on your personal items and sacred paraphernalia when you get back on home.

The natural tobacco was acrid to the taste, so powerful it took all I had just to keep what little I did inhale within me. Enveloped as in a cloud of its vapours I could yet make out my sibling's kind words: "This is all meant to help you along at your school, brother."

And indeed, it did. After I returned from the break, my supervisor let me know that now my efforts were at the very least acceptable Thus, ancient traditions carry on.

From Life to Land!

O ut of the ashes of family, Tradition! The ancient figure lumbers out of eternal waters, to find the one spot on the beach to lay its eggs. So, too, we make our initial fumbling attempts to carry on what we can recall of times past.

One spark from these ashes came out of what the old Navajo man does with his corn pollen of a pre-dawn do, making offering to the coming day.

As we all do, he, too, had his story. A life for the land could not have been more closely tied. He had served in the US marines, having used the initially forbidden language, Dineh, as a Code Talker, to eventually help save democracy, in the Pacific theatre of World War II.

One thing always in his fading memory was that sometimes his late wife would tote a small leather bag of corn pollen to make these daily early morning offerings.

I dreamed of my old hunting buddy, Gene Rabesca of Radelie Koe, Fort Good Hope. Especially at the times we were travelling hundreds of miles from town in the dead of a sub-sixty-below winter he spoke of 'The Last Mile', when you have to gather whatever strength you can still muscle, to make it to where you are going,..

> One of our elderly grandmothers
> Pulled from her bag several items
> She had somehow saved. . .

Gene said that these few things we had were more than enough to make our lives again. After the devastating ruin of the Canadian residential schools, its attempt at cultural genocide, those of my generation who managed to make it through the foreign flotsam of high school found our true Dene selves back to our Indigenous ceremonials, with the Sweat Lodge Ceremonies.

For good reason it was the first time we really met.

Quite a number of decades later, when I was already well into my second youth, past forty, I found myself in the Japanese city of Nagoya, with a small group of Northern artists, to help in our government's attempt to get more tourists to come to Canada.

As often happens to me on these trips I felt restless, unable to sleep.

I told my room-mate, Dene drummer Michael Cazon of Liidli Kue, Fort Simpson, that I would go outside to offer some tobacco.

As it turned out this was the Hour of the Morning Star.

In a park across from the hotel, there were a large number of tents that the city had set up for the homeless,

I found a large tree in a far corner and did this ceremonial, in memory of all the American soldiers who never made it home from Vietnam. As it turned out, Japan was a staging area for troops sent there.

And as it turned out, my home Sahtu area figured into the history of Japan, too, when our Dene prophet Eseh Ayah gave forth with events which ended when the bombs dropped on Hiroshima and Nagasaki.

> Again, history and its fumbling attempts
> To push we human turtles on.

First Travellers

ACCORDING TO THE OLD-TIMERS, the first to arrive in our part of the North came from the Northwest. After crossing the mountains, there they stood on the shores of the Duhogah, what is now the Mackenzie River.

> The old woman, carrying a child
> Became the Dene.

> A pack dog carrying their goods,
> Didn't like what was there, so turned back,
> To the land of the Gwich'in.

> Beaver traveled on, to the East,
> Becoming the Inuit.

> It is said the child carried by the old Dene woman,
> Is now full grown,
> Our southern relatives,
> The Navajo and Apache.

Ehseh at his Deshigohgi

Tʜᴇsᴇ ᴇᴀʀʟɪᴇʀ ᴛɪᴍᴇs ᴀᴛ ʜᴏᴍᴇ, the early sixties, marked a major turnaround for our Dene Peoples. The Canadian government wanted us off the land and into these stifling northern towns. We children only had two months of the year at home from residential schools, so at least we got to spend days like this in comfort.

Here is my godfather, Antoine Kelly, dutifully planing a new set of marten and other stretchers, for winter furs. With no electricity there were only hand tools. In this case, I wanted to do a painting of one of these deshigohgi, wood planer. Straight lengths of spruce were cut, depending on the size of the animal you were after, usually marten in our treed country.

What really makes this come to life though, are the two children to his side, really enjoying their times with this man. Even though he seldom spoke, his granddaughters, Dora and Angela, took great delight in his company. In childish play, the old dry-fish tent in back becomes their castle, with brother Archie as royal guard, behind. The mass of fine wood shavings before them becoming tiny butterflies taking wing.

Also in back is their mom, Alice, hanging bedsheets to air, and grandmother, Henrietta, sizing up her moosehide stretching frame for possible use when their son Gabe returns from the hunt. Very likely, the other two sons, Leon and Edward, are out with him too.

Meanwhile, all the days and weeks in the Land of the Midnight Sun slowly loll along, making as in a dream.

Yamoria and the Eagles

"When our father returns there is
lightning and rain
...Mom comes with a short hailstorm."
—*from "Yamoria and the Evil Eagle"*

IN HIS BOOK of collected legends and stories of the Dene, Elder and statesman George Blondin (1923–2008) told of an ancient time: *When the World Was New.*

Our culture hero Yamoria (Travels Across the Universe) spent all his time making life safer for future human society. When news came to him that Eagle was eating people, he travelled up the mountains to its nest.

Finding only two young ones there, he asked them to tell him what happens when their parents come back home. When the female young would not answer, he killed her and lay in wait with the boy-eagle, who gave the right answer.

When the adults arrived, Yamoria clubbed and killed each parent in turn. He then led the young eaglet to the shore and taught him to fish, with strict instructions to eat only these and other small animals and no more human flesh.

He then squeezed the eagle to its present size.

Eagles have since avoided humans as prey.

When he lived in *Somba K'è*, Yellowknife, for a number of years in the early 1990s, George Blondin would tell me many of these legends, with the thought of my illustrating them someday.

I have... a few.

Trapper's Flag

Growing up in these trappers' camps, one of the first things you'd always notice was the stark black mass of marten furs, suspended on a fur pole, leaning on the back poles. These were the winter season's catch proudly on display and keeping the prized, precious furs fresh. The large clump would catch even the slightest of breezes, making for the 'flag' waving above. It was also a sure sign that the trip back to town for Christmas was only a week or two away!

In our *Kasho Got'ineh* area of the Sahtu, Great Bear Lake Region, marten was always the most numerous, especially right after a forest fire and new growth to attract them. The day's catch would be brought in after the trappers made their rounds of several hundred traps, often taking several days. If they didn't bring a tent, a simple *Mehkoih*, lean-to brush shelter was warm enough for the arctic night.

Various furs, including fox, wolverine, otter, and even beaver, were brought in to thaw out, carefully skinned and stretched on wooden frames. Different sizes were made from spruce to fit whatever was caught. Leftover wood shavings made fine kindling for the next morning's fire.

While a Coleman gas lamp hissed along with the Rayuka Northern Lights outside, rows of these stretchers lined the upper drying rafters, the constant heat from a woodstove drying them overnight. Taking them down, the trapper would make a big show of carefully smoothing out each hide, lovingly blowing on each, fluffing them up.

By the time the Christmas season came along, many trappers would have several hundred of these marten, along with whatever else fetched top prices at the fur auctions to the south. I recall that we had quite a number of other furs, but I think they were stored separately, on a stage in back of the family tent, along with stores of frozen meat and fish. These kept any marauding predators at bay.

At the very top of our spiritual animal totem, the polar bear, intently keeps guard over all who make the winter camp home for several months. A mother lovingly cradling her infant in turn gets a blessing from a past relative, just above.

The ONLY Indian

You're the Only One Who Looks Like One!

EVERY TIME WE MET, before he passed on, Freddy Doctor, of Tulita, used to tell me this about my braids: that everyone else called themselves Indian, but I was the only one who was proud enough to wear them. He had a good point, too.

One of the columns I wrote in *News North*, beginning back in 2003, was about this subject. If a UFO were to land in any of our Northern 'Native' communities, they would simply assume we were a ball team with our short hair and baseball caps!

There was a true and suppressed story from the Vietnam War era, which goes to show how important our long hair was to our Indigenous culture. Special Forces from the US Department of Defense were sent out to the different Indian reservations to search out and recruit young men who were especially gifted in tracking and survival. Once they were in the army, it was found that they all lost these special skills once their hair was cut to regulation length. Others in their place were allowed to grow and keep their hair long and proved themselves in combat, serving out their tours of duty with dramatically lower death rates in the ranks of their assigned platoons.

When personnel were sent back to Indian Country to talk with the Elders, they were told that in the old days a person's hair served as a kind of sensory antennae, to be able to somehow 'know' where to find the enemy and to sense when danger came close. Hair in braids is a symbol your entire Being—your mind, body, and spirit all formed into one. Some tribes believe it is worn in this way to ensure rain and healthy growth for your People.

The Elders often describe me as being "more Spirit than person," although I believe this is more personal than directed at my hairstyle.

Like my mom, I never did care much for things of this world.

There was, though, a deeper evident divide apparent to some, like our Elder Lucy Jackson of Radelie Koe, Fort Good Hope. She made it a point to mention that she did not like the term Indian Time and what it really meant. She said that living on the land meant that for some things, there was a very short window of time, like to catch the grayling fish run, for instance, and in general, if you went by this Indian Time, you are simply not able to survive in the North, really.

When we first started our Indian Brotherhood political movement in the early seventies, this long hair was also a simple badge of honour.

We just did not trust anyone with short hair.

As time went on, this kind of dedication to The Cause died off. When you did see the long hair it became the style to have it as a single braid down the back, as if the wearer didn't want you to know you were talking to an Indian until it was too late! Sad.

The corporate world took us over.

Like the coin with two sides, I also had to decide whether to cash in on the craze for Native Art, back in the early eighties, just getting done with art school in Toronto.

It became the thing to do, after the Anishinabek Group of Seven broke trail for young Indigenous artists to make a name for themselves.

Even though I had had art shows with the best of them—Norval Morrisseau, Art Shilling, the Kakegamics, and so on—I chose not to even have people assume their Woodland style of painting was also mine.

Today, I encourage our young Native artists to find their own style. Of course, it is much harder for them to relate to a land-based life. Theirs is about the internet and cell phones. They get lazy and don't even want to go to a real art school, choosing to take a few lessons from TV shows. As a result, they only deal with tourists, not the best of visual judges by any stretch!

All the trees are the same, fields of snow with not a single animal track on it . . . like you're looking at the 'Native' painting through a pane of glass.

Overtaken by a corporate world.

In N. Scott's House

"It is the mark of an educated mind to be able to entertain a thought without accepting it." —Aristotle

ONE OF THE ESSENTIALS OF LIFE in the sixties, if you were radical, was to be well read. We spent countless hours in heated debate on how to bring the Man, the Establishment, down, long into the night on our versions of one communist manifesto or another, peering through hazy smoke of hash pipes and cheap wine goin' 'round.

There were other just-as-important literary works of persons such as N. Scott Momaday, a Native American author, whose Pulitzer Prize-winning *House Made of Dawn* was all the rage. The fact that this singular honour was accorded to a Kiowa author made it all the more important.

Unlike the fiery oratory of political jargon-embellished screeds for social change, the Kiowa words were like a fine quilt laid gently upon the land, allowing you a second appreciation of Mother Nature. Too, it evolved into a damning indictment of today's degrading industrialization of the only lands we have left.

Featuring an engaging writing style and gifts of compilation throughout, N. Scott Momaday, in his book *The Night Chanter* effort-lessly lends a universal ear to whatever each individual chapter, and even page, is about, even when anonymously written.

> I am the Turquoise Woman's son.
> On top of
> Belted Mountain,
> Beautiful horse—slim like a weasel.
> My horse has a hoof like striped agate;
> His fetlock is like a fine eagle plume;
> His legs are like quick lightning.
> My horse's body is
> like an eagle-plumed arrow;
> My horse has a tail like a trailing black cloud.
>
> —*Author Unknown*

It all fairly reaches out and caresses your longings for freedom, no less. Going back far enough you surely sense the roots of Indigenous movements like Idle No More and the protests at Standing Rock, alive in N. Scott's House.

> Once upon a time . . . there was
> the simple understanding that
> to sing at dawn and to sing at dusk
> was to heal the world through joy.
> The birds still remember
> what we have forgotten,
> that the world is meant to be celebrated.
>
> —*Terry Tempest Williams*

Hooking for Sorah

SUMMERS IN TOWN would find a whole bunch of us little guys sitting on the Police or Nursing Station dock, fishing for those smaller ones. To this day, I am not quite sure exactly what kind of fish these were, but very likely a kind of chub. They rarely showed up in the fish nets and didn't look like the cisco, whitefish, or coney usually caught in the nets.

With a bit of patience, you would feel a mighty tug on your home-made willow and line outfit. That kind of time was not hard to come by, under the 24-hour Midnight Sun, where the day would go for like six weeks. You would let it go just a bit for the right catch and then yank all the way back, tossing stick and all as far back on the shore as you could, so you wouldn't lose your precious *sorah* with everyone around you getting splashed and soaked.

The talk would never be about anything important.

On a hot day, there would be women down by the water, too, scrubbing their wash or smacking wet clothes against bigger rocks.

The really lucky children would go zooming by in dark-green canvas-covered freighter canoes, pushed by eight- or nine-horse Johnson 'kickers', outboard motors with the gas tanks right on top.

When we'd cooked up our catch, the serious fun of driving our little hand-carved poplar boats, tied to a stick with a line, little motors of their own, Copenhagen Snuff can tin covers for props, would start . . . You would just walk along making a "Brrrrrrghhhh . . . brrrrghhh . . . beeer-rrrrgh" kinda sound to go with your adventure.

Evening would find us on the same shore, picking up driftwood (gohtoneh) for the summer fires at home. At many homes, a common-enough sight were the women hard at work on their moosehides, scraping, stretching, or smoking them to a golden brown. It was so hot in July that many homes just had a big wood camp stove set up outside, with an oven for roasting bigger fish.

As our southern Navajo Dineh relatives were infused with a much-more spiritual expression of life, our Northern version had more to do with survival skills, in the coldest part of the world. Simple sorah fishing eventually turned into the actual hunt, being able to put food on the family table. For the girls, sewing started at an early age, and in the following years they created wonderful outfits for the entire family.

Upper: "Hooking for Sorah"
Lower: "Sa-Ra ahyileye"

Sa-Ra ahyileye

WHOEVER in government came up with the idea of taking us Indians out of homes, forcefully, in the fall of each year knew what they were doing. We boys missed out on the moose hunt when we could prove our worth to Community. The girls were hundreds of miles away when they were expected to learn how to care for home and family. The painting recalls those days, at just such, the brilliant Northern Sa Ra-ahyile, out in force for the summer. Our time at home, away from the dreaded residential school was all too short.

A young person stares point-blank at you, one hand protective of hair, knowing it will soon be shorn off, like sheep, the other turning into bear claws in protective desperation! *(See lower painting, previous page.)*

Just the idea of 'Porcupines and China Dolls', what the others jokingly called each other, when shorn of hair, rankled Pearl to no end. Supple willows, along the river's high bank, intertwine with her hair, a note of inner strength and resilience.

I've added Dutch artist Vermeer's famed pearl earring, with its stead to perfection, incorruptibility. Too, symbolic of the moon as a feminine, protector, its portends for the future hidden.

All the while, our mighty Duhogah flows on forever past the places Aklavik and Inuvik, where these institutions of cultural genocide once were. To Mother Nature anything once standing, only shifting sandbars.

Summer of Tough Love

"In our sleep, pain which cannot forget falls drop by drop upon the heart until, in our own despair, against our will, comes wisdom through the awful grace of God."—Aeschlyus

THESE WORDS, commemorated by Greek poet Aeschylus (525–456 BCE) and publicly spoken by another soon-to-be martyr in the name of freedom, Robert F. Kennedy, could also serve well as an epithet to all the social calls to arms of this seminal year.

The occasion, the brutal slaying on April 4, 1968, of civil rights leader Dr. Martin Luther King Jr, one of a handful of sane voices in those turbulent times.

At the time that we at the elitist church-run Grandin College were happily lulled and numbed by colonialist forces, the outside world was going through some catastrophic changes, mainly with the efforts of youth. In most places, the only voice daring to be heard was that of the youth, who in many ways had nothing to lose but the certainty of the status quo. In Germany, Spain, France, Mexico, the USA, and elsewhere, students rose as never before to rid society of an archaic way of setting the standards for life. One particular group that rose to prominence in this drive for change was the Students for a Democratic Society (SDS).

An example of the increasing dissatisfaction with the influence of the military on campus and in Vietnam was the April 1968 takeover of Columbia University in New York City. One feature of this action was that the school was planning to build a segregated recreation facility to extend into the Harlem community. Although there was a dispute over tactics, this resulted in at least a de facto coalition with the Black students and the occupation of separate buildings. The week-long event ended with the violent removal of students by the New York Police Department, but not before gaining worldwide attention.

The Weathermen, a radical wing of student demonstrators, put them on the FBI's Most Wanted List after a number of government-owned buildings were bombed and targeted for more violent action. They eventually had to shut down public bombings after a number of their members accidentally blew themselves up making explosives.

The Black Panthers, an outgrowth of the Civil Rights Movement, was definitely not non-violent in practice, as the movement had been until then. The average age of their members was seventeen, speaking to the commitment young people had at the time to a social cause. Young as this age was for reawakening, there were first, frail calls for change…

The spark knows not of the Fire
This nor the Next Time

…were in time turned into a tumultuous, highly visible scream of indignation over our blinded psyche.

No longer would voices like theirs fall silent
…but not before many fell silent in our midst, valiantly
Echoed in a meaningless Tomb of an
Unknown America, Once, So Blessed

Magic Trails of Colour

Like a diamond sparking in a dark, neglected corner…

FROM THE VERY FIRST, I felt a kindred spirit with the place. Art's Sake was an alternate school set up to just allow for the latent talent of its students to shine forth. There, I was to meet my lifetime mentor, Diane Pugen, one of the founding members of this institution of learning, on the third floor of a factory in Toronto's Queen Street Garment District. My friend from back home John Turo was already a student there, so the idea was for me to go there too.

It took several months from when I arrived in Toronto, but with the long-distance help of James Ross at the Dene Nation's Education Department I enrolled at Art's Sake. Although the place could be viewed as more relaxed than other more-formal settings, there was no doubt that we were there to learn the basics. To the great credit of our instructors, who were themselves all professionals, for the first year, we were not allowed to touch any brushes or paints at all.

Of course, we did so on our own, and the presence of the Nishnawbe Group of Seven helped us to see the familiar world in a very different way. The teachers I was most influenced by at Art's Sake were, of course, Ms. Pugen in anatomy, Gord Rainer, Ken Lywood, and a fellow First Nations artist from the Six Nations, Bob Markle, who passed away too soon.

That first year, being a real keener, I would make it a point to spend every lunch hour with ol' Dem Bones, a real-life skeleton I would pull out of the closet and just draw, draw, draw, trying to get the proportions right, the ghastly face grinning all the while.

A part of the crowd, which spent a good deal of time at the Black Bull Tavern, at the corner of Queen and John, was Zbigniew 'Ziggy' Blazeje, a very gentle soul. It surely was our Northern version of the Eagle's 'Sad Café', where we made big plans for our art careers over beers we could hardly afford.

John Turo and I were the exceptions, though, riding a wave of a popular interest in First Nations Art just then. The others took to calling us The Bank!

It was Bob Markle, though, who kindly advised the class, "If you want to do this, drink in the Black Bull or the Wheat Sheaf farther west. You have to 'do the other,' that is work hard and 'sell your paintings.'"

Luckily, our instructors were all professional artists themselves, so they well knew the life. Other popular spots were the Beverley Hotel, which featured different kinds of music on each floor: blues in the basement, rock on the first, and folk, I believe, at the top of the stairs.

On Spadina Avenue there were always some laid back beats at Grossman's and, of course, the notorious Silver Dollar, your average Indian bar. You came in, lost your seat in five minutes, and just boogeyed on!

When we formally started in with colour, I recall that it was Graham Coughtry who really drilled it into me that I simply needed to relax my brushstroke, to make full use of a wider, looser range of expression, and to vary my images.

Other well-known artists associated with the Art's Sake were Dennis Burton, Deni Cliff, Ross Mendes, Robert Hedrick, Joan Van Damme, and Paul Slogett.

One thing for sure is that we always got the best of that day's music, and for good reason the Artist/Rock Band Talking Heads!

From time-to-time other artists joined in, like David Ruben, an Inuit carver from Paulutuk and my residential school days.

To this day, I believe it was Art's Sake's insistence on these fundamentals that allowed me to realize so much potential in the four years I was there, experimental or not.

I don't recall anyone ever having it made it big on the art scene from Art's Sake, but then again, that would've defeated the purpose of the place. We definitely did not want to have the same kind of commercial drive as OCAD, the Ontario College of Arts and Design, just around the corner.

In its very own way, Art's Sake was like that ray of brilliant sunlight you come across after a rain shower on the lake, your boat somehow suspended for a seemingly endless moment, in mid-air…

Somewhere between
grim reality
and the REAL WORLD.

An Olde Familiar

High above it all, ball in hand

IN AN EFFORT to improve my basketball game as best I could at the third and last residential school, Grandin College, I began to just spend a lot of time dribbling and would shoot the ball, right- and left-handed, on the empty court later in the evening.

I also patented a move in which I spun the ball on a finger, ran to the basket, and laid it on up in one smooth motion. Another had me make a rail with my arms, roll it forward, and catch it behind my back. All moves to add dazzle and sparkle on the court on game night!

One of my knees had always pained me from late childhood, but it was just one of those things I chose to keep to myself. It was excruciating to land on it. Perhaps as counterbalance, there were nightly dreams of being able to float forever, away above the puny court, basketball in hand, in a heroic pose.

Once I got used to being in that one noisy gym, which picked up each and every sound and echoed it in every direction, I also found out that it was the one place I could get back to what I once did as a very young child in the mountains.

Only this time, instead of allowing my eyes to get out of focus from the just-so-blue snow-laden willows, I could now get right up close to the smooth walls of the building and concentrate on the one thought—Institution.

After a while and as before, these varied answers came whispering back at me from the very bowels of the imposing but sterile walls:

I also long to be far away
and yet we two are close again
As if we were meant for each other
I do not fear you
Nor should you!

One thing I began to realize was that—like in a desert much later on—there is much power one can have over any situation you find yourself in by just letting go and allowing the place to open up to you.

Upper: "Seven Moon Sleep"
Lower: "HIS Shield"

Seven Moon Sleep

Bear, healer, even when in deep slumber.
Able to dig and find different kinds of
plants to fix its wounds.
We watch and go out and harvest these
in order to
make ourselves better.

MY PAINTINGS at this time were still quite influenced by the works of the Anishnawbe Woodland School, the Native, or Indian Group of Seven including Norval Morrisseau, Daphne Odjig, Alex Janvier (a Dene), Jackson Beardy, Carl Ray, and Joseph Sanchez.

One in particular who took me aside was Eddy Cobiness from Buffalo Point, Manitoba, who simply told me to "forget whatever you think you know and just be your Indian self."

Having hung out with John Turo, the 'Second Benjamin Chee Chee', I was even invited and took part in various art shows and public exhibitions of this elite group when in Toronto for my first training in the late seventies.

We were all in good humour, heightened by the antics of one Art Shilling, who took great pains to let it be known he was there for some special entertainments.

The paintings I did were of memory of winters spent on the land, when our days would only be lit for about five hours.

Evenings were spent under the glorious Rayuka, Northern Lights. We would take out various types of sleds—even the kind made of hides from the legs of moose and caribou, which were very slippery indeed! Down steep hills we would go, laughing and tumbling in big, merry heaps.

All the while, the Spirit of Bear and the land itself would remain in a deep rest under blankets of snow . . . awaiting the times of summer yet moons away.

The main and abiding purpose of the school I was in at the time, Art's Sake, served well its purpose to simply create art.

HIS Shield

Lᵢᴋᴇ ᴀ sᴋɪᴛᴛɪsʜ ᴘᴏɴʏ in her father's herd, Autumn Leaf found herself jumping at every strange sound. *Gone are the days,* she thought, *when the world I knew was as solid as the ones before.*

Now on a high hill a little removed from her People's camp, she felt the weight of the war shield she carried, a wayward autumn breeze catching at its rounded shape, swinging it away from her tattered dress.

The dishevelled way her blowing hair kind of matted in patches told of her present state, that of mourning, crying for a lost someone.

Her man, Green Tree, was one of the more outstanding of the tribe's warriors, having earned every white tailfeather now fluttering along the edges of the shield. In his honour, she carried it along on her daily wanderings in the late-fall hills, hoping for a sign from his departed Spirit for what to do with it.

Of course, she so wanted to keep it, or at least hand it off to someone new, but this was what her Uncle Bear Doctor instructed her to do: find some high-up place, quiet, for it to put at rest her departed man's Spirit. As men would, little more was ever said about the shield itself, although it was certainly very central to her man's life. So high was its value that two fine ponies were exchanged to the Pipe Carrier, who fashioned it from the tough buffalo hump hide passed along to him.

Yet she gladly accepted these duties, even wandering aimlessly alone in high country, where any enemy might spot her. *There is enough reckless bravery to go around amongst the warriors,* she thought, as her endless search continued. The irritating scratch of thistles and thorns on her legs reminded her of this present ordeal. The implement of war moved in her firm grip as a penitent but, yet, wayward son, seeming, yes, to set her free of his memory, but bonded to habit.

Things must be looking up too, she thought, for every once in a while, she would catch the distinct drift of scent from Sweetgrass, even here in the sandy highlands.

Her grandmother had told her that Mother Earth had her ways of reaching out from the Great Mystery to reassure her children in moments of doubt. Autumn Leaf really needed these reminders to somehow return her to the Circle. These last days of late summer felt as if she was already aged beyond her late twenties, like one of those elder-lies who can't seem to know what to do, nor even where they are. Even a close relative got the blank look.

Just now, she really had to reach to remember the melodic flute tunes he would play for her, way back when they were both newly in love's playful hold.

> Too, she hoped for even a bit of female rain,
> . . . a light water shawl
> waiting for the sun

These parched hills felt as she did—all out of play.

She longed for the days her grandmother fondly recalled when as a young girl, she would just run and romp through fields of spring flow-ers, shouting and singing for joy!

Now her People wandered, as she now did, these foreign hills south of their northern home.

More, Autumn Leaf could better relate to the great but old stump she came upon—it once threw a majestic shade for all who sought its cooling comfort.

Just needing a bit of rest, she lazily flopped into its tired arms . . .

> Distant mountain peaks reached out
> Beyond the miles it would take
> To Know them

Now at least comforted by smaller memories, she recalled how her man would sometimes toss and turn in their night robes, even mum-bling incoherently about a lightning-struck tree . . .

Could this omen have somehow led to his untimely death?

With Shield now rested between her and Tree, she could feel a growing hum in the small of her back, in a way so much like Drum, sounding in His memory—drumming the coming storm . . .

> Now starting—faint rumblings, like a deep Voice.
> Thunder slowly, insistent, made its way through valleys . . .
> Of this, her tree
> Catching its echo

Passed through aching ribs, to a waiting heart, into Voice, Autumn Leaf
now hummed . . .

> HIS Shield, she thought, *not only keeps, but sings,*
> Of things past, yes,
> But, too, to Be . . .

As if in answer, the winds from afar brought the light mists Autumn
Leaf craved, even as a salve for her aches.

Now weary of bone, yet light in heart, she carefully placed the shield
in the sheltered hold of the ancient stump, along with some mountain
tobacco, gratefully turning to the arms of village and family hearth.

Too, the distinct sound near her light-footed pace, a sharp snap.
Now fully out of the months-long mourning reverie, this reminded her
of the turtles she had heard of, to the North and West, and the thought:

> This Land, so powerful it has now
> Loosed its hold on me . . .
> Playful minnows of mist
> Mingled with newer Life within

Good Doctor Thompson

"This place is like the Army: the shark ethic prevails—eat the wounded."
—*Hunter S. Thompson*

HOWEVER OUTRAGEOUS, his statement fit the times. Following
the good Doctor Hunter S. Thompson's sixties call to arms I had
always thought that this take on Julius Caesar's battle cry, *"Veni, vidi,
vomiten,"* (I came, I saw, I threw up) characterized my lifelong anarchic
view of what we as the Youth had to do, to turn our world, around.

The American journalist, Hunter S. Thompson had his early professional start in California, Puerto Rico, and Brazil, finally settling in
at Aspen, Colorado, to a life of mostly political and social commentary,
with a good dose of self-imposed madness and mayhem.

In a world of individuals, the good doctor became something of a
counter-culture standout from the early seventies on, virtually inventing his New Journalism, Gonzo Journalism, casting the author on centre

stage. *Fear and Loathing in Las Vegas: A Savage Journey to the Heart of the American Dream,* serialized in *Rolling Stone* magazine, served to give warning of the failure of the 1960s counter-culture movement, as if the death and violence at the 1969 Rolling Stones concert at Altamont Speedway was not enough. As an itinerate politician, Thompson made some unsuccessful attempts, running for Sheriff of Piktin County, Colorado in 1970, under the Freak Power Party banner.

Among other notable writings was *Fear and Loathing: On the Campaign Trail '72.* Richard 'Tricky Dick' Nixon was a favourite target for his venom, whom he characterized as standing for "that dark, venal and incurably violent side of the American character." Of the book's subject, Senator George McGovern's bid for the American presidency, his strategist Frank Mankiewicz said that Hunter S. Thompson's was "the most accurate and least factual account of that campaign." On the flipside of that madcap equation, English Artist/Illustrator Ralph Steadman brought much of the good doctor's bizarre writings to a generation expecting nothing but the finest to top off a daily menu of high-grade fun-filled antics, to say little of Thompson's erstwhile sidekick, the Brown Buffalo, a 350-pound Mexican lawyer and another real-life sixties warrior, Oscar Acosta, in Gonzo-guise. Due to public demands on his rising popularity, Hunter S. Thompson's literary output declined from the mid-seventies on. His increasing use of drugs and alcohol no doubt contributed. He committed suicide at sixty-seven, leaving uncounted writers in his debt.

I have my own thoughts on his untimely end. The part of you wanting for a hero dies a bit with the way it actually happens in real life, maybe even to the point when you eventually realize that true heroism is something you already have the seeds of, deep within, brought up to the surface each time you see it in action.

> The Idea, then, is to begin showing it,
> in everyday acts
> with no other thought ...

Yet again, who am I to know, much less judge, the personal gargoyle muses who stood jealous guard over the good doctor's visions, only to turn and exact their pound of earthly flesh when the music faded?

As with a good work of art, every person is somehow trapped within a certain set, in style, a mold, if you will, until a newer version is called forth by time itself. All I can say is that for that desperate time, at least, we all needed a beacon. When the waves grew the most horrendously overwhelming, Hunter S. Thompson shone a rare and courageous light into our fragile cages.

And again, what could be more real, than listening to Pink Floyd "A Saucerful of Secrets" at 3:30 a.m. under the light of a blue moon, tucking into the good doctor's *The Curse of Lono* about a writer on his way to cover some story in the Hawaiian Islands, striding unsteadily back from the john, with one arm bright blue up to the elbow from that one chemical they use to keep the in-flight can clean.

Searching out some lost treasure?
…and that is just the Start of the tale….
The rest, as they say, is history
And, *yes,* by gum, interesting times Indeed!
And over for some precious few,
All… too… soon

The Power of Teresa's Love

"So now faith, hope and love abide, these three;
but the greatest of these three is love."
—*Corinthians 13:13*

THE BIG CITY OF TORONTO presented a lot more wonders for a little ol' Dene country boy. One of them happened in the early 1980s to be Mother Teresa herself at Varsity Stadium right downtown, at the University of Toronto campus. Her presentation was about the Power of Love, and easily held all twenty thousand of us in her gentle spell for a good two hours.

She took us baby step by step, proving that love in its greatest power has the potency to hurt you, and as badly as you have ever experienced, to be the real thing. In her words, "This kind of love has to hurt you so bad that it is the only feeling you have, and one you are sure you cannot survive from."

Yet this is what you need to "Love the Poorest of the Poor." These words from such a committed person hit me where I really lived, coming from a residential school background, which took me all the way to the brink of insanity and dropped into an abyss of an inhuman vacuum. Of course there was no way that the absolute and officially sanctioned trauma we had experienced back then had anything at all to do with love, affection, or even common decency.

But in its way what this sainted person had to say struck a chord with some of what we of the First Nations believe, that the act of giving has to contain an element of personal hurt to mean anything at all. The humble nun must have made some telling points with the traditional people on stage with her, for they crowded around her in appreciation after she got done, one removing his big breastplate and ceremonially placing it on her. She was so tiny that the sheer bone weight of this gift brought her entire frame down a notch or two.

Seven Songs Coming

OVER MY TIME in *Lutsel K'e*, on the East Arm of the *Tu Nedhé*, Great Slave Lake, beginning in the mid-seventies, I took it to heart what I heard them say, that one could pray for the songs.

I once joined a line-cutting crew for a new road for the town's water supply. We had plenty of time just walking between sections of the road to work on, and I recalled some saying that little streams, especially, had a "lot of songs in them" and so do the little breezes sent to cool a furrowed brow.

Having been in a high school rock band helped, for we had even then made our first attempts at writing tunes. I had also continued with these, right after graduating and in the years after.

Now the songs made their way through the warm summer winds that blow across the *Tu Nedhé*, Great Slave Lake. The first had to do with the thoughts of Black Elk, following along with, in his words, "all over the sky a sacred voice is calling." Over the years, this one proved to be the most meaningful to other members of the Native American Church.

One after another, I was given a total of seven ceremonial songs for the Native American Church, and even one to acknowledge my grandmother calling us "very poor people who just knew how to pray."

Any artistic ability always manages to find its way to the surface.

Rodin's ADAM

Does man have free will, at all?

THE PURPOSE OF ANY ART is to at least allow you a moment to pause in your daily walk of life. The meaning is often a very different matter, for good purpose. Such is the case with French sculptor Auguste Rodin. As with and especially the very rudimentary in Van Gogh, we are presented with seemingly contradictory visuals. Too, there is always a direct connection between this Frenchman and that of the immortal Michelangelo, a visual mix for the graceful male.

The massive block of Rodin's *Adam*, for instance, fairly exudes the power we often see in this sculptor's work. However, this one is also somehow quietly contained in the stationary stance of a tortured man's quest for meaning of his time here on Earth.

As with every artist at work, surely Rodin, as with Michelangelo, could feel with every blow and careful scrape of his tools, the 'inner meat' of his ideas taking shape. Taken further, the very personal image of the figure itself brings to mind the utter nightmare we sometimes have when we try with every effort to at least move on, or in this Adam's case, run, but cannot.

He runs too, yes, but also from some unseen terror. His legs, so close together, serve to hold the image in place. Oddly, a formed boulder supports one foot, as if our place in the universe is a temporary one.

The sheer beauty of this is that an internal dialogue also goes on, the figure forever frozen in place, as if the Creator, God, holds himself to account. Does man, then, have free will at all?

Take, for instance, the odd angles of the original Man, his head stiffly tucked into a protective shoulder. From an artistic point of view, one cannot help but imagine an invisible wind coming not from in front but also from above. Man chooses to buffer an ulterior scheme of destiny.

Of course, there is much more we cannot know, for an artist is one person who carries the real with themselves.

Yet the questions for us are surely enough.

For now.

Eagle in Hand

"Hold that feather STILL!"

THERE WERE A NUMBER of our southern Navajo Dineh I spent my time with when I first arrived in Denetah, the Navajo Nation. I arrived at the border tourist town of Page and stayed with a Mola, a Bilagaanaa White man called Sky, and Garrison Yazzie and family.

One man who came around a lot was Leonard Claw. He and his wife, Charlene, and small family made me feel right at home and introduced me to Dineh hospitality, a laid-back way of living with not a lot to worry about, although real cash money wasn't always easy to come by.

I also got to know Frank Tsosie who didn't speak a lot of English, but we got along just fine.

There were actually quite a number of other people in my small circle in the months I was there. Ervin Frank and family—he was probably one of the most generous people I ever met.

There were also the Begaye brothers, Andrew and Lorenzo, who really taught me the art of patience. This was at a time when sobriety was new to me, early 1990s, and I still had some of that needless impatience, wanting to get it all done right now.

The young fellow, Lorenzo, really made me smile one time, though. He really wanted an especially long eagle wing feather I had, so I passed it along to him. He was so proud of it that he made a special box just for it, and made quite an impression, taking it out at one of the ceremonies. It looked for all the world like he was busy pulling out one of those old US Army cavalry sabers or as if he were Zorro! He did it with quite a flourish too and held it like a swordfighter would or a Marine on parade, maybe waiting for the right gleam to catch on its edge before using it.

But in all that time, there was one who really stood out. Deedee Sands made it a point to take me all over the neighbouring Big Navajo Reservation to prayer meetings of the Native American Church.

Every First Nations man has an innate liking for any bird of prey, eagles, of course, being the most sought after for their majestic bearing and noble features. We also believe that these of all our Winged Relations fly closest to the Great Ones Above.

Like everyone else, in those early days, I wanted a fan of my own for these all-night ceremonials. From my travels back home, I eventually returned with a loose set to have made into a prayer fan. These sacred paraphernalia are said to act as a shield, to protect you from all harm.

At the first meeting I went to with Deedee with this new fan, I was eager to do what the others had a habit of, that is to hold my feathers aloft and wave it around a bit, to show off, in other words.

But my bro there right next to me must have read my mind, for he leaned close and sternly whispered to me: "Hold it right there, Bro, and don't move it at all. I'm a veteran, and I know for a fact that this here bird had to die to be in your hands now, so you show him the respect he deserves. Your body should move more than the fan in your hand does. Remember that."

Again, such artistry in practice.

So, I learned right from the start to always handle whatever feathers I have in this way, held with the feathers straight up as intended.

When I do choose to pass one along to someone close to me to use, and I notice them wanting to wave it around, I just have them return it to me, for this very reason, whatever other feelings are involved.

Tu Nedhe Idyll

At times, when the sky matches
the colour
of the water on
Great Slave Lake
you are floating on Creation . . .

THERE WAS NOTHING I would rather do when I had my boat on the crystal-clear lake than to just jump in and go on out there for the day. In the early 1990s, I had bought an 18-foot Grummond from my brother-in-law Bob, and with a 25-horse Yamaha, I could be planing right on top of Back Bay, on my way to the islands in no time.

Pretty well everything in the Somba K'e, Yellowknife area is rock solid granite, so someone like me used to the muddy Duhogah, Mackenzie River, learned pretty quick that you had to watch out for the reefs, which you simply cannot see on a clear day with that dazzling sunlight right on the surface.

But from also going on out there with Chief Fred Sangris, I got to know where all the trouble spots are.

I made a habit of seeing what the big birds, eagles, were doing and learned to spot their nests from a distance.

In bear country, you always have to have a gun close by, but most of the smaller islands were pretty safe . . .

I would land and tie up my boat and just wander around, trying to spot a 'live' feather, one that had fallen off the bird. Many of these were still in good shape.

We use these in our Native ceremonials.

When the 'golden hour' came along, that window of about twenty minutes in the day perfect for taking pictures, I would just seek out some good angles and compose images for painting later.

This worked out perfectly for what I also got into the habit of doing at the time: painting right on-site, at the Northern Images Art Gallery.

Colonialist Disconnect

With lies you can go on in the world,
But you can never go back.

ASIDE FROM THE NEW MUSIC coming out in the mid-sixties, there was very little in the way of art for me during these earlier residential school years. One rather glaring point earlier on was a book I was awarded, probably for doing some noted writing of my own. This was *The Wind in the Willows,* by the Englishman, Kenneth Grahame, first published in 1908. This children's classic, set in pastoral Britain, was definitely one I could not associate with at all. Very likely the idea was to replace our traditional Dene culture with this comparative drivel.

Although I am sure the intention was a good one, the level of where my teachers were at in Sir Alexander Mackenzie School—SAMS—was a world away from my Dene upbringing and consciousness.

For some odd reason, one book that definitely did connect with me was the *500 Hats of Bartholomew Cubbins,* a 1938 Dr. Seuss classic. Its author, aka Theodor Geisel, was on a New York commuter and saw a businessman sitting stiffly in front of him. He thought, What would happen if he simply took the man's hat and threw it out the window?

As Seuss, he set the story in feudal times, with King Derwin ordering Bartholomew Cubbins to doff his hat in obeisance. The citizen does so, with the surprise of another popping up in its place. This goes on all the way to 500 hats, each more beautiful and opulent than before.

Something about the magical nature of this tale impressed me at the dreamy time of these early residential schools. Maybe with its hint at other, alternate possibilities.

Over the years, I too took to the habit, like author Geisel, of collecting headgear, hats, in particular.

It should be noted that the worst of the three residential schools I was subjected to, besides the initial traumatic immersion at Aklavik at the tender age of seven, was the notorious Grollier Hall. In later years, when the world was ready to hear of Canada's contribution to cultural genocide, the place turned out to be the site of numerous cases of outright criminal sexual assaults.

For the time being, though, I started winning trips 'outside' one to the big southern city of Edmonton, Alberta. Along with the trips I was taking to represent the North to races in Quebec, my eyes were certainly being opened to The World I was forever craving.

Like everyone else who had half a mind to what was really going on in the world around at the time, MAD magazine was the place to go to for an escape of sorts. I especially loved the art of Mort Drucker.

But it was not until I somehow picked up Nina's Book by the American Eugene Burdick of *The Ugly American* fame that my so-far innocent eyes were really opened to the real possibilities of the writing craft. Up until that time, in the late sixties, I was more or less being guided as to what to say. The setting in Nazi Germany, a love and an anti-war story, was something into which I could sink my eager intellectual teeth.

'Round about this time, too, I heard for the first time Led Zepplin and Janis Joplin and her band Big Brother and the Holding Company. My poor old grandma must have surely thought the world was coming to an end when I stuck it on my record player at top volume! Up until then, she and the rest of our little town of Radelie Koe, Fort Good Hope, had been lulled to half-sleep with the heartbreak and sorrow of the likes of country singer George Jones.

Meanwhile, the wheels of torture back at Grollier Hall just kept right on turning, poisoning the souls of close relatives, planting the seeds for their abuse of their own selves and their children. With its covert aim at cultural genocide, the residential schools had a profound effect on each and every one of our First Nations families. By forcing each member apart, our emotional ties were severed, many never to regain the traditions built up over some thirty thousand years of our history in the Americas.

In our case, with each year of the education I needed, the gap between myself as the oldest child and the rest of my siblings became impossible to maintain.

It started with my oldest sister, then worked its way down the line, through all the rest of my sisters, to my brothers Robert and Fred John. Traumas collected deep within each survivor, came out both as neurotic and dysfunctional. Now every time I came home, I was a virtual stranger. For want of a more understandable target, I had to bear responsibility for this loss. Without knowing why, our parents set me apart for what life they could continue with.

The saddest result was that on a community level, probably in about every northern Dene community this became accepted as 'normal.'

Even after the residential schools became an issue, the Church itself found no reason to apologize but kept right on with what they called the Word of God.

To this day, my People still keep right on spouting religious dogma, the path of least resistance, more or less.

Nails in our collective coffin.

Sprinkled

A true gem,
Though worn
and tossed to the last of Light

Needing naught of polish
nor even waned utterance.

Only moonlit memories
and bits of
Promised
Sunlight.

O'er these
S*p*a*r*k*l*i*n*g
Days.

E'en to faded past
She befits
Her coat,

So many Lives!

Choke-Hold On

Always have been partial
to a Choker
I wear one from time to time
'Round people . . .
. . . Special events
And when I do, I put it on
REAL T-i-g-h-h-T

To remind me
Of My People
The Way they Watch
-n-
Keep You true
To Our
Old Way

Conceptional: Beghon Rat'setih

THE SIBERIAN RUSSIAN REPUBLIC, commonly called the Altai within Russian borders, just north of Kazakhstan, Mongolia, and China, reminds me a lot of my own home in the Canadian North. There is an enduring sense of a primordial past here, lingering over the high country of the Altai Mountains—no more evident in spirit than in the swift waters, which cascade down into an otherwise empty land.

One can spend a lot of time seeking out the hidden places, which whisper strangely of eons ago, when dinosaurs roamed and life was always on the brink. This, too, is part of my People, the Dene's history. Even today, I get the distinct sense that I have been here before, once even having five separate déja-vu's in one afternoon!

The last time I was in these borderlands of Mongolia, we took a guided exploration with a native of the Altai Mountains, Svetlana Shupenko, who for some reason has never left this area.

Among the many places with petroglyphs we toured, was the one painted in homage to women in general and one which those who cannot conceive go to leave offerings in pilgrimage. On a stone wall, a little off to the side of the main altar, is one that clearly depicts the moment of conception when the sperm enters the female egg. This from a time centuries before the invention of the microscope!

As my sister the linguist noted, these ancestors had a power we cannot possibly imagine, even today.

To Read the Mind of GOD!

"$E=MC^2$" looks simple enough, with a total of the five odd characters, closer to code, which probably goes a long way to appreciate how the word 'genius' is now most often associated with its founder, Einstein.

His mind was such that he could simplify the complicated, the mysterious.

The theoretical version of the space-time continuum in studying the speed of light explains how time appears to slow down when the traveller is moving closer to the speed of light, from the traveller's point of reference.

Light as a constant made it a given that time is relative for each person. The added feature that at the speed of light time stands still is mind-boggling as a theory, with stupendous, even time-travel implications. Yet on the outside there was anything but the incandescent shine we now associate with the man. He didn't mind study but hated school, dropping out to study on his own.

The German-born Jewish theoretical physicist is best known for his work in the field of science. His "Relativity: the Special and General Theory," published in 1905, yet stands as one of two hallmarks of modern physics, the other being quantum mechanics, which he also worked in. Einstein received the Nobel Prize for Physics in 1921 as a result of his years of research, beginning with expanding on Newtonian mechanics.

The scientist was visiting the USA when German dictator Adolf Hitler came to power in 1933, and as a Jew, he prudently stayed, becoming an American citizen seven years later.

Clearly understanding the dangers of the Manhattan Project, which resulted in the atom bomb, he and British philosopher Bertrand Russell signed a manifesto denouncing the use of nuclear weapons.

Too, it must have seemed so maddeningly odd to Einstein that he would personally be so mortally condemned by the Nazis for simply being a Jew.

And at the same Time,
Holding the Keys
To the UNIVERSE!

Although he never was directly involved with the production of the atomic bomb, his one lifelong regret was that it had all begun with his discoveries. In a letter to American President Roosevelt, Einstein wrote: "Had I known that the Germans would not succeed in producing an atomic bomb, I would have never lifted a finger."

An early supporter of civil rights and peace, Einstein offered to testify in court as a character witness for American civil rights activist W.E.B. Du Bois, a founding member of the National Association for the Advancement of Colored People (NAACP). Du Bois and three colleagues were federally indicted as Soviet Agents because he had circulated a petition against nuclear weapons. The case was eventually dismissed in 1951.

Einstein's work in science and theory also touched on and opened up a myriad of fields, carried forth by the likes of Swiss psychiatrist Carl Jung whose 'synchronicity', for instance, explained how two or more events can be meaningfully but not causally related.

Perhaps because of his heightened illuminations and support for the downtrodden, Einstein was certainly no fan of capitalism. Rather, he saw it oppressing both society and nature. When encouraged to compete, humans turn on each other:

> The necessary sense of community no longer exists
> And individuals are socially crippled.
> Life becomes a 'lonely struggle'.

Einstein's findings when viewed in terms of synchronicity, for instance, correlates to Indigenous holistic Ways of Knowing. What we like to call coincidence, was also touched on by Cree musician Buffy Sainte-Marie, in her 1992 album *Coincidence and Likely Stories*, which to me is all about our collective body of knowledge, paradigms, and how as individuals we fail to appreciate the power we have. Or not.

Indeed, to an Indigenous mind, Einstein's theory of relativity is closely akin to the way our traditional teaching tool, the Medicine Wheel, in its way, opens up many avenues for correlation. For instance, the Indigenous concept of ceremony as an expression of Spiritual renewal is in lockstep with synchronicity.

One Indigenous scholar, the Blackfoot Dr. Leroy Little Bear, goes on to quite some lengths on how Indigenous science relates to quantum mechanics. As he notes, tied into the concepts of, say, cybernetics of complexity, the interconnectedness of whole systems, too, is that these are best understood in very general, inter-related terms, or patterns. Indigenous Ways of Knowing are thus ideally suited to making and linking human elements.

Broadening the field even more is his theory that "Imagination is more important than knowledge. For knowledge is limited to all we now know and understand, while imagination embraces the entire world, and all there ever will be to know and understand." In application, take for instance, how at one point, we thought that things of everyday use, like the home phone, the landline, would simply always be there. Now it's already a relic of the past.

The possibility for this scientist's work can also include the field of sports, where one would apply how certain superstars speak of being able to slow down time itself when the action warrants it.

Applied to more real-life situations, complexity, for instance, can even be understood in how emotions, for instance, change. Think of the time it takes to heal past slights, strong feelings, or events in general. Suddenly, seemingly out of nowhere, a door opens, welcoming you into new worlds of the possible. The situation itself hasn't changed, but your perception of it has as you evolve.

A Divine Order, if you will, or at least a logical one eventually becomes evident from the intricacies of science proper.

Poetic, too, is the way Einstein saw learning:

> Education is not the teaching of facts,
> It's rather the teaching of the mind
> To think.

An Indigenous leaning towards non-interference that is to allow nature the upper and final say combined with an intimate and immediate connection to the natural world, makes us the definite force for educating a needy world.

Indeed, given in total, the recent paramedic swings away from science as we know it to what the Indians have been saying all along that the rise of Indigenous Knowledge will certainly take on new meaning as our needs for survival arise.

It is also a curious enough fact that Einstein's study of light was carried on artistically and about the same time by the French Impressionists such as Renoir and Monet who figure in *Child of Morning Star*.

> Just as clear, his prophetic down-to-earth views:
> The world is a dangerous place to live;
> not because of the people who are evil,
> but because of the people
> who don't do anything about it.

Curiously, the study of light by the Impressionists mirrors that of duty, no less for artists, to challenge all our complacency.

In Light of Renoir

A S MOST DID IN THE SEVENTIES, I could have easily stayed with the Woodland School of Art, which had suddenly grown popular in the country. I did spend a good deal of time with this group, including Norval Morrisseau, since we shared a common interest in doing things in our own Indigenous artistic way.

Many people just wanted to own something of the new expression, so it was also an easy way to make money if that is what you wanted. In particular, I definitely did not want to use these traditional Anishnawbe forms as my own upon returning home to the North, as many later did.

I too was in the bona fide art world of the alternative Art's Sake school to learn and found myself pulled towards the Impressionists, particularly in the use of colour. They were a group of nineteenth-century French artists who simply wanted to get away from the former, rigidly constraining Romantic Age of painting, everything being so static and dull of expression.

I would spend hours just poring over whatever I could find on Pierre-Auguste Renoir (1841–1919) for his absolute lyrical use of light and delightful use of tones. His sun-dappled outdoor scenes taught me to see my own world, as in my *Dans la Lumière de Renoir*, in a new and vibrant way.

What I started doing right from the start is as my lifelong hero Michelangelo wrote in one of his sonnets:

> The marble not yet carved can hold the form
> Of every thought the greatest artist has,
> And no conception ever, comes to pass
> Unless the hand obeys the intellect.
> —*Sonnet XV*

Thus, my own art has been an invitation to the thinking person, one who allows the powers of colour and form to free the other senses.

Peace Willow Flats Studio

The little guy just soaked it all in

IT SURE WAS A PLEASURE to have Devon Allooloo from next door over to my little cabin studio as a student. I have worked with gifted artists before, in a long series of presentations and workshops at various schools, but none like this eight-year-old neophyte. He just took whatever I told him without so much as a question and went with it.

In about early 2007, his mother, Cathy, simply sent him over whenever I had some spare time, and she made these lessons a part of his home-schooling. We started with simple depictions from photos of animals from magazines, and young as he was, he was able to add whatever he already knew from going out on the land with his canoeing family. From these sketching exercises and works in paint, he quickly moved on to his own designs on cards, cups, and such.

By the time Christmas rolled around and he had been part of a few arts and crafts sales, his father marvelled, "The little guy has more money in the bank than I do!"

The little cabin in back of the house and family of the Allooloo's was a newer and real home of sorts for me. Just like back in Radelie Koe, Fort Good Hope, I was never made to feel any kind of way—just go into the kitchen and help myself.

In terms of this my second book, the simple situation of being part of a family again ties in so closely with newer beginnings. As I mentioned in my first book, *From Bear Rock Mountain: The Life and Times of a Dene Residential School Survivor,* as a group we didn't actually begin to recognize each other until it was all over, and we began to willingly drift back to the Circle, to our Indigenous ways, through traditional ceremonials.

The idea of the Arts and 'Community', was still a very real puzzle to try to piece together. The younger generation of today is not the only one that has lost the human connection.

In a very real way, each succeeding generation has to reinvent itself to fit into our changing times.

This kind of resilience has always been, and no less, the hallmark of Indigenous societies.

The Beauty Way

Art is borne
Planted aloft . . . Set asail,

Finding mused wing
Past inertia universe

. . .

Just so, we the Dene believe
In reincarnation

A soul recently passed
Like young beaver in spring

Wants for the warmth
Of Home

Whilst painting
I watch in wonder
. . . Hand, brush, and colour

All around . . . forming

. . .

Colours of Life

Spirit Stonechild

The rattles flew everywhere in the dark Cree Sweat Lodge,
bonking various ones on the head.

A FIRST NATIONS NAME is a soul treasure and to have it first pronounced is a living blessed. Mine was the last generation born right on the land, each given a genuine Dene name at birth, or soon thereafter. This defined the person so deeply that among some tribes it was considered downright dangerous to simply give your name out for public knowledge, lest someone take a notion to harm you with its use.

It wasn't uncommon, either, for a person to have a number of these forms of identity, some in recognition from other tribes. One of some twenty given to me came from the Tłı̨chǫ of Behchokǫ̀, to do with being the son of a Big Chief and friend thereof.

Other names have me as being especially able, with great power over women . . . the owner of four guns . . . part of the Eagle Nation, and on to some earned for some valorous deeds . . . almost ten in all, not counting the puny Mola, White man name, Antoine Mountain.

At the time, around the early 1990s, of one of the annual Spiritual Pilgrimages to Desnethé, near Fort Reliance, a Cree Sundance Man requested a special Sweat Lodge Ceremony, which turned out to be one to bestow me with a special name.

He had a number of handmade rattles, which, without warning, began to haphazardly fly all around the lodge, hitting a number of people, including myself. The man running this Sweat sternly told us that this happened because we were not paying the Spirits our proper respects.

The following day, when I went to visit the Elder and his wife at his camp along the beach, he calmly laid out his collection of rattles and asked me which one I thought had hit me the day before.

I searched out a likely suspect . . . and was presented with it!

I thought this to be a fine addition to go along with my new name.

Monet's Sense of Place

He surely must have watched with Vision

A FTER RENOIR, Claude Monet (1840–1926) was the main Impressionist to catch my attention. It was he who began this group of French artists away from the rigidly organized annual Salon de Paris, which invariably favoured the same established set from before.

Over time, he purchased some property in Giverny, where he produced all the outdoor *plein air* landscapes from his sprawling gardens, lily pond, and the now-famous little Japanese bridge.

He also became known for his series of the Rouen Cathedral and, of course, the haystacks. These were done to feature the changing play of light and different seasons.

Another important figure amongst these painters, Édouard Manet, was a pivotal figure in the transition from Realism to the new style they invented, Impressionism.

As for how this form of the Arts related to the North, the warm Mediterranean light the Impressionists were after didn't exactly exist as such in the Far North, but the preference for living colour did.

It did take a while for people to get used to it, but to their credit, they eventually did. If nothing else, they identified with Monet's free use of colour and the outdoor setting.

> Without quite knowing it
> I was not Learning to fit myself
> With a cloak, a shining suit, of Beauty
> The same way
> A willow stands to the strongest gale
> Without breaking.

I also actually managed to win quite a number of Artists and People's Choice Awards at the annual Great Northern Arts Festival in Inuvik over the years.

Mad Trapper of Rat River

*Even people who have lived all their lives on the land
say he was one tough hombre!*

Although the exact identity of this man, whom some call Albert Johnson, will likely never be known, all agree that by outrunning the law for over a month, over 150 miles (240 km) on foot in the dead of winter, is one superhuman feat.

He emerged from the gold fields of the Yukon innocently enough, coming out at the Peel River, near present-day Fort McPherson, on July 19, 1931. After building himself an eight-by-ten-foot log cabin, he settled in.

In the late fall, a Gwich'in trapper complained to the Royal Canadian Mounted Police that someone, probably this strange man, was disturbing his traps, springing them, and hanging them from trees.

The stranger refused to answer the door when Constable Alfred King and a guide, Joe Bernard, went the sixty miles (97 km) to question him. When they came back with a warrant, he still would not speak but, without warning, shot Constable King right through the wooden door. The officer recovered, setting off a major manhunt with nine men and forty-two dogs carrying 20 pounds (9.1 kg) of dynamite.

The Mad Trapper took flight on foot after his cabin was blown to bits.

In pursuit, Constable Edgar Millen was shot through the heart by this marksman, killing him.

With the dim Arctic twilight barely making sight visible, trackers meticulously crawled over the ice for even a trace of the man's presence, and the chase continued.

When the authorities were sure they had their man cornered, he miraculously climbed a 7,000-foot (2100 m) peak, using an ordinary axe as a pick, once again setting off the chase in the bone-chilling -40°F cold.

With the Yukon border within range away up in the foreboding Richardson Mountains, a post-war air force ace pilot, Wop May, was called in, flying a ski-equipped Bellanca monoplane.

The desperate fugitive was finally caught on February 17, 1932, in the middle of the Eagle River, Yukon Territory, where he was killed in a firefight, but not before wounding another police officer.

In the end, the emaciated Mad Trapper, face frozen into a defiant other-worldly devil-dog wolverine death mask, forever scoffs at mere human likeness.

Among the puzzling questions still remaining is why he would have been found with $2,000 in American and Canadian currency on him.

From my own readings, I found that a distant relative, a trader by the name of James Mervyn, married to Judith, the sister of my grandfather Peter Mountain, Sr. hired this mysterious Mad Trapper of Rat River to run a trapline near Mayo, Yukon, over one winter.

In a way these mysterious connections are all about us too, a little bit of a rebel, outsider. . . Northerner.

Degas, Master of the Mark!

The bubbles seemed to float right in the air before me!

Such is the power of the French Impressionist Edgar Degas (1834–1917) that I stood transfixed in the Art Gallery of Toronto's presentation of a few works of his and Monet's, with a few by Van Gogh. The painting in question was of a woman in her bath, with these exquisite multi-coloured bubbles miraculously appearing out of the water.

One of the founders of the Impressionist Movement, he was a master draughtsman, as well as a painter and sculptor, famous for his standing sculpture *The Little Dancer*. A favourite subject was the ballet, which accounted for over half of his art.

Just then, in the earliest years of photography, he became adept at capturing movement and produced many works featuring new and different perspectives.

Edgar Degas also featured psychologically complex works and those to do with human isolation.

Upper: "Waitin' on the Sun." The Mad Trapper
Lower: "Degas, Master of the Mark"

Scientific Politico Machiavelli

Like the hapless poet Dante Alighieri before him, Niccolo Machiavelli (1469–1527) found himself on the wrong side of fickle local Florentine politics. Judged guilty for crimes against Medici family despots, he was imprisoned and suffered the dreaded strappado: cruelly dropped a number of times, with the full force of his body held up by only his chained wrists.

Little doubt on each way down to a sudden lumpen stop, poor Niccolo would've regretted each of the six extra-large slices of pizza ordered, casually ordered from the *'ria,* so oft before. Over the next fifteen years, the exiled Machiavelli took to a daily habit of appearing for work in evening formals, to compose, among others, *The Prince,* a learned study into history's continual need for and process of what we now know as political science.

He hoped that an eventual Medici ruler would use this treatise as a guide to drive out foreign powers and as a job application of sorts. Though neither dream came true in his lifetime and with not much to stand in their way, both Spain and France especially ran rampant over the entire Italian peninsula, waging outright war over entire regions.

In practical terms, and with a brigand's mind, the budding political scientist sought to set aside the traditional concept of a 'good', rather than a pragmatically successful ruler.

Machiavelli must surely have been referring to Jesus Christ himself in the chapter to do with the certain fall of 'unarmed' prophets, but there was a case in point conveniently at hand: that of the Mad Monk, Savonarola, whose call for the fall of the Roman Catholic Church was dramatically answered in Florence's Piazza della Signoria, a civic government square, where he was hanged and burned at the stake, on May 23, 1498. Moreover, at a time when the Christian Church held a stranglehold, especially over the thoughts and beliefs of ordinary citizens, it took this new Machiavellian and secular thought to help change the future of realpolitik. Inscribed over political philosopher Niccolò Machiavelli's tomb in his native Firenze's Basilica of Santa Croce are:

TANTO.NOMINI.NVLLVM.PAR.ELOGIVM:
"To so great a name, no epitaph can do justice."

Comanche Chief Quanah Parker

—One of the last to surrender—
This man's story could not be made up!

IT ALL BEGAN when his mother was captured by the Indians from the family's ranch in Texas when she was eight years of age in May 1836. By all accounts, she blended in well in her adopted Comanche home and even married a chief, no less, of one of the six bands.

Her son Quanah surely inherited whatever independent streak ran through Cynthia Ann Parker's veins, leading war parties and becoming chief himself in his twenties. The times being what they were during the Indian Wars, he fought to keep his people free in their vast buffalo hunting range, finally surrendering to save the women and children in 1874.

Quanah Parker did all he could to help his band of Comanches make a transition from hunters to a life on a confining reservation, going on to become something of an oil company and cattle baron.

He even owned stocks in a railroad and served as a circuit court judge. Judge Parker was rather strict with his own people, even hanging some for minor offences to prove that they needed to change their former rowdy ways.

He must have indeed been a man of means, having a total of eight wives and many children, all with their own rooms in his 'Indian White House', with its thirteen stars on the roof.

Early on in his raiding days he was gored by a bull in Mexico and brought back to health by a Brujo Medicine Woman who prescribed peyote for him.

He remembered this and would make long arduous horseback trips on over the border all the way from his home in Oklahoma just to build up a ready supply of the Holy Medicine.

He became a Roadman, an equivalent of a priest of the Native American Church and was instrumental in having the use and transport of peyote formally recognized in the Constitution of the United States, making it part of a bona fide religious faith practice of communion.

Michelangelo's Pietà Comes a-Calling

*She now stands sentinel to our dearly departed,
forever cradling her son in protective arms*

THE PIETÀ OF THE MADONNA sheltering Jesus in grief has had quite a history of its own. As the second in a long procession of masterpieces by the Italian sculptor, this magnificent marble depiction immediately following our Lord's crucifixion was brutally attacked by a crazed hammer-wielding man in Rome's Saint Peter's Basilica in May 1972. In typical Italian fashion, workers meticulously picked up even the tiniest missing sections of Mary's shattered head and shoulders, eventually restoring it to its former glorious form.

This surely took some doing, for the wonderful glassy sheen on the Carrara marble alone took the artist's assistants a good six months of patient polishing. As usual, I kept a mental note of each of my artistic hero Michelangelo's works, having been to Italy for my third art school year (2009–2010) and back again for a seven-week visit during the writing of this book, six years later.

After completing my studies for a master's degree, I spent my usual summer at home in the North, working with the Youth. One day, while thinking aloud about more possible works for the community, I just mentioned to the caretaker of the church, Sister Joan, that the famed Pietà would make a fine addition for our relatives sleeping there.

A group of teenage paddlers came to my log house to view my paintings. While there, they helped me to stretch the canvas on a prepared frame for this tribute to our relatives gone to their new home.

The work itself took a number of days, at the invitation of Bonnie Bergsma, renting the very home of our late Adeline Tobac, just in the back of Wilfred and Lucy Jackson's home. Using various depictions of the Pietà, one can truly marvel at the divine Italian's artistic gifts.

Each section of the work can be appreciated separately: the folds in Jesus's mother's voluminous dress, each compositional angle, down to the smallest detail of an extended grieving hand.

I took long moments at the site where the work would be eventually displayed, thinking of the many relatives we've known and how, as with this work, all things come to a passing.

So too, with each person buried in our community's graveyard; every person in their part, going all the way back to when Radelie Koe, Fort Good Hope, first moved here, the parts make up our magnificent present whole.

Of course, any kind of work of this size doesn't happen by any single person, and I was greatly assisted by the Band Council jack-of-all-trades, Enos Ellton, and his crew, to carefully select the right spot for the visiting Pietà.

As is also the norm in northern small country life, it took a while for the outdoor mural to be installed, but on the day all of the materials were ready to go I took a walk farther south, to the Point.

Walking down the old creek sideroad, I was thinking, *This is the way the Big Birds think.* And there, waiting for me right on the trail just down from the foot of a large Eagle Tree, was a 'live' feather, as if in thanks from my mother, who passed away a few years before from cancer. Back at the graveyard, on the mural's other side, was a fresher grave of a niece, part of this country's tragic and inhuman legacy of Missing and Murdered Indigenous Women and Girls.

Through it all, with our Duhogah, mighty Mackenzie River nearby, ever-flowing north to Mother Ocean, we each, in our way . . . carry on.

Antonio in Italia

My eight-month school year of 2009–2010 was not without hijinks I lived on Via del Inferno, Hell Street, just off the spacious Piazza della Repubblica in Florence, the former no doubt in reference to the artists and the rest of the damned of the past who lodged there. In testimony to the local builders, for whom simply putting buildings up is a year-long passion, even the third-floor apartment had one solid stone wall in the bedroom, as was the entire floor. The aesthetics of why this would happen so far off the ground can only have an Italian reasoning.

Regardless, to go with the name Hell Street, August was a demonically hot time, calling for a number of showers every day just to cool off.

One of the first things I had to get was a cell phone. Being of a rather non-technical and decidedly individualistic bent, I chose a unique ringtone, of course. Later, walking around with a severe case of culture shock, I was absolutely delighted to hear an ice-cream truck cruising nearby, just for my benefit! Or so I thought until a number of people kept pointing to my butt. It took me a while to realize that someone was calling me on my cell!

There were people who became stopping points for my daily routines. One ran an eatery on the way to where the Ontario College of Art and Design had its Italian studios near the train station downtown. He patiently taught me a catchphrase, which in his words would open every Italian door: "Conosco e mie polie, I know my chicken."

One door it did open, to the grand Pizzeria Piccadilly on Via della Santa Maria, between the famous Duomo and the River Arno. Its owner, Romano, whom I took to calling the Italiano James Bondo, must have been surprised when I right off showed an interest in some nutritious eggplants he and a Cuban worker Anna had on display.

Of course, I could take some, along with just about any dish I wanted on my evening stroll, all for the same price as it turned out. In true molto genteel Italiano manner, he also made sure to have the cream for my espresso always warmed up . . . just so. I already began missing the place an entire month before leaving.

Wanting to remember . . .
The warm twilight breeze over the River Arno,
Church bells ringing off the red-tiled roofs,
Storefronts decorated anew every week or so

The down-to-earth people
Who would literally walk into each other
On seeing a real live Indian! Trying to maintain balance
On uneven cobblestones

Gelato, with real Fragola. Market stalls with free samples
For Antonio della Montagne. Everything about Heaven on Earth

What made the parting at least bearable was meeting Peter Porcal, our Art History teacher, for espresso here and there to compare our mutual interests in times gone by. He sadly went on to join these famed legions a few years later, to be forever missed by his hundreds of students who took the Florence Italy Program since the mid-seventies.

Maestro Porcal

R IGHT FROM THE START, our Art History teacher Peter Porcal had no problem holding us twenty-five Ontario College of Arts and Design University students of the Florence Italy Program in his thrall.

He had a theatrical sense all his own!

Many were the early mornings he would lead us through this sixteenth-century artistic paradise, recounting in great detail a Renaissance world he made come alive. And with such a pointed irreverent touch, commenting on the great number of penis-shaped acorn adornments these Italians were so fond of.

He would adroitly and with boasted aplomb include the population of one of the thousands of small country villages with the exact number of cats and dogs, including and in fine detail, their dastardly contribution to its cultural street life!

So beloved was this molto genteel, very gentle man that members of other touring groups nearby would join our class for a time, just to share in his love of life!

He took to calling me maestro, master, which to this day I deeply treasure. We met in private a number of times, so he could give me a more personal direction from his mastery of how all culture, any culture, is intrinsically tied in with art. And to, of course, give free rein to his own ribald thoughts on grand masters such as Leonardo da Vinci, whom he sorely tortured on his own devious rack!

Knowing my fondness for Michelangelo, Maestro Porcal, to his discreet credit, kept his wicked mental meanderings to himself in our frequent stops for espresso.

One of the many lessons our Maestro Peter Porcal taught had to do with how the independent Vatican City's massive St. Peter's Basilica, the largest Christian church in the entire

world able to easily hold fifty thousand with room for another million or so out front, could not possibly compare with Firenze's tiny church Santi Apostoli, close onto the Piazza del Limbo, for the simple reason that a smaller house of worship is "much more pleasing to the nature of the Holiest Spirit."

Another, and one we heard right from the start, had to do with the value and relevance of discipline, which in the study of history, for instance, we as students of life have to objectively allow for what has happened in the past to act as a guide, even within our private selves.

As our Art History teacher and in his inimitable way, Peter Porcal pointed out how the artist Michelangelo on his own, broke down the various thematic underpinnings for the Sistine Chapel into two: the possibilities for mankind in "The Creation of Adam" and our eventual fated downfall, with the one I chose to portray, "The Drunkenness of Noah."

I also ventured another, from the massive two thousand square foot "The Last Judgment" behind the altar for the historic Sistine Chapel, as an assignment for Sylvia Whitton's class, in a puny, by comparison, four-by-five feet size. Her official response was an 'A', which turned out to be the only one she had ever given in over a quarter century of teaching in the Arts, a truly humbling experience!

After a number of decades with the Florence Italy Program, this great man passed away in his expatriate home and was interred in one of the historic places he was so fond of, no doubt with his merry cupid angels now for company.

Into a Wondrous Abyss, Dante's Inferno

"All Hope Abandon.
You Who Enter Here."

BEGINNING WITH "Through me is the way to the City of Woe. Through me is the way to sorrow eternal. Through me is the way to the lost below," words to this effect graced the top of the cave-like entrance to Hades, hell, which the Italian poet and philosopher Dante Alighieri (1265–1321) composed in a lifelong personal quest, over two decades, before his death in 1321, in exile for political reasons.

What makes this epic poetry so impressive, be thee ever mindful, is that *The Divine Comedy* was written over a hundred years before the invention of the printing press.

No doubt the descendants of the Mongol overlord Genghis Kahn would have been given pause by the screeds the Italian poet proffered as an oracle to the wise.

Dante's Italy would not even enter into prominence for hundreds of years with the Renaissance, yet he was revered by the French for insisting on Italian, rather than the traditional Latin, for his prophetic call to humankind.

In format, the story goes that poor Dante fell for another man's wife. She died, leaving the lovelorn scribe, pen in hand, to find his eternal love, first through the thrusts of hell itself, into purgatory, and finally throughout the heavens.

Much of the initial purpose of these early writings had to do with bolstering the Roman Catholic religion. I don't have much to say about that ecclesiastic favour, although there are voices from within to cause pause: church officials gone awry in their respective priestly, nunnery, and frock-monked duties.

At present, although Christianity's sincerity can be brought to question, we have somehow gone past the stage of official denial, with the 2008 public apology from the Government of Canada for abuses caused to First Nations Peoples by the residential schools. Yet a more specific party at fault, the Roman Catholic Church, is yet expressing indignation and outright anger for being challenged on various forms of abuse.

There was a time, a bit ago, in February of 2013, when Pope Benedict XVI actually resigned, presumably over official Irish government inquiries into sexual abuse and child abuse amongst the clergy itself. From Dante hundreds of years earlier:

> More than a thousand at the gates I saw
> Out of the Heavens rained down, who angrily
> Were saying, "Who is this that without death
> Goes through the kingdom of the people dead?"
> And my sagacious Master made a sign
> Of wishing to speak with them.

In company with Roman poet Virgil, the Florentine goes on to witness violent sinners against nature and art, the fraudulent, panderers and seducers, hypocrites, fraudulent counselors, makers of discord, and falsifiers.

The ninth circle of hell is reserved for the treacherous to kindred and country. Again, if any of this be true, there are no doubt plenty of spaces now occupied by those charged with our care in the residential schools. Dante reserves particular ire for prelates and even pontiffs of the Roman Catholic Church found to be guilty of simony, that is, guilty of selling church offices and roles.

In the Third Bolgia of the Eighth Circle of Hell, we thus find Pope Nicholas III, chief sinner, headfirst in a hole with flames licking highest:

> Out of the mouth of each one there protruded
> The feet of a transgressor, and the legs
> Up to the calf, the rest within remained.
>
> In all of them the soles were both on fire;
> Wherefore the joints so violently quivered,
> They would have snapped asunder withes and bands.

Joined in such rank would be Julius II, in Michelangelo's time, who also saw fit to afford clerical status to those generous to the church.

Another favourite instituted by this pope was Indulgences, that of pardoning a suitor and whomever of his relatives' and ancestors' time in purgatory—for a price, of course. According to popular reckoning, the period of such a spiritual wait would go on in purgatory for 9,000 years, although I would judge several hours to suffice any roast, to public or privileged parts, and certainly no more than your usual of twenty concerted, hermetic spa-moments.

As it turned out, these practices, begun to shore up assorted funds, were the straw that broke the Reformation's Martin Luther's faith. In perhaps some wise of saving grace, thus-damned Nicholas III foresees more future popes to be found guilty of this crime against God.

Amongst a myriad of other sinful wrongs, this one of gluttony, it is said that one pope, in particular, had a fondness for, of all things, chicken breasts. Such a liking for the whitened, in fact, that he was struck dead upon attempting one breast over the goodly amount of twenty-eight!

Truth be told, here in the Western world, these various vices in toto may prove to be fewer sins of the human condition and more to do with outright official policies of cultural genocide.

The Bible itself could well prove to be an instrument of these 'sins against nature', with its meaningless dogma bent on promoting man's ambitions over science and evolution. The power of Dante's visions well over a millennia ago goes far beyond a mere literary classic, which his *Divine Comedy* certainly is.

It is no wonder he penned this masterpiece while in exile from public office and his native Florence, Italy, where his writings yet reverently echo through the stone walls of the Italian city to a grateful world. Stirred by a lifelong love lost too soon, Dante's *Inferno* can also be likened to a soul's eternal search for a loved one through the very fires of Hell. *(See artworkW on back jacket cover.)*

Even in the visual arts, Dante Alighieri was to greatly influence other cultural giants, like Michelangelo and Botticelli, and those others of letters, namely Petrarch, Chaucer, Milton, Shelley, William Blake, Yeats, James Joyce, Ezra Pound, and others.

And T. S. Eliot: *The Divine Comedy* could be compared with "nothing but the entire dramatic work of Shakespeare."

Sling *that* to Arrow, Bill!

William Wordsworth Longfellow was so moved as to refer to Dante Alighieri's works as a "medieval miracle of song."

Small wonder, indeed, with such endings in poetic visions of lofty Heaven as "the love that moves the sun and the other stars."

Sublime Terribilità Michelangelo!

*Of course, no artist worth his chalk would not attempt at least
a number of sketches from this man's work.*

T AKEN FROM choicer morsels of a typical free-wheeling rendition of
our Art History teacher, Peter Porcal, on a class trip to the Vatican
City's Saint Peter's Basilica:

> When he overheard some ragged-robed, pompous fool in a small
> crowd of admirers from Lombardy before his newly completed *Pietà*
> say that 'our Gobbo, Cristoforo Solari, the hunchback from Milan'
> had done this splendid work, Michelangelo stood to listen, getting so
> furious that he later stole into the church in the dead of night with his
> tools and signed '*Michel. Angelus. Bonarotus. Florent. Faciebat*' (Latin
> for Michelangelo Buonarroti, the Florentine, made this), to a band on
> his *Pietà*, to settle that question.

I can still see the great Ontario College of Arts and Design University
man holding forth to help forge another, the divine Michelangelo
Buonarroti (1475–1564), into context.

Not that the Italian Renaissance sculptor, painter, architect, poet,
and engineer would ever need much more to be ensconced in his rightful honour as the greatest artist of all time and certainly a Renaissance
Man for the ages.

Two of his most famous works, the *Pietà* and the quintessential
David were done before Michelangelo turned thirty. In fact, his professional career began rather early, at a time when your usual artist had to
study for a number of years at the service of a master, who took credit
for every work his group of acolytes did.

As it turned out, there was no appreciable share of *amore*, love,
between him and his first teacher, Ghirlandajo, who had to submit to
the teen's corrections of his drawings!

At fourteen, Michelangelo fell into questionable league with a
rather dishonest merchant who convinced the young artist to make a
copy of the popular figure of art collectors just then, a *Sleeping Cupid.*
The finished piece was covered in dirt to make it appear to have been
recently rescued from an earthly grave.

Sublime Terribilità Michelangelo

Roman Cardinal Raffaele Riario was convinced to buy the supine figure. To his dismay, the duped church official eventually learned of this fiendish forgery but was also duly amazed that a mere lad rendered this magnificent piece. One thing led to another, and the church official invited the young man to be his guest at his villa.

There, this Italian artist completed arguably his most magnificent work, that of an anatomically perfectly proportioned, if not slightly drunk Bacchus, God of Wine, comically attempting a dance step at a festival.

The patron, Roman nobleman Jacopo Galli also had the northern sculptor render yet another priceless work, his famed *Pietà*, oft graced in this chapter's intro. The sculptor's demands were such that the work was painstakingly polished by a special team for no less than six months!

This Christ was far removed from the one later about to cast *Last Judgment* over an unsuspecting world, with a protective Mary tugging at his robes to forgive misjudged or forgotten souls.

In his long and illustrious career, Michelangelo went through a total of thirteen popes when the Church was the one sure backer of the Arts. He began with Julius II, whom he convinced he could do over forty life-sized sculptures for his massive funeral tomb. With five different contracts for this work alone, the artist only completed a handful of these statues in solid marble, including a magnificent Moses and various struggling slaves.

Terribilità Michelangelo and Il Papa Terribile Julius II were destined to butt heads, both being as stubborn to any task, human and otherwise, Twin Towers of Cheek to Jowl Terror, ill-jested the joust, if you will, artist and ecclesiast, noses frothing and flared, fairly aflame with heated hosts of will-o'er-might!

Two of Michelangelo's defining works, the *Sistine Chapel* and *The Last Judgment*, took a total of well over a decade to paint, and very likely caused him his most severe physical ailments later, for the dim lighting and the awkward way he had to hold his aching body in order to transfer his gigantic images to the fresco just above.

No stranger he, the Florentine, to the grand statement, the surface of the Pope's Ceiling covered over ten thousand square feet, just under the size of a basketball court, proper perspective alone presenting a herculean task in an unfamiliar medium, not only of painting, but the added delicate frescoes which, only allowing for a minimal amount to be attempted per day, stretched him to the breaking point.

The wonder of it all was that only a very small area could actually be done in a single day, for the punctured outlines to be later painted in fresco. The complicated frescoing process involving highly corrosive chemicals could only be done a little at a time to allow for the drying process. This was at a time when even the paints had to be hand-ground from various stones. Despite the mammoth job, an average of a five-foot-by-five-foot painting was done every single day!

Though easier for Michelangelo to work on, *The Last Judgment* on the vertical wall in the back of the Sistine Chapel actually took the artist longer to do, a good quarter of a century after the ceiling, with fewer architectural divides and more spatial interruptions within the work's space. Little wonder, for the chapel's ceiling now contained almost three hundred biblical figures. Preparations included a thousand sketches and drawings, foreshortened, for viewing from the floor sixty feet below.

Michelangelo much preferred to work alone and, in fact, sent packing or ignored all his assistants and the church officials hand-picked to help advise him on the theological philosophy behind the biblical works commissioned. Although his surviving works would astound millions throughout the ages, this bent for personal independence, dubbed "lonely as a hangman" by fellow Florentine Raphael, set him apart, largely by choice. This he could well afford to do, owing to sitting at the Medici table in Firenze, with regular guests including the brightest Renaissance minds, giving forth on the new Humanities, away from paganism. The artist in him added a decided touch to antiquity, going all the way back to the ancient Greeks for inspiration.

From direct experiences in these early times of the Medici and as a devout Catholic, Michelangelo was also heavily influenced by the Mad Monk, Cirolama Savonarola, a zealous Dominican friar, who almost single-handedly overturned the then-modern Church itself, except, of course, for his skyrocketing career being abruptly shortened: he was extensively tortured, strangled, hung, and then burned at the stake for good measure, a Bonfire of the Savvy, if you will, in the city square, Piazza della Signoria, Firenze, 1498.

At one point, utterly determined to have the pope's permission to begin on the Sistine Chapel, the artist caught up with the Vatican army, with its pontiff riding before, as general, and spread his large drawings out on the ground before the pontiff.

When asked why this could not wait until after the present military campaign was over, Michelangelo's reply was, "Just in case your Holiness does not make it back alive!"

When it was all said and done, though, the artist must have surely thought of himself in a time warp. From his Old Testament prophets on the completed Sistine ceiling to the majestic figure of Jesus Christ passing judgment on our entire mankind with a wave of his arm there were absolutely no reference points as if we sinners did our due diligence in a candlelit *Twilight Zone*, Rod Serling in robes intoning some echoing refrain:

> Picture yourself falling,
> falling from the heavens,
> never to return to harp and veil
> to grim fated coals below . . . in . . .
> the Hades Zone!"

. . . and ol' Buonarotti's ghost going, "Good grief, Rod! *I'm* the one in the time warp here!"

These and more sombre thoughts must surely have left the artist in a quandary. On the one hand, here depicting a Christ casting final decree on some of the self-same human jackals he could see still plainly cavorting in all manner of seriously unchaste splendour not fifty feet yonder, but to step over to at least take a leer or two back would mean a deadly drop to the sobering cold solid flooring below!

. . . Suddenly turning around, mid-stroke to some saintly beard he goes—

"NoAh! Awhm talkin' to you, Boi! You Know you done those grapes, man! Done laid you Right OUT, they did!" (Back to divine Whisks)

. . . And again, "An You, Adam . . . First man! I know I didn't give you much, but you should have kept that ol' fig leaf ON! Stayed in the GarDen!"

Ah, the trials of God's Chosen!

Given these kinds of psychic shenanigans abounding within the Sistine's walls, small wonder it often took months for the cardinals to pick the next bearer of the papal seals here!

. . . "Well, y'know, sir, there IS a Lotta smoke comin' outta there. None white, mind you, but some kinda mass gigglin' too! But, ah, still no vote."

Such vile jesterly cheek-by-jowl, the artistic significance that is the Sistine Chapel, rendered in an unfamiliar painterly and frescoed medium, entombed within a relatively small papal prayer room within the vast Vatican complex itself, bespeaks the grandeur, no less, of the eternal artistic person Michelangelo, a vision no doubt wrought of an earthly Roman citadel.

Still, this man of the arts had to yet again contend with another after his throne, wanting for ensconced within the princely artistic pinnacle of the visual world; his contested bouts with Leonardo da Vinci a thing of a bruised past, Michelangelo now had to vie with Urbino's Rafael, every bit his equal as a painter and with a gentler, human touch, evidenced with a good number of renderings of the Queen of Heaven and child Jesus.

They both fought for especial favour of the pope of the moment, for costly commissions and to be named papal architect for all of

Rome. These challenges for the title of the greatest, though rancorous, lacked nothing for recognition. In his magnificent fresco "The School of Athens," Rafael saw to at least include his dejected rival afoot the lofty stairs of knowledge, morosely reworking his sketches. (No doubt of Rafael sporting a hangman's noose!)

Mere earthly pontiffery aside and wanting to be remembered for his directly 'Divine' artistic gifts, Michelangelo took and methodically burned all of his drawings, which must have taken some doing to destroy over twenty thousand of them over some time. He did an average of over one hundred sketches for every figure completed. Today, even a small sketch by this master would easily fetch a royal ransom.

Mere divinity aside, it is rather doubtful this man even thought to any extent of his genius being in the totality of his talents. In medieval culture, not placing any value on the concept of originality, the term wouldn't become novel for another three hundred years.

Not that visually small was anywhere even near onto shadow of this Italian visionary's ken. Even his avowed non-talent, painting, both the Sistine Chapel and "The Last Judgment" contain hundreds of figures, and to add layered puzzle, the ceiling is a curved surface, needing additional perspective allowance.

The figures of Christ and Mother Mary on the chapel wall, for instance, had to be rendered in gargantuan size, owing to their further distance from the viewer.

Questions of dimensions aside, even from the length way up a far wall, we are treated to this particular artist's superior understanding of human emotion, like opera, effortlessly transcending all bounds of language: almost three decades after the Sistine Chapel, and before casting his final say over humanity itself, the now vengeful Christ is seen to dramatically turn away, even from his own mother's plea-filled entreaties on behalf of those souls in the balance, somewhere betwixt heaven and hell, which, after all is said and done, is our imprisoned *Homo Erectile* experience, no?

In an astounding show of artistic might and humane largesse, at over seventy, the indomitable maestro took to rebuilding no less than the gargantuan Saint Peter's Basilica itself, volunteering his architectural surveys gratis, free of charge, in the hopes of absolving his earthly soul, recreating the grand temple in the name of the original holder of both keys to the basilica and the Pearly Gates, although scraggly beard and matching fashionable footwear would grant Michelangelo easy access!

Unless, of course, said mass-o-facial hair was a ruse to get by a nosy pope and a prophet or two and all the while attempting to bargain St. Peter at the gates, key to the Eternal City's church for a turn past earthen bonds, for wings of his own.

Whatever the posthumous guise, well soul-bargained with demonic impresarios, this would prove to be, for the artist spent almost twenty of his final years struggling at Vatican City with poor workmanship and corruption in building materials.

Now nigh on to ninety years of non-stop fatigue, with many monuments of the Arts to bolster his legacy, the only thing that killed this great man was falling off a horse and catching pneumonia to boot!

Upon his death, the Church sealed off his apartments and made it a point to count the money in his bedroom.

One chest alone contained in today's currency some $275 million in gold, well over what The Beatles made in their entire touring career!

And finally, a tribute like no other:

> *The effect of the capital works of Michael Angelo*
> *perfectly corresponds to what Bouchardon said*
> *he felt from reading Homer;*
>
> *"His whole frame appeared to be enlarged,*
> *and all nature*
> *which surrounds him,*
> *diminished into atoms."*
>
> —*Sir Joshua Reynolds,*
> *Discourse on Painting and the Fine Arts, 1778*

Indeed, in Michelangelo, as in no other, we can trace a direct Humanist awakening from medieval slumber, first from the Romans, then all the way back to Grecian antiquity, beginning, innocently enough, from a simple feisty replica of a sleeping cupid.

Artist as Thug—Caravaggio

With mayhap only Conan the Barbarian for kindred spirit,
sword in hand, this knavish rogue strode Roman streets,
seeking out mayhem.

AMONGST A GALAXY of Renaissance, Mannerism, and beyond, certain ones would bid for more of your attention. Given the vast store of influences possible, I gravitated to Michelangelo, of course, Bernini, and yet another Michelangelo—Michelangelo Merisi da Caravaggio (1571–1610)—the Baroque painter whose realism and dramatic use of lighting gave forth chiaroscuro, bright to dark with no intermediate value between.

So apt, too, that his villainous conceits would naturally morph their way into a visually darker measure. Yet again, his particular spark of genius sought a newer and more exciting form of realism from what he saw as sour, bucolic Mannerism.

Oh, how we each, in our way, seek to out-tread even the worn and naked paths before us.

In a medieval world of earth-shattering events, with even an ambitious pope riding at the head of a Vatican army, Caravaggio's was especially marked and matched with the same drama he chose to portray.

Others settled for depicting a violent world. Caravaggio lived it.

When not forced to work simply to survive, a typical day had him going from one sporting event to the next, sword and armed bodyguard at the ready, seeking combat and creating mayhem, even at home. True or not, it was said over time he was guilty of six murders most cruel.

In a time, too, of being a favourite of those in papal power for commissions, it was tempting to overplay artistic sport a bit, given free rein for subjects as models, often with religious themes.

For the artist in me, it was his way of simply picking ordinary citizens right off the street for his portrayals of otherwise biblical and divine scenes he was to do. For the first time, you would see these characters as they really were, with dirty, soiled feet, and scraggly beards, especially and subtly festooned on women he despised.

Caravaggio also packed a personal life of violence and heroic paintings thereof into his short thirty-eight years, including torture by lashings, a whipping in a Roman prison he escaped from, and a number of other cases of serious attempts on his life and having to flee town for his safety.

Yet for all these adventures, it may have been simply a lowly but lethal malarial fly that brought him to his fated end in seaside Tuscany on his way to receive yet another official and timely church pardon from a death warrant for murder. It did not help that it involved the slaying of a police officer.

Though his death for the most part is shrouded in mystery, one account has him being found by some monks, dying on a lonely stretch of beach north of his adopted home in Rome, still reaching for questionable freedom.

Then again, with this artist's grim past, and as is suggested in director Paolo Pasolini's 1975 film, it may have been a murder most foul by other brigands he entrusted. Only the sand below his body knows the true grain of it. His favoured smiting hand in a death-grip on the hilt of his blade, crabs and lobsters furtively scurried to shaded palmy fronds nearby.

. . . and a final filial, though edgy venal blast from forlorn Conan: "CROM! I was just getting' some jist an jest of Ol' Carav!"

Either way, poor Caravaggio was buried in a humble monastery nearby. What struck me as an artist was to learn that he was such a great draughtsman that he painted, as I do, directly onto his canvas without the aid of a guide first worked in.

Michelangelo Merisi da Caravaggio's art went on to influence no less than Bernini.

"Ribera, Vermeer, Georges de la Tour,
Rembrandt could never have existed without him.
And the art of Delacroix, Courbet, and Manet
would have been utterly different."

—*Roberto Longhi, Italian Art Historian (1890–1970)*

Judith Beheading Holofernes

My depiction of Judith beheading Holofernes

A S WITH MANY of Italian painter Michelangelo Merisi da Caravaggio's paintings, this one is particularly gruesome, clearly showing the brave Jewish widow, Judith, in the act of killing General Holofernes to save her people.

But once you get past the great gush of bright red blood shooting out of the surprised general's throat, you begin to appreciate this one artist's sheer and undoubted command of human emotion.

His Judith especially shows deep psychological insight into both her determination to do the grisly task at hand and her revulsion for the man she must kill.

Too, her maid Ambia, standing eagerly ready, holding a sack for the hapless general's head, shows a manic delight in these midnight proceedings. As were many major works of the Renaissance times, this one was no doubt started, with a royal model, Roman courtesan Fillide Melandroni for Judith.

In a violent age, there was also the public execution of Beatrice Cenci, a few years before, as a gruesome reference. After a life of derring-do and outright murder, the artist Caravaggio died at only thirty-eight but is remembered for a lasting legacy of drama and visual mastery.

Right about the time I began writing this book, I also took to doing a sketch or two each day, one of which is included here.

From my drawing classes at the Ontario College of Arts and Design University some years before, I recalled one teacher, Peter Mah, saying that he started the practice of doing this some forty years before and continued. (His was a curious blend of bloods, of Chinese and some Mongolian horse people, I believe.) I too found this daily sketching a good way to compare my progress as a visual artist, doing the same image a time or two further down the line and having a look at the two.

It also brings a smile, a story Peter told us about staying late to sketch at some church in Europe. By the time he was done and was aware of the failing light of day, he also realized, to his horror, that he had been locked inside the holy building!

It took him some time, banging on the windows, to get someone's attention to call a priest, who finally let him out.

He didn't say if that act of kindness prompted him to drop a coin or two into the collection box to the side.

Whirling Dervishes in Firenze

The planets spun; Sun immobile in their midst

ONE OF THE MORE interesting people I met in Florence, Italy, was Giulia Scarpa. She also turned out to be a Sun Dancer who went abroad from Italy for the annual traditional cultural events in North America. When she mentioned a group of dancers all the way from the home of the Whirling Dervishes in ancient Persia in early 2010, I jumped at the chance to go along with her, not to spin a measure, mind you, but just to be there.

Before the actual dance began, an announcer explained its significance. What we would be witnessing was a representation of the universe, no less, with each dancer in turn one of the celestial worlds, revolving, at first slowly and picking up tempo around one man all in black, the Sun. The dancers maintain their balance by tilting their heads to one side, or else they would surely lose their balance at such increasing speed. One hand is held aloft to gather spiritual energy from the heavens, passing through their meditative body and bestowed to us below with a drooped hand. A conelike hat is meant to be a tombstone.

The music of stringed instruments, drums, and flutes pick up tempo with the sublime regal movements, to tread so bold progress to the divine within, heightened by verses by Sufi poet Rumi.

The Sufi religion is still banned and harassed today in some countries for its more humane approach to the Muslim faith.

Of course, we were spellbound by this performance, and I, to the point of doing a painting based on what I had been lucky enough to have been invited to.

Ghost Beads

He was rushing to catch up.

WITH OLDER BROTHER 'Antone' on his way back North, Kelleroy just wanted to go ahead and leave me something. He was all out of breath by the time he was at the open door to the family van taking me away from our two-storey Hogan up on the little rise, about twenty miles out of the Arizona tourist town of Page.

"Here," he panted, "this here necklace is for you—for making us them . . . bows and arrows . . . an' for taking us out to catch rabbits. All of it." In his one outstretched hand, he held a curious-looking string of organic dull brown beads. When I asked what they were, he simply said, "These here are Ghost Beads . . . for you, brother. Just put 'em on if you cain't get the good sleep."

With that I thanked him kindly and put them away

Later in that summer of the mid-1990s, my ol' hunting pal Joe Martin and I were taking one of my lifetime friends my Arts mentor Diane Pugen and one lady she brought along, to the site of an Annual Spiritual Pilgrimage to Desnethche, near Fort Reliance, way over the Tu Nedhe, Great Slave Lake, from Somba K'e, Yellowknife.

Our boat trip on this big lake was very long and tiring.

We had to camp on the way at Lutsel K'e to resupply and check in on other people bound for the place of T'seku Dawedah, Woman Sitting

Up There, where there is said to be the Person of the Lady at the Falls.

When we finally got to the site at the mouth of the Lockhart River, we were exhausted, having had to unload and replace the entire boat-load over a portage. We still had to set up camp in the early morning, and I thought for sure I would have a bad dream or two after all that.

Just then, I thought of the Ghost Bead necklace my younger brother Kelleroy Zahne gave me way back when.

Not thinking more of it, I found it and put it on.

As I drifted off to rocky sleep from the continuous waves of the past three days, I was greeted by all of these Disney cartoon characters: Mickey and Minnie Mouse, Daffy and Donald Duck, Porky the Pig, Pluto and all the rest merrily dancing in a jolly circle, all their arms waving in greeting, making for some welcome and joyous greeting indeed!

I have used this Ghost Bead necklace since, and certainly every time, I think I will dream of my exes!

A Clear Mind in Rocky Boy

You always get the best, just dropping in.

ON ONE OF MY FIRST annual trips down to the American Southwest in the early 1990s, I happened to stop in Rocky Boy's Chippewa/Cree Reservation, north-central Montana. I had heard quite a number of people talking about the place, and besides, I only intended to stay for a couple of days and move on down from there.

But these Chippewa/Cree have their ways, and my host, Earl Arkinson, brought me to a Sweat Lodge Ceremony they were having. One of the first people I met there was Theron Small, who everyone just called Doggie because he liked following you around. As any ambitious young man would, he asked me if there were any good-looking women where I came from, in the Far North "way over by Alaska," as he put it.

"Yeah, man," I answered, "but you need to know how to handle three things before they wanna meet you."

"Oh? You don't say. What's that?"

"You have to know your way around a knife, an axe, and a gun."

"Well, y'know, bro, funny you should mention just those three . . ."

(Here I knew something was fishy, Indian style)

"'Round these here parts, ain't no one better with a knife. I can skin and take apart anything needs killing, and I can shoot whatever be moving out there, with any kind of gun you give me to go and hunt stuff with. Why I'm known as Grizzly Adams hisself in these parts!

"And besides that, here in Rocky Boy and in other places, they been takin' to calling me da Chippewa/Cree Paul Bunyan, on account of I know my way around an axe and any piece of lumber or timber!"

Well, needless to say, this went on for some time between the two of us total strangers before we were called in for the second 'round' of the Sweat Lodge. When we got all settled back in, the covers were pulled shut, and the Elder, Ol' Tom Arkinson, Earl's father, who was running this 'inaugural', first Sweat, said he had himself a few words to say before we got started up again. His deep-chested, gravelly voice is what made people want him to be in charge. His gruff ways belied a military past.

"Okay, guys, men, I wanna clear up a few things I got in mind right now. We's in here to have what I call a Clear Mind; a Clear Mind in Rocky Boy. I don't want no messin' 'round here in God's House, and especially none of that loose talk I know someone's been doin' 'round this Sweat!

"Take fer instance, I heard me the name of Grizzly Adams. Now, who in the Hell is *that?*" Someone pointed out to the old man that it was just Doggie bragging to a new visitor.

"Well, y'know," Ol' Tom took on up again, "we here Cree people we surely do love our kinfolk, relatives, and visitors. But I gotta tell y'all once again, and this time's for real. We are here for a Clear Mind . . . a *Clear Mind* in Rocky Boy . . . an' none of us here know no Grizzly Adams! Man's crazy enough anyway! And Doggie, I know you are 'round in here, somewhere, sniggerin' to yerself. You cut that out right now!

"We are here to pray to Almighty God for a Clear Mind, and no more of the Grizzly Adams talk 'round this here Sweat House!"

Such was my Grand Introduction to a Clear Mind
in Rocky Boy's Chippewa/Cree Reservation!

I also knew right then that I wanted to stay for the rest of that winter, which I did, and in the company of Ol' Tom Arkinson himself.

Magic Bilagaanaa Wand

A BELAGAANA, White man, music teacher in Navajo Country had been with his class for a few months. One day, he told his class of Dineh students that they now knew enough about his kind of music to play some, but it wasn't really fair because he didn't know much about them or their culture.

"If there is something cultural going on amongst your people, I'd like to know about it," he said.

One of the pupils said that, yes, there was going to be a ceremony of the Native American Church right that weekend, and if he so chose, he was welcome to attend.

"Is there something I can bring?" the music instructor asked.

He was told that there would be food, so he could help out with that, if he wanted. Come the night of the Thank You Meeting, it was a joyous occasion, with the water drum (an old-fashioned type, with a hide strung over) really going ninety and the people in the teepee in a singing mood, chanting along with every set of songs.

The teacher himself was in fine form and was so moved by all the rocking sounds that he took out his little conducting baton and got busy directing what he thought to be a First Nations version of an orchestra!.

At the very end of the all-night event, the Roadman, the equivalent of a priest, told the congregation that they were now free to go "but not to wander off too far" because there would be food served in a bit.

As the music teacher stepped to the front of the now open teepee door, he chanced to see a sheep corral in the distance, with the animals milling around, making hungry sounds.

The Belagaanaa man thought, *As a holy man, I must tend to my flock.*

With such thoughts of messianic concern, he stepped into the sheep enclosure, let himself in the gate, got down on all fours and slowly worked his way to the puzzled goats, ewes, and lambs, doing his best to blend in and make like one of them.

His "baah-AH-ahing" all went for naught, as his flock got all bunched up from what they must have surely thought to be a crazy man coming at them with questionable intent.

As he got close enough to make his final pleas, a pair of legs of one of his students told him that he should have listened when told not to wander off too far from the rest of the gang and that it was now time to eat anyway.

Galileo—Science on Trial

Eppur si muove . . . "and yet it moves," was written on the walls of the dungeon where Italian astronomer and philosopher Galileo Galilei (1564–1642) was summarily cast by the Inquisition. This is in reference to his continued strongly held belief in heliocentrism, which is that the Earth was not flat, as the Roman Catholic Church's Vatican made into formal doctrine, and more, the Earth revolved around the Sun, and that mankind was not at the centre of the universe, ruling over all he should survey. And convert!

Before universities made knowledge part of our everyday musings, the Roman Catholic Church had a firm grasp on all information, largely used to control the ignorant masses. Even Europe's universities limited themselves to ancient texts from the time of Aristotle, some two thousand years before. If that wasn't bad enough, there was a marked tendency for these places of learning and the Church to interpret the works of the ancient Greeks to their own purposes, just as the Church still does with the words of Jesus Christ.

Like Copernicus before him and peer Englishman Francis Bacon, the Renaissance's Galileo faced a sea of doubters during what amounted to a scientific revolution.

Unlike Aristotle's set and immovable body of knowledge, these free thinkers insisted on conclusions reached from personal experience and experimenting to reach conclusions from nature. Strangely enough, it was actually an epiphany of balls, falling balls—hailstones—that made Galileo begin to question Aristotle's original claim that it was the weight of an object that determined its rate of falling; that is, those heavier balls arrived first from the heavens.

Thus, it remained to nature to prove whose balls held the most weight: Galileo's or the Greek's, scientifically speaking, of course. After some concerted effort, of knitted brow and properly aligned sight, the Italian won out, holding, if you will . . .

Great Balls of Knowledge!

O NE CAN BEGIN to realize what this use of Reason could mean in the name of Freedom. For instance in a court of law, the role a witness plays in answering questions put forth. And, of course, in the fundamental idea that given free rein and a bit of training, the human mind itself can be made to comprehend everything in the universe.

No doubt now that the age of Humanism was over, this simple and fundamental stand away from fundamental Christian dogma and institutional format put Galileo the 'revolutionary' at grave odds with the Roman Catholic Church, which even to this day relies on what apostles and others understand of what their founder Jesus himself said.

The ultimate idea that the Earth stood still, with Man, in the form of the Roman Catholic Pope at its very head, was now up for question. Like a modern-day Moses, Galileo stood at these very imposing ramparts, alone to challenge doctrinal equation, ready to part a celestial sea of ignorance, and let flow . . .

Pure Waters of Reason

A FTER A DECADE of struggle and with some of his work having gone public, Galileo finally appeared before a salivating Roman Inquisition. Failing to recant and take back his carefully controlled scientific findings he was found "vehemently suspect of heresy" and spent the last nine years of his life under strict house arrest. This Father of Scientific Reason died at seventy-seven.

One more note that should be made is that as a lifelong and devoutly religious Roman Catholic, Galileo teaches us that it is the duty of a rebel to ask, yea, demand ethical answers to set the world to its rightful and heavenly order. In a stilted time, as a discerning scientist, he had indeed dug his own grave and with in-depth research that put him at educated odds with even his own religious beliefs.

For its part, the Church saw fit to involve itself in a biblical *Star Wars* of its own making, outright claiming spiritual dominion over the heavens. All this at a time when the most advanced 'telescope' to study all the above consisted of two handheld centre-rolls from toilet paper, with a studious . . . "Ah, okay, Uranus, over to the left . . . jes . . . a . . . bit."

Followed by, "Holy Crap!"

To put a little counter-spin to these proceedings, were he alive at the time, the Godfather of Soul, James Brown, could've enlightened ol' Galileo on a Thang or Two about the Laws of Motion, step for step! I can just picture that ol' Italian scientist sashaying up to the guys with the glowing tongs, resplendent robes a-flowin', goin'—

"Hiy! Hiy! Ain't no drag, y'all.
Papa's gotta Brand New Bag!
Brotha James sent Meh! Hurt MeH!"

As it was, Galileo Galilei was buried at the Basilica of Santa Croce in Florence, Italy, the middle finger of his right hand on exhibit at the Museo Galileo, forever giving the finger to a stupid world.

All jest aside, the world of knowledge, paradigms, owes some serious debt to these giants, Galileo, Copernicus, and Newton, for putting the lie to all the former Laws of Absolutes. No doubt others and especially Einstein, made the connection between scientific curiosity and stellar imagination as the very spearpoint of knowledge.

They have fair braved the way to what we now have before us:

Indigenous Knowledge!

From Lascaux to the Sistine

Both are a cave-like presence

THE STORY BEGINS in 1940 with a French teen's dog having fallen through a hole. When Marcel Ravidat returned with two friends, they discovered to their wonder what eventually turned out to be a total of some six hundred cave drawings and paintings! The hapless dog had fallen over a past of 17,000 years to a time when cave-people dwelt amidst shaggy prehistoric bison.

Even the wisest of sages fail to fathom these eons in dog years! Suffice it to wager that the best guess would be to such records being dog-eared up to the neck of historical recall. At present, the curious creatures masterfully fair festoon their underground sanctuary, along with a variety of horses and deer. Of equal grandeur are those rendered on the Sistine Chapel by the sublime Italian Michelangelo, over 400 years earlier. To be certain, the thousands of years separating the two represent leap years of artistic effort, drawing close in themes of culture and community.

Some binding the two had to do with an intimate knowledge of their relative ways of life. For its reaffirmation of humanity there is no doubt that the animals depicted in the French caves were those familiar to the people who left their marks.

Michelangelo's work is largely regarded as a benchmark of all the artistic in us. As a devout Roman Catholic, he also drew on his memory of sitting at his early Medici benefactor's table, listening as experts held forth on religious doctrine. In fact, when the Pope assigned a group of Vatican theologians to draft out a workable method for the artist to go from, he summarily fired all of them choosing to forge his own way.

The fiery bombast went even further, choosing to rid his workspace of all the artistic associates he had handpicked to work on the painted ceiling. And this at a time when you had to grind your colours yourself.

As a singular work of art, both the Sistine Chapel itself and the altar wall, which took several years longer to do, is testament to what the energy of a single man is capable of.

For instance, the physical act of the work itself, painting whilst standing on a rickety support, leaning so far back that his paints spattered all, face, beard and body, must surely have an excruciating physical exercise, aside from the creative process itself!

Having produced quite a number of murals myself, the visual guide would have been impossible to do, in Michelangelo's case, with any workable viewpoint blocked by the scaffolding for the work itself.

In his time, though, individual artists rarely got the recognition they deserved. In fact, there is only one major work he himself signed, the *Pietà* and this because of a public argument he overheard of who exactly did the magnificent statue.

Teens who were found to have enough talent signed on with an established master who saw to their professional training. This, of course speaks to the fact that there were set groups of masters with their apprentices for patrons like the Church to go to for what needed doing.

On the other hand, individual cavepeople some thousands of years ago, like at Lascaux, probably well saw themselves as simply wanting to leave a mark for future generations that this was the work of a human, who had both the time to hunt for the group and to make representations of their achievements, beyond mere survival.

Whilst the Italian master struggled to keep his paints out of a scraggly beard, the earlier cavemen no doubt had little choice but to hearken to the hungry howls of wolves they had outsmarted on the hunt!

All considered though, what is left to us is that culture and community can be seen as both an individual and group effort.

A Life Stranger than Fiction

J. D. Salinger's Holden Caulfield struck a chord in a generation

THE POWERLESS AND ISOLATED student was one many of us felt to be, trying to make sense of the sixties times we were caught up in. When *The Catcher in the Rye* was first published in the early fifties, little did I know that in many ways, it would come to define me, both as an artist and a First Nations person. There was no doubt that this masterpiece would also leave many wondering about the strange disappearance of its author, J. D. Salinger.

Perhaps it was being born rich and well-educated that he eventually turned away from it all, choosing instead military school, where he first began to put his talents to writing. Unlike many who did the same, he drew much of his inspiration from real life, being there at D-Day, storming the beaches at Normandy, and for a total of almost a year, in combat. Salinger also met his hero Ernest Hemingway, who turned out to be a literary peer.

One reason why I would identify with this one author is that as an artist, he was always true to his nature, even going so far as marrying a German Nazi when the army expressly forbade it. It turned out to be an impossible situation for his Jewish family back in New York, and they were divorced after only a month back stateside USA. Salinger remarried in 1955 but was such a recluse, even at home in Cornish, New Hampshire, that this bond also ended in divorce.

He did make various attempts at publishing his reported prolific output, namely in *Franny and Zooey* (1960) but had to contend with some rather severe criticism, not the least being that he was too "engrossed in his own image", "too much philosophy," and just a plain ol' 'crackpot'. His estranged wife noted him to live in a 'fantasy of innocence', the characters in his books being more real than life to this strange person.

Many now believe that the cliff he famously guards is one of adult-hood, a Peter Pan with a magic quill to hand. Salinger's last published work was in 1965 but would inspire the Hippies of the sixties and seventies. In a very real way, the famous author's shunning a well-deserved public life mirrored the way we dropouts viewed our contribution to society, a way of survival when you really think about it.

Catcher in the Rye gained him some notoriety, having been found at the scene of the crime when Mark David Chapman shot Beatles legend John Lennon to death in New York City. It was again quoted by John Hinckley for his sole reason for almost killing then-President Ronald Reagan. All drama aside, there are elements of this man's life that strike particularly close to home. His obvious signs of Post-Traumatic Stress Disorder (PTSD) from a time at war and an avowed professional life writing for himself are at least two traits that make him a like Spirit in a parallel universe we share. The virtual shot-in-the dark of his one best-seller, *The Catcher in the Rye,* reminds me of my lifetime of writing and only now, after retirement, looking to publish my own book.

Then again, my First Nations roots are basically an oral one, with an almost aversion to seeing our life in print. *The Catcher in the Rye* still proves to be a standout, though, with some sixty million copies sold and a quarter of a million a year yet. Sadly, J. D. Salinger took all his lifetime of writing with him, along with the slight hope that we will see some of it finally, after his passing in 2010.

PART TWO

A MONTH OF

BLUE MONDAYS

SUN Calling

To stand alone before one's Father takes a long road, full of twists and turns, and back to that one, early dawn, a dozen years back now, waking up on the side of that forlorn stretch of road with no memory of even a recent past. The strangers came along with at least some food and a worn sense of direction. Each time Sun shone was a memory from that start.

Even the most clouded of days
Now brought at least its silvery lining.
And always now back to the light, of yon and distant
Yes, reach. Reach

With every straining hope, for a day, now never out of touch.
. . . and leave behind. Thin veils

Shrouds, from distant Turin.
To reformed gossamer wings.

Yet each step, somehow, like that of the condemned.
Tradition
Yet holds an idyll,
Out of humane
And ethical reach.

"A Good Day to DIE!"

*I felt like one of the thirty-eight Santee Sioux men
standing at the scaffold,
waiting to be hanged the day after Christmas, December 26, 1862
by Lincoln's Presidential Order, at Mankato, Minnesota.*

A T A HEARING of the Federal Court of the Government of Canada, I brought forth my case for severe abuses suffered in residential schools. Rather than having to swear on the Bible, I asked a Nishnawbe Elder to come in and do a Sweetgrass Ceremony, after which I assured the Crown's judge and lawyers that I was now sworn to tell the truth and nothing but the truth.

Over the day it took, we went all the way back to when I was continually strapped and punished for daring to speak my own Dene language and all the time being severely abused. At the very end of the long day, I quoted a First Nations warrior who said words to the effect:

We were never afraid of your guns, nor your bullets.
We have but one life to give.
We were most afraid of the one who would not tell the truth.

The "Good Day to Die" was uttered by Ponca statesman, Chief Standing Bear (1829–1908), explaining that every day in the service of the people is a good day to meet one's Maker. In its true form, the Good Day to Die is not a defeatist way of seeing being. More, it serves to address the very purpose of life itself.

Chief Standing Bear was made to suffer through a degrading civil rights trial to find out whether he was a 'person' or not. At the end of the trial, the Judge asked the Chief to make a statement in his defence. The Chief's words were solemnly delivered:

"That hand is not the color of yours, but if I prick it, the blood will flow, and I shall feel pain. The blood is of the same color as yours. God made me, and I am a man." Judge Elmer S. Dundy ruled in Chief Standing Bear's favour on May 12, 1879, at Fort Omaha. That landmark ruling set the legal precedent that "an Indian is a person" under the law and entitled to its rights and protection.

As a lifelong student of history and especially that of my own Native Americans, I am always of the mind that being so close to nature went a long way to make us natural actors of life itself, able to expound on the essentials of the soul.

Buffalo Dreamer

The Look comes at you from over the Ages

IN AN UNCERTAIN TIME, when the Plains Indians' food source may well have taken another migration route, the people had to make every insurance to have fate lend a helping hand. Thus, the Buffalo Dreamer would be implored to make medicine, to know where Tatanka might be found.

In the late seventies, when I was invited to a number of showings with Norval Morrisseau and the Nishnawbe Group of Seven, these were the kinds of work I had to offer. My work then was much more graphic, with larger blocks of colour, more static, structurally.

We did so well that the rest of the students at our alternative Art's Sake art school took to calling me and my fellow tribesman John Turo "the Bank." Little did we know that with all the ready money to be had, coupled with an accumulation of swallowed and held-down abuses beginning with the residential school, also clearly had us set for a downward spiral.

One definite stabilizing force was the social scene we were still a part of, with the likes of Jimmy Dick, Vernon Harper, Duke Redbird, and Gordon Six Pipes, who always somehow knew what we needed to do to raise our voices in a positive way.

From too, the heart of this story, the old man offering his corn pollen to the Morning Star is a kind of seer. Even though he, as a Medicine Man, would often discern the cause of a specific illness, as an ordinary man, he too, like the rest of us, had a life to live. Without a pass, if you will, for a guaranteed full life, he had to deal with things that just happened the way they did.

One tradition that did follow was that his own son could now claim the honour of being a war veteran himself, having served two terms of enlistment in the United States Army with an honourable discharge.

As part of an upcoming end-of-army-contract ceremonial, he had to get a buffalo hide. After going through a purification procedure, it was stored in the Hogan.

The old man immediately noticed a change in his dream patterns that now came along a number of gruesome ones. Something was charging into his normal lazy presence, forcing him to take note that all was not well. Once acknowledged as the boss' though, the hide took on a more protective role, the veteran's visitations from the other world more pleasant.

So strange, thought he, *that something at first so forcefully 'removed' from modern times, at first cold to the touch, would, with care, assume it's normal place in a reconciled home.*

Even a newer attention to detail came at rest within,
As a vital ceremonial tool.

Spirit of Tatanka says, You mortal
Ask for your son,
But what are you willing to give
Of Yourself'

Yet, though, when he resigned himself to have 'Come Home', of one dream in particular he did take note:He rode out on a buffalo hunt with all of his former hunting buddies and members of his army platoon, whooping for joy as their runners, horses trained to dodge the dangerous horns of their prey, darted in and out amongst the mass of meat.

After all of the butchering was done and the people came to share in the hunt, after the feasting and dancing, his very best friend took him to his lodge. For a time, they recalled past times and what the future might bring, marriage and children. Now his friend said that he had to go and rest, sleep, and that he could just stay as long as he wanted.

The distant haunting sound of a passing train woke him. Upon waking, he also thought of his long hair, how he was taught that the Holy People placed a "power" within, which surely pulled him out of that long jungle rainy battle.

It then came as no surprise when he heard of a special military project. Some soldier scouts were allowed to keep their long hair, serving as excellent scouts and helping in the survival of fellow troops under their watch.

When questioned the Indigenous Elders back on the reservations on their reservations said that the warrior's long hair acted as a sensor, a sixth sense, to let them know of any danger close.

For all of it, what had served the old veteran well in times of deepest stress, always awake to terrors at hand, now left the doors to even an everyday life a bit too open.

What had imperceptibly changed over time was definitely away from his discharge from the army. Then, though, especially, the PTSD molded him into a stranger even onto himself, or at least what he could recall of a freer childhood.

The new life at home was now even more foreign than the devil he knew, one in which he knew what was expected of him.

Somehow, too, these Buffalo Dreams were at least a way for him to reconcile with an earlier reality, when his people lived in the same place, yes, but a more familiar normalcy.

For the time being, all he knew for sure was that these early morning offerings to the Morning Star had something to do with his daily life and that the blessings offered to the world by the Holy Ones, often in the form of stories, had something to do with his return.

In its way, this also brought a strange reason.

Buffy's Wisdoms

Now if I were the queen of all the world
I would go in chains just to see you free
Of the ropes that bind you, And the role you play
And the pride that hooks you, While the big ones get away

—Buffy Sainte-Marie, from "The Big Ones Get Away,"
Coincidence and Other Stories (EMI Europe, 1992).

BUFFY SAINTE-MARIE, more than most, was made to pay her dues for being an artist in the true sense of the word, the price of truth in a statement of position.

From the late sixties on, with her unflinching "Universal Soldier" she was pushed to the side in favour of more palatable entertainers, much in the way many others of our socially conscious era were sidelined—the Muhammad Alis, the Malcolm Xs, the Mandelas.

She always continued to set the bar very high for any thinking person, First Nations or not, to sift through and simply try to read at the level intended.

Her music touched you the way only experience can. Her songs, both haunting and poignant, grew on you from within.

In her album of the early nineties, *Coincidence and Likely Stories*, for instance, she revisits the plight of the American Indian Movement (AIM) activist Leonard Peltier, then going on two decades of very likely wrongful conviction and imprisonment, while "The Big Ones Get Away."

In terms of paradigms and what former spokesperson for AIM, John Trudell, had to say about the imprisoned political prisoner—who may never, ever, be set free in our lifetime—her words bear some scrutiny.

Activism or any kind of an ideal that spawns it often comes with some very human frailties attached. For instance, members of the SDS, Visionary Michael Albert, author of *Remembering Tomorrow: From the Politics of Opposition To What We Are For,* said that Students for a Democratic Society, would go out from the cities to learn to shoot at tin cans. To brace themselves for coming hard times, they would intentionally cut themselves to learn to suture and stitch up wounds.

At the end, when three members of the Weatherman Underground

"Buffy's Wisdoms"

accidentally blew themselves up in the early seventies trying to construct bombs to make their political point, we see the price of these kinds of attempts to reach out to a deaf, dumb, and blind public.

In gauging these temperatures, in the chapter, The Action Faction, about this faction of the sixties unrest, Michael Albert, from *Remembering Tomorrow*, wrote, "As I look back at it, many of the best minds and hearts of my generation got caught up in spirals of anger that took them far from relevance. Revolution is not a tea party." In that chapter, Albert quoted Dickens:

> *It was the best of times, it was the worst of times, it was the age of wisdom, it was the age of foolishness, it was the epoch of belief, it was the epoch of incredulity, it was the season of light, it was the season of darkness, it was the spring of hope. it was the winter of despair.*

—Charles Dickens, *A Tale of Two Cities*

In a very real way, revolutionaries often forego the technical disciplines necessary to be effective in terms of the end result. The rage and anger necessary, as Buffy Sainte-Marie puts it in her song, for "the role you play, and the pride that hooks you," leaves little room to be effective, "while the big ones get away."

What John Trudell is getting at with a seemingly pessimistic and doomed view is that along with being concerned enough to act out our beliefs, we also have to accept the fact that the change we have in mind is not going to happen in our lifetime, and for very good reason. It is already a very real part of human and evolutionary destiny that there has to be a series of sacrifices on the Altar of the Times in order to make it all come about, which is the real value of these songs for Freedom.

They serve as guideposts along the way, no more, and certainly no less. History, then, is no less than the tide going out, leaving us reminders of what took place, and coming back in, with another episode. Much of this book makes direct reference to the sixties and seventies, for very good reason. To a very great extent, these were interesting times, largely missing now from our detached, homogenized modern lives.

And it just didn't all happen in song nor some distant country. We had close personal friends who could not resist but take the easy way out, starting out as leaders "to the bitter end" but along the way found a way out to pay the bills and just never came on back to our original purpose, which is to work for the People. Of course, as with all things human, the same kind of history has its way of carrying on.

One of the most blatant miscarriages of justice in Canada was the 2016 murder of young Colten Boushie in Saskatchewan. Among all the blaring and wilful ignorance of the facts and evidence, a close *Mola*, a white friend, Leora Harlingten, sadly remarked that at the trial for the supposed wronged farmer, Gerald Stanley, there was clearly a racial divide: whites on one side and the Indigenous people on the other.

The court workers made every attempt to keep that clear separation in place, but the Boushie family claimed Leora as a relative, allowing her to show close support.

~ While the Big Ones Get Away ~

Our (NWT) TEST Ski Team!

Top row L-R, Coach Father Mochet, John Turo, me,
Coach Dave Sutherland, Gloria Allen and Harold Cook.
Bottom row L-R, Fred the Kelly-Express, Margaret Steen, John Ross,
Eva and Janette Tourangeau.

Pictures bring back a lot of memories. To represent the North as we did, for the first-ever Canada Winter Games, winter of 1967, we had to go out in the freezing minus 30–40 weather, almost every day, to train, under the Northern Lights. For me, it was a chance to get away from the soul-wrenching residential school, the notorious Grollier Hall. I know that at least one other member of the team felt the same way.

Our coaches, Father Mouchet and Dave Sutherland were very strict but fair, putting us through our paces, trying to let us know early on what to expect. Because we trained in such low temperatures, we weren't used to what we thought of as balmy weather when we raced in the 'outside', the South. People there could not believe it when we took part in the gruelling cross-country runs in our t-shirts!

Of the nine athletes pictured here, four are from my hometown of Radelie Koe, Fort Good Hope. To this day, our local athletes are superior, often coming back to decorate the high school gym with a growing number of winning banners and new additions to the trophy case. The two Tourangeau girls makes six of nine from the Sahtu, Great Bear Lake

Region. I am third from the left on the top row, with the late John Turo next to me. He was also a well-known artist from the late seventies on.

The one team member I was always the most impressed with though, was John Ross, in the centre of the bottom row. This young man from Fort McPherson just showed up one day, and we didn't see a lot of him in the races. You knew for sure he was at the starting gate, but after that, it was anyone's guess where he might be at. He didn't have a lot of the precise technique required to cover a lot of ground fast, but he had that indomitable Gwich'in heart and determination you just don't see a lot of, anywhere, anytime!

Janette did the best of our team at the Canada Winter Games, putting the North on the sports map. Five, including the Firth Twins, Roseanne Allen and myself, made it all the way to the NWT Sports Hall of Fame, with one coach, Father Mouchet.

This man skied almost every day of his long life. One belief of his which I have always shared is that, in his words, 'Nature is the Church!'

"Here I Stand!"

"I can do no other!" Martin Luther when faced with the might of Pope

A T THE COST of religious groups like the Roman Catholic form of Christianity, of which there are close to thirty, being the only Word of God, we have the story of the original Martin Luther (1483–1546).

This former Augustinian friar first fled the altar upon realizing the immense responsibility of being the person of Christ on Earth at the moment of lifting the holy sacrament. Upon returning to clerical duties as a professor of theology, he began questioning and rejecting several Roman Catholic teachings and practices, one being confession. He decided that it was enough to accept Jesus Christ as one's saviour and not to have to seek heavenly forgiveness for each human wrong committed. At the time, too, the Church was heavily in debt, with the Pope himself riding forth at the head of its own army. The practice of purchasing Indulgences for the forgiveness of sins was created to make it possible for Catholics to buy their way to salvation, along with relatives, even those long dead.

"Saving the Dene in us"
Upper: With Frank and John T'Seleie.
Lower: On the river in winter

Voice in Stone

The child you are,
Turned to Mute,
. . . To the Vacuum

(This balloon, the air,
Somewhere, all gone)

The World out there,
Lifeless, but expectant
of Mirror-Talk

Will not let you
Learn the Real You

Only the mountains,
Akin to Wind,
Know your tongue

Speak in ME, too . .

Untouched by Mere Time: Bernini

Cold, unforgiving marble was butter in the hands of Bernini.

WITHIN THE PRE-EMINENT stone palace of worship, the largest in the entire world, Saint Peter's Basilica in Rome's Vatican City, Gian Lorenzo Bernini's stupendous baldacchino's four massive bronze columns spiral some 30 m (90 ft) to a suspended canopy, eternal guard under the divine Michelangelo's majestic dome, hovering over the tomb of St. Peter, far below.

Not only could this Italian post-Renaissance man humble a viewer, as this church's chief architect, Michelangelo's spacious square directly out front even now regularly and easily, makes room for half a million pilgrims, whilst creating its own spectacle for audiences worldwide. His "Ecstasy of Saint Teresa," begun in the late 1640s, fairly dazzles the very mind's eye, proclaiming a devout heart of faith in all manner godly.

A decidedly gleeful angel of God readies an arrow, yet again, poised to pierce the prostrate Spanish nun, herself in the throes of communion with heavenly forces. The setting, too, displays Bernini's architectural genius for his first-ever combining of the varied Baroque era disciplines of sculpture, architecture, and painting, set as it is in the dark recesses of the Raimondi Chapel in the Church of San Pietro in Montorio, Italy.

From somewhere high above, thin golden shafts miraculously carry light to illumine the two figures caught in action, fairly afloat upon thine supine gaze. Another, "The Damned Soul," portrays the last terrified human expression of a soul about to be cast into the fires of Hades, a look of both utter disbelief and horror at a past forever questioned and a future encased in doom!

Too, this sculptor's "David" is a study of strength held in check . . . a boy about to unleash upon the giant Goliath, grim in determination, power secured. He also left a number of memorable fountains, including the "Fountain of the Four Rivers," designed for Pope Innocent X.

Over his eighty-one years and before passing in 1680, Bernini left a lasting legacy of creative wonders, not the least being "Apollo and Daphne"W, at the very moment she transforms into a tree. Bernini had a distinct knack for capturing the exact most dramatic moment in a sculpture: witness the startled expression on the Greek god Apollo's face when he realizes that the chaste lady he pursues, Daphne, is turning into a laurel tree just as he catches her . . . with her fingers and hair becoming leaves and sides a tree trunk with her feet taking root. It is this timeless, effervescent quality that sparkles so in this master's work.

Buddha

For a number of years, he lived on a single grain of rice a day.

CENTURIES BEFORE the likes of the original Protestant, Martin Luther, was the Indian Mystic. A holy man like Saint Francis after him, the Buddha or Siddhartha, actually came from a rather rich and powerful family, born in present-day Nepal, between 6 and 4 BCE.

He lived his first twenty-nine years as a prince in the household of a chieftain of a tribal confederacy, groomed for such a life and shielded from worldly cares. The man who would become the Enlightened

One even married at sixteen and fathered a son. However, upon seeing real human conditions, illness, and death from his sheltered life, he renounced his material surroundings, taking instead to wandering as a monk, begging for his food as he went.

Now, as a monk, he practised yogic meditation. However, his search for the Truth turned to the point of severe bodily mortification, on the edge of starvation. With the advice of common people, Siddhartha discovered the Middle Way, a path of moderation, between sensual indulgence and the former severe asceticism.

At thirty-five, after six years and still determined to reach his ultimate goal, he vowed not to leave his meditation under the Bodhi Tree, and finally achieved enlightenment, rising after a period of 49 days.

The Nirvana he valiantly strove for would lead to teachings as a sage, leading his followers over many millennia away from ignorance, greed, hatred, and other human afflictions.

For his remaining forty-five years on this earth, the Enlightened One, the Buddha, travelled and taught, and died at eighty.

Of his many sayings, this one:

As the rain falls equally on the just
and the unjust,
Do not burden your heart
with judgments
But rain your kindness
equally on all.

Far from the basically singular East Indian spiritual reach for enlightenment, we in the North, as in most poor countries, were made to somehow survive the sustained onslaught of a narrowed version of the zealous fire and brimstone of the Roman Catholic version of Christian terrorism.

Even today, with this 'faith' having largely failed in its mission of producing priests and nuns, we yet face a major psychic hurdle to overcome over four centuries of psychological abuse.

Depths of Brotherly Love

Soul on ice, he entered the courtroom proceedings
with a satchel full of guns.

I N TODAY'S super e-connected, but humanly disjointed world, I like
to recall the following story when doing student presentations:
In what later became known as the 'Marin County Incident', August
7, 1970, Jonathan Jackson, brother of Black Panther Party member
George Jackson (a Soledad Brother political prisoner at San Quentin
State Prison from across the bay from San Francisco) entered the Marin
County Hall of Justice in the Civic Centre with a number of automatic
guns belonging to activist Angela Davis. In a bid to free his older brother
from San Quentin for his birthday, Jonathan and three prisoners in the
courtroom took Superior Court Judge Harold Haley hostage, looping
a wire attached to a shotgun over his head to ensure his capture. Also
in tow were Deputy District Attorney Gary Thomas and three female
jurors. A shootout ensued in the parking lot as the total of nine—five
as hostages—drove off in a van, Jonathan Jackson at the wheel. After a
brief shootout, four lay dead, including Judge Haley, Jackson, and the
two prison inmate escapees.

In various classroom presentations, I would later recount this true
story as an example of the kinds of events commonplace in the late
sixties and early seventies and to point out the serious commitment to
cause, right or wrong, entirely absent from our present corporate world.

In death, Jonathan Jackson was only seventeen years old, about the
average age of a black panther in the wild.

Noam Chomsky, the People's Champ!

T HE UNUSUAL NAME, in a casual and inspired betting moment, con-
jures up a plodding heavyweight contender tender of foot sure, but
with anvils of steely fists, magnetic to glass jawry. Yet the sports enthusi-
ast would have to be punch drunk or otherwise halfway loopy to ignore
the fact that this single man was voted by *Foreign Policy* magazine in

2005 as the "world's top public intellectual."

As an analytic philosopher/activist Chomsky is mainly associated with his career at MIT, the Massachusetts Institute of Technology, where he began in the late fifties and in a very public forum, of course.

From an early introduction to anarchy, he was influenced by Anarcho-Syndicalist Rudolf Rocker and the better-known English democratic socialist George Orwell of *1984* and *Animal Farm* fame, which continues his widespread influence on popular and political culture to this day.

One of Noam Chomsky's closest associations was his involvement with the New Left in opposition to the Vietnam War, in 1967, for which he was arrested a good number of times. He continued in this vein with his anti-Iraq War stance and as a supporter of the Occupy Movement.

No stranger to controversy, Chomsky was largely misunderstood and paid the price, career-wise. As no other, he continued to see to the very heart of every issue he bravely challenged.

In 1979, he authored two volumes comparing US media reaction to the Cambodian genocide and the Indonesian occupation of East Timor.

Both conflicts resulted in the utter turmoil of bloodshed and outright human injustice. Yet because Pol Pot in Cambodia was an American enemy, it was summarily condemned, while East Timor as an ally was completely ignored in the news.

A film documentary, *Manufacturing Consent: Noam Chomsky and the Media,* is a history of *The New York Times'* coverage of the occupation of East Timor by profit-driven corporate media, furthering the agenda of elite groups in society.

When he chose to defend the freedom of speech and expression of historian Robert Faurisson in his controversial stand, Noam Chomsky was roundly condemned, mistakenly deemed as siding with the Frenchman's Holocaust denial. In its haste to judge, the media simply chose to ignore the fact that this man previously made many one-sided stands for his Jewish people.

As for the impact of people like Noam Chomsky, much of the background for his thinking, for instance the works of Orwell, were required reading in the rebel sixties and seventies, certainly not being available as such in our official schooling. No doubt the lasting appeal of these philosophies harken back to the roots of our communal humanity.

Cops Run Amok

"The Whole World is Watchin', The Whole World is Watchin'!"

A LL EXCEPT for our sleepy little southern NWT high school in the town of Fort Smith. At the squeaky-clean Grandin College, we were being groomed for a Northern elite of sorts, after all.

In the US, the Democratic National Convention was held to replace President Johnson, who had suddenly announced that he would not be seeking nomination or re-election to head the party for a US presidential run. This followed an entire year of intense unrest and violence the country had not seen since the Civil War, a hundred years before.

Well-loved civil rights leader Martin Luther King Jr. had been assassinated in Memphis in April 1968, as was Senator Robert F. Kennedy in June of that year, just after declaring for his run for the leadership of the Democratic Party.

Chicago Mayor Richard J. Daley not only failed to maintain order, but instead brought in 23,000 police and even the National Guard, who wantonly and savagely weighed into outnumbered peaceful demonstrators, running mayhem, swinging on all in sight with billy clubs, teargas, and mace. The police riot was clearly caught and beamed all over the globe, in front of the Hilton Hotel, with crowds chanting "The Whole World is Watching!"

One end result was that the leadership of the National Mobilization to End the War in Vietnam, the Youth International Party (Yippies), Students for a Democratic Society, and even the Black Panther Party, the Chicago Eight were brought to trial for conspiracy and incitement to riot. The Chicago Eight was later called 'The Chicago Seven' when Bobby Seale's case was severed from the others.

Of these, Abbie Hoffman, Jerry Rubin, Bobby Seale, Tom Hayden, David Dellinger, Ronnie Davis, John Froines, and Lee Weiner were sentenced to prison terms of two and a half months to four years.

They were later all released on appeal. The appeal judge ruled there were multiple errors by the trial judge, including never asking potential jurors about their political or cultural beliefs, something that now features prominently in jury selection.

"Attica, Attica, Attica"

Tʜᴇʀᴇ ᴡᴀs no doubt that these were the most volatile times, with sparks for human rights being lit everywhere you cared to look. The Attica prison riots in upstate New York took place on September 9, 1971, for political rights and better living conditions.

This was only a couple of weeks after the killing of Black Panther leader George Jackson at San Quentin State Prison in California and a part of the Prisoner Rights Movement. Almost half of over 2,000 inmates rebelled and seized control of Attica, taking 42 staff members hostage. Authorities agreed with almost thirty demands after tense negotiations over the following four days, except for complete amnesty.

By order of Governor Nelson Rockefeller, police took back control backed by armed state troopers, in the bloody process leaving almost fifty dead, including ten correctional officers and 39 inmates. Contrary to the official story, that all hostages had their throats cut by their prisoner captors, every single one killed, inmates and hostages alike, were shot down by brutal law enforcement. Millions of dollars were eventually paid in restitution. Many people felt that the prisoners at Attica were heroes, martyrs in the struggle for justice.

One other direct response came from the Weathermen, setting off a bomb at a New York Department of Corrections facility, calling out the American prison system, as an example of "how a society run by white racists maintain its control." It also blamed Nelson Rockefeller for not even going to the place himself to resolve matters.

> In the process of regaining our humanity,
> we had to make an effort to know
> what others were going through.

I have never really thought of myself as a political person as such. I slept through most of the all-night group harangues so much a part of sixties and seventies counterculture. Then again, when you are the only red face in a white crowd it soon becomes very clear who 'They' want you to be. The choice then becomes where you want to stand.

The question too, in a book like this, about the Arts and Community is what you have to overcome in order to set it all straight again.

The Weather Underground Organization

"You don't need to be a weatherman to know
which way the wind blows."

This Bob Dylan lyric from his 1965 *Subterranean Homesick Blues* spawned at least the name of the 1969 radical left organization, a faction of Students for a Democratic Society. The goal of this clandestine revolutionary party was no less than the overthrow of the US federal government, in the name of a classless world: communism.

Specifically, in opposition to the Vietnam War and the invasion of Laos, the Weather Underground began with a demonstration at the trial of the Chicago Seven in Chicago, December 8, 1969.

They also began a series of bombings of government buildings and banks in the mid-seventies but took great pains to leave evacuation warnings beforehand to ensure public safety.

One incident that pointed to their incompetence as a strike force was an accidental explosion at a townhouse in Greenwich Village, New York City, March 6, 1970, which killed three of its members.

The appeal, though, of outright revolution sparked the political imagination of many, making even artistic statements, like Jimi Hendrix's, subject to loyalty to a cause, in his case the Black Panthers, an expression of civil rights.

The raison d'être behind the Weather Underground's existence came into question in 1973 with The Paris Peace Accords, officially titled the Agreement on Ending the War and Restoring Peace in Viet Nam, and by 1977 the movement had faded from public awareness.

This information came from a movie *The Weather Underground: The Story of America's Most Notorious Revolutionaries* directed by Sam Green and Bill Siegal in 2002.

Soul Bro's Guru

. . . a body so pure, it took fully three weeks
to show signs of physical decay . . .

THIS STATE of "perfect preservation" is how Indian guru Paramahansa Yogananda was described after his death on March 7, 1952. For his part, my good friend Ted Huff from my Confederation College days in Fort William (present-day Thunder Bay) turned me on to the ways of this holy man born in Pradesh, India, in 1893.

His brother Sananda described Yogananda as having an awareness and spiritual experience "far beyond ordinary."

After a lengthy search, Yogananda met his guru Sri Yukteswar Giri at seventeen, instantly feeling a deep and abiding kindred spirit who "knew God and would lead me to Him."

Yogananda founded a school for boys in Dihika, West Bengal, combining modern educational techniques with yoga and other spiritual practices.

In 1920, Yogananda moved to Boston, Massachusetts, founding the Self-Realization Fellowship to spread teachings on India's ancient practices and philosophies of yoga, along with the tradition of meditation.

This holy man also met with Mahatma Gandhi in 1936.

On the must-reads list for our sixties and seventies generation of ne'er-do-wells was Yogananda's *Autobiography of a Yogi*, published in 1946 and translated into thirty-four languages, attesting to its global popularity.

He founded another hermitage in Los Angeles, California and lived in America until his death.

One vivid memory I have is of being summarily cast into the deep end of the sixties culture, going to a party and hearing for the first time "21st Century Schizoid Man" by Space Rock's King Crimson! These were the fun parts of suddenly being cast free to post-secondary student life after twelve years of psychic torture.

A decidedly more confusing one was trying to relate to people like my new best friend Ted, having only the prolonged institutional experience. He and almost everyone else there had no way of knowing that

"Into Your New"

I had already been through a lifetime of intentional cultural genocidal immersion, through three different residential schools, each geared to mold some kind of a perfect Canadian Catholic out of the Dene me.

However, to my delight, these Freaks or Hippies simply didn't want anything to do with that part of it, and some in fact, like Ted, simply chose to 'drop out' of the system. He later became a follower of Paramahansa Yogananda at an ashram in California.

Among Indian mystic Yogananda's many followers, was Steve Jobs, the famed founder of Apple Inc.

Shakespeare on Activism

All the world's a stage
And all the men and women merely players.
They have their exits and their entrances,
And one man in his time plays many parts.

Ⲓ N THE VOICE of a melancholy Jacques, Act II, Scene VII of *As You
Like It*, lists the seven stages of a person's life: Infancy, Schoolchild,
Teenager, Young person, Middle-aged, Elder, and Dotage and Death. It
serves as well to play out encounters with imposing figures of authority,
for instance . . .

When you hear the inevitable siren, slow down to a stop, roll down
your window, remind it not wise for thee to blast right on into an instant
royal edict on the poor guy doing his job, with choice observations on
intimate relation to mother and swinish kinfolk.

(Balming Sigh, with portent to Bliss Rewarded)
Rather, in vain o these plaints of our English bard, upon one's way and
pulled aside . . . Breathe deep a drought of humility,
what finds you at centre stage

Now, else the ol' black leather-cased book makes presence felt,
This be thy chance to exercise with will of Job's cow
He/she acts out the tough arm of law and just desserts
Thee but a humble driver misshaped of chance

And foresook devilry
Thou livith to traverse 'nother league . . .
Or put simply, from ol' Bill himself

"Strong reason makes strong actions."

One other and notably opposite phenomenon in these times of
action worth noting has to do with collaborators. In times of strife, even
when you knew you were in the right, there were those who take advan-
tage of this world's stage to get a pass.

Probably the most glaring and blatant in recent history involved the Nazi collaborators, in places like France, divided, one part under German control and the other French.

Perhaps the closest one can come to understanding the mind of people who turn on their own was set forth by Nobel Laureate and Pulitzer Prize winner Czeslaw Milosz, in his book *The Captive Mind.* Commenting on the 'pleasures of conformity', the Polish poet speaks of the turncoat's need to return from the alienation of mission, back to the masses: "He eats with relish, his movements take on vigor, his color returns."

Patty/Tania's Syndrome

M1 carbine in hand, she stood with the other bank robbers, shouting commands.

THIS, following the kidnapping of nineteen-year-old Patty Hearst, granddaughter of publishing magnate Randolph Hearst, in a radical group's bid to free an arrested member for murder, in February of 1974.

Initially blindfolded and in handcuffs for a week, she was gradually indoctrinated into thinking of herself now as Tania, a bona fide member of these political extremists. She started making propaganda statements for them.

In a bizarre turn of events and while the search went on for her, the heiress next showed up two months later as urban guerrilla Tania, of the Symbionese Liberation Army (SLA), weapon in hand, robbing a bank in San Francisco. She took part in a number of illegal activities as a part of the SLA and was captured almost two years later. After being found guilty in 1976 and serving a prison term many found to be unjust, Patty Hearst's sentence was commuted in February 1979 by then-President Carter, and she was released on parole with no civil voting rights until she was finally pardoned by President Clinton in 2001.

What had occurred to Patty Hearst is now termed 'Stockholm Syndrome' a psychological condition in which the hostage gradually learns to show empathy, sympathy, and even emotional feelings towards their captor, a form of defensive traumatic bonding.

Thus, the aggressor ceases to be a threat.

The first case came to light after a six-day hostage standoff during the Norrmalmstorg bank robbery of the Kreditbanken in Stockholm, Sweden, in August 1973. Within a day, the victims became emotionally attached to their captors and defended them, despite being threatened with death by their captor.

One telling quote from one of the two Swedish bank robbers, Clark Olofsson, brings to light the entirely human extension of what the Nuremberg Trials of 1945 revealed of ethics and the matter of consent. Hearing of his release from the penitentiary, upon demand to join cohort Janne Olsson at the bank standoff, Clark's responded: "I had absolutely nothing to run to, but a great deal to run away from."

This sense of being out of the frying pan into the fire is a familiar one to my survivor-of-residential-schools self.

Along with the real legacy of the residential schools, Post-traumatic Stress Syndrome (PTSD), we survivors surely shared in the fate of those left after these dramatic incidents. When the priests and nuns who were charged with running these modern-day concentration camps even chose their "pets" from our numbers . . . those who took the easiest way out, acting out our weakest collective persona, somehow making our ordeal more palatable for the Canadian colonial system to succeed, years before it came to a public and conscious mind.

Severely traumatized children grew into adulthood only wanting to be 'good Indians', playing it safe. I had close relatives who did not want to be a part of our political work to wake up our people, fearing the *Mola*, White backlash and others who made it a point to let it be known they were loyal British subjects . . . anything to avoid having to face up to and turn around the process of the brainwashing forced on us so many years before.

A more personal response to being free after twelve years on imposed rule was not being at all prepared for a world which expected me to be able to make life decisions on my own behalf.

It actually took quite a number of years of alcohol and drug abuse to finally awaken to my true Dene self.

Even today, decades after the last of Canadian residential finally closed the majority of our Indigenous Northern communities are still reeling from intergenerational residential school trauma, acting out a dysfunctional reality.

An Eclectic Bunch

One group going out from the North,
the other wanting country life.

THE SEVENTIES, then, made for about as different a group as you could get. Ours included for the most part northerners who, for one reason or another, wanted more from life than your usual sleepy little village or town.

When not busy with the rigours of the Movement we helped create in the Indian Brotherhood, we simply hit the road in summer, usually to Vancouver. The move to free political prisoner Leonard Peltier was one rallying cry!

We certainly looked the part: braids and tough talk. But true risk-it-all revolutionaries on the order of a Fidel Castro we certainly were not. Once the threat of a pipeline was over, we were content to just carry on with life. Some retreated to an Evangelical version of a Christian past. Others became consultants or just fat cat politicians or outright sellouts to the government we originally fought against.

One time, we found ourselves planting trees on Vancouver Island, getting around in Earl Dean's big ol' truck, all the way from Hay River in the NWT. Of course, most of our efforts ended up floating down the streams, but the party continued on unabated.

Back in Lutsel K'e, where I was spending most of my time, my pal JC got to settling down, at first with a young lady from Alberta we called Chico. Of necessity, life in a small Northern community revolves around the family, and that's the way it was there. JC and Chico, Evelyn Desjarlais, had a daughter, Prairie, and life carried on.

Over the years though, things changed, and the couple became estranged for personal differences.

JC took up with a German Beaver-volunteer named Hanna, which brought problems to a front.

Chico must have somehow learned some ancient Cree medicine from her earlier years, because she started to act very strange, to the point that people got hurt.

Poor Hanna got the brunt of this damage and ended up very frail for such a young person for a number of years.

Nelson Small Legs, Jr.

IT MUST HAVE taken some superhuman effort and more, to go through, for we of the First Nations hold all forms of life to be the Creator's most holy expression . . . but the young Cree protestor simply saw no other way out but to lay down his own life in a personal statement against the way he saw our People being treated by the Canadian Government.

This was also a very volatile time, with one of the main leaders of the American Indian Movement, Leonard Peltier, sent back over the border to face trial in the United States. And not long after, Anna Mae Aquash's body was found on a forlorn corner of the Pine Ridge Indian Reservation, shot dead, execution-style.

Nelson Small Legs, Jr. had been on this earth less than a quarter of a century, a suicide only a few days after testifying to the Berger Inquiry, the only measure he saw to make his point about Indian life, or the lack of it, in Canada. There were others too, in fact, a growing list of residential school survivors, some even close relatives, who were in effect MIA, Missing in Action, of Canada's genocidal war against its First Nations.

Some attempts were made to deal with these dead-end conditions.

In the late sixties, Chief Smallboy set up Smallboy's Camp in the Kootenay Plains of the Albertan Rockies, an alternative to a soul-drenching reservation life.

There was another, MacInaw's Camp, which our small group overnighted at, on our way back from the Crow Indian Agency's First Indian Ecumenical Conference, in the summer of 1970.

Yet the haunting memory of Nelson Small Legs, Jr. returns, a sad refrain, to remind us that our country has a long way to go.

On certain
Deep Alberta moonlights
A warm Wild Rose breeze
Surely caresses
A little clump of sage
Where his Spirit holds
A certain special
Naheyawin Seedling.

High Country Magic

The Dempster Highway runs between Whitehorse in the Yukon, north to Dawson City, and all the way to Inuvik in the Western NWT, with an extension to Tuktoyaktuk on the Arctic Coast completed in 2018. Many tourists use this all-season route, especially in summer, to enjoy the season of the Midnight Sun, when one day goes on for a total of sixty, from mid-June, all of July, and halfway into August.

Either coming or going, this trip is an artistic feast, with a new and spectacular view around every turn along its winding route. Along the way, one can see grizzly bears or porcupine caribou and plenty of *ts'e-lih*, ground squirrels. Early September is easily the best time to be in the Richardson Mountain Range, with the ground bearberries' bright orange and red, mixed in with magenta hills and dwarf birch to dazzle every eye.

The ever-changing light adds rare drama as brilliant shafts of sunlight play along distant ridges and vales in a visual concert of colour.

There is a history of the region, too, going back all the way to Beringia, when giant mammoths roamed these high, arid lands, bridging the Americas with Siberian Russia. Over the years, I have travelled my fair share in both regions a number of times.

A Spirit-Filled People

Being new to these ways when first there in the early nineties, I would marvel at my new relatives, the Navajo Dineh. The ones living right out on the Big Navajo Reservation, especially, had grown up all their lives right on the land, around sheep, most without running water nor electricity . . . and very set in some ways.

Following one all-night Native American Church ceremony, the young fellow to my left, Kelleroy Zahne, showed me some genuine arrowheads and told me where his family lived on the reservation. I found my way there several weeks later.

There, I met my future adopted mother at their two-story Hogan to have a look at what I supposed to be no more than five or six arrowheads.

What Alberta showed instead was an entire tabletop of these, set in rows on a white bed sheet all laid out. As it turned out, she had been told by her mother that she should "just collect these, for one day she would meet the *Dine Nahdloh*, relative from the Far North."

When I was invited to stay and learned that I was adopted into the Zahne family, it was like I was in a different world, although the tourist town of Page, Arizona, was but twenty miles (32 km) north, close to the Utah border. I was told that an Elder would often take and offer corn pollen to the first sign of the coming day, the morning star, at about four, with it all being still pitch dark out.

There were, of course, certain taboos to be strictly observed. Firewood blackened by a lightning strike would not be used at all and there was a deep-seated aversion to any sign of death and/or snakes a coyote crossing one's path was a major omen, depending on the direction, calling for an immediate offering.

Too, the dreaded Skinwalkers, evil people who got together of a full moon, donned the hide of a wolf to go and terrorize unsuspecting families. Even a seemingly routine chore, like emptying the stove of its accumulated ashes, would not be done during the day.

Some events were downright mystical in nature, a coming mist, seen as the Spirits of visiting Holy People, who could be talked to and prayed upon. Thus, every waking moment had its times to be mindful that Life is a sacred blessing to enjoy.

This kind of closeness to nature could not help but show up in anything needing an artistic touch. Right from the start, in fact, I was much impressed with the way any of the Navajo Dineh could put a personal touch to whatever was at hand. A small round pebble I'd brought from the North ended up balanced in a Dreamcatcher, which still hangs over my bed, wherever I live.

Right at the time, too, I was making a serious attempt to sort out my own life. Neither did I want to get to depend on any foreign 12-step program to get back on the Circle of Life.

These new ways were as foreign to me as a step back in time to our former Indigenous ceremonials. But I slowly came to realize that the only way back to my own Indigenous World was through these ceremonials and to recreate my artistic self.

For the time being, I was immersed in just being Dene/Dineh.

Holy Man's Mad Dash

He was not about to be denied his chance at FRUIT!

My pal John T'seleie has an eye for what goes on behind the scenes. Or, in this case, before our very eyes. We went in his boat to the Annual Spiritual Gathering at Desnetche to the Site of T'seku Dawedah, Woman Sitting Up There, the site of a Chipewyan Dene woman whose spirit dwells at Perry Falls, up the Lockhart River about twenty miles (30 km), near Fort Reliance, east arm of the Tu Nedhe, Great Slave Lake.

This particular year, the crowds of people were much larger than usual, with about seven thousand who made the long trip by either boat or bush plane. One of the main events called for a feast.

In traditional Dene fashion, before anyone could so much as touch their food, the Elders sitting in a row in front of all had their chance to speak about our way of life, of hunting, trapping, and fishing.

Needless to say, this could take up to several hours . . . and then a prominent Eelder would be summoned for the Opening Prayer itself.

It finally got to that point, and as the appointed person began lengthy incantations, the cooks decided that the children should be given at least a taste of something to keep them in order while the waiting throng held back. With this in mind, boxes of apples and oranges were set up for them on the side, and they were allowed to have their go at them.

Noticing this commotion with a lifetime of hunting eyes, the old man suddenly cut his lengthy prayers short, and made his way pushing and shoving the children aside to make sure he could get at least a couple of handfuls of the precious fruit into his pockets!

After all, the closest grocery store was at least a day's journey away.

I think these kinds of sports keep that permanent twinkle in *She Leh*, my friend, John's eyes!

Baby Steps and Art Mentoring

*That year was like just fully expecting to step into
a Black Hole and disappearing whole.*

F ROM WHAT I learned later from people who had quit the use of
drugs and alcohol, this is a common feeling after putting it all to the
side. Yet I had to pick up on my Art somewhere, and I was granted a
mentoring, one which took me all the way back to my stompin' grounds
of Toronto to learn at the hands of my lifelong mentor, Diane Pugen.

I did this for a number of months and thus began to feel more
confident about what I could pick up and do again with some sort of
confidence.

It did take a while, but some work came along, such as a contract
to do a mural for Weaver and Devore's General Store in Old Town,
Yellowknife.

My art also graced the cover of Northwestel's phone book in these
sketchy early 1990s.

Over time, I was even selected to represent the North to Her Majesty
Queen Elizabeth II herself in Yellowknife on a cultural visit.

When Mountains Meet

F OR SOME REASON or other I was in the nation's capital, Ottawa. With
some hours for certain leisure, I thought to go to the new Museum
of Civilization over in Gatineau. My oldest sister Judy back home had
told me that they commissioned her to make a traditional Métis outfit. When she added it took her six months to embroider with silk, I
thought to find it there if I could.

From outside, I took some time to marvel at Cree architect Douglas
Cardinal's grand, flowing designs, actually to mask the fact that I couldn't
find the front door! Entering, I joined a line-up to register. I was greeted
quite cordially in broken English by a nice young Francophone lady,
who pointed out that I wouldn't have to pay the five-dollar fee were I to
simply go to yon desk and show them my Indian status card. She also
took a moment to compliment me on my traditional moosehide jacket,

fur hat, and fancy mukluks, made by Gameti's Mary-Adele Chocolate.

Strolling to the main lobby, I casually cast my gaze up and up, craning neck muscles to properly take in all of Dene artist Alex Janvier's colourful Medicine Wheel designs, fair to stagger the culturally uninitiated and making a mental note to maybe borrow a few choice sections as soon as I was alone and inspired again (ahem).

It took about an hour of getting past a vast forest of totem poles and then some to realize that, no, this was all too much to even try to find out about one Métis coat from ages past. Saying as much to a helpful staff member, I was informed that the museum only actually put out about five per cent of its collection at any one time for display

Upon receiving such sentiments, I had had enough of being impressed with it all for one day's share of memories anyway, so I recomposed myself and made my way through the maze and back to the front. Amost at my destination, I happened to spy the same nice young Francophone lady still on duty, directing culture-seekers, of whom I may as well be one, once again.

With that resolve I joined the same line towards her smiling face and shining teeth, proffering, "Excuse me, young lady, have you maybe seen my twin brother come in?"

"Your what, monsieur?" A baffled brow furrowed to three-quarter alert, one finger furtively searching out a possible emergency button just under her dais in case.

"My twin brother . . . looks exactly like me. We were supposed to meet here about half an hour ago."

"Why, sir, that is *impos-si-ble!* There is no one could look like you, with these bee-a-u-tiful ah, deer hide vestments, fur 'at, and fancy galoshes!"

Again, I averred, with a slight pleading wince, "You do not understand, mademoiselle, our mother, she dresses us two exactly the same, every day!" "Oh, mon dieu . . . I . . . I . . ." She just sorta mumbled some apologies, I suppose they were en français and kinda ambled her officious way out through a velvety side curtain . . . high heels giving way now and a step . . .

With a nervous yet haughty, "Harummph!" I left it at that but could not help but notice once outside, the ambulance pulling up to the same side of the building she had exited from.

"Very strange people!" I concluded.

Feeling "Somehow"

BETWEEN THE first and second time the Medicine Peyote goes around the teepee, in the all-night Native American Church ceremonial, you get that ol' 'somehow' feeling, like when you suspect someone owes you money, but you can't quite recall who.

It was all familiar, but in a long-ago kind of way, Indian 'in the blood', as the saying goes.

When I first began my visits to our southern Dineh relatives, the Navajo, in the early 1990s, I made it a point to go to a good number of prayer 'meetings'.

Twenty-six of these followed one after the other, from October to February, some as 'double-headers', two nights in a row, with no sleep from the morning of the first day, as prescribed by tradition.

A new member is cautioned to always pay respect to the Medicine Peyote and "not to turn your back on it," physically and in practice, to remain faithful to its ability to help.

Going through a genuine and serious commitment to change my entire way of life was a gradual step, which was helped along by my new and extended Native American Church family.

I was simply told to just pay attention to the way the ceremonies were done and not get side-tracked. People who went into it looking for 'visions', the way the Hollywood movies have it, were said to have a 'weak mind'.

Almost all Indigenous ceremonials have a fire in there. The idea here is to keep your attention on this, our relatives who have passed on, trying to teach you lessons for a Good Way. Eventually, I learned that the feeling that went with the Peyote Spirit would carry on into my daily life.

This it did.

But it all had to start with that "ol' somehow feeling."

The Other Rasputin!

He humbly stood
In a Maze of Masterpieces
Each one so different
And yet from the same miraculous Hand

THE FIRST TIME I was in Siberian Russia, in the early 2000s, some five years before, there were signs of a superior quality of art on display, but nothing like *this!* Vladimir Rasputin lived a relatively simple life, with a spacious studio, as many Russian artists do, supported in good part by the State. One interesting feature setting this man apart was his headband, from the cuff of a pair of jeans!

As a very discerning artist myself, I had a difficult time just trying to select the number of his paintings to have for my own. From past experience, I knew Customs would take some concerted doing simply to have the works I did select make it all the way overseas to Canada.

Yet choose I did, from the great variation on one of his central themes, taking one back to the very beginnings of Siberian life and even back to the time of the Vikings.

One thing I did notice later was the quality of the materials available, from the coarsest of simple gunnysack, to what he produced, a glasslike surface, was like taking a moment's inspiration and effortlessly jumping a leap year into the rarest of artistic airs.

One work depicts what Vladimir describes as the Princess of the Dragonflies, a young lady standing amidst a wondrous and magical field of these insects, which we Native Americans, too, consider at the door between this world and the next.

> Another, of a stately Asian woman,
> Astride a road-weary steed,
> Boldly forth, to a new land,
> Eagle held aloft.

> That kind of muse simply does not exist
> For most,
> So elusive when She does
> Deign to torture
> Some fortunate Soul

From Woodstock to Altamont

"If your train is on the wrong track
Every station you come to is the wrong station."

—Bernard Malamud

IF WOODSTOCK'S "3 Days of Peace & Music" was the high point of the Love Generation, then Altamont, only a few months later, was the absolute low. The free concert, featuring the Rolling Stones at the Altamont Speedway in California, was touted to be Woodstock West, but with its escalating violence, it was anything but. The main reason was the presence of the Hell's Angels Motorcycle Club, paid off in beer for security.

An attendance of 300,000 virtually guaranteed mayhem, coming close enough with one person, Meredith Hunter, killed right on camera for all to see (film, *Gimme Shelter,* 1970).

Another sobering incident two years later, the Manson Murders, signalled more of the downright sinister. A career criminal with fully half of his life spent in various correctional institutions, Charles Manson began with a quasi-commune in the California deserts, fueling underage disciples with LSD and 'Helter Skelter', a supposed racial apocalypse from the Beatles song of the same name, signalling an apocalyptic race war.

Whilst last-week preparations for Woodstock were in the works, the "Manson Family" carefully planned and executed the murders of occupants in two residences, including actress Sharon Tate, eight-and-a-half months pregnant at the time, and a couple Leo and Rosemary LaBianca. These killings, amounting in total to seven, were done in the hopes of precipitating a race war, whites against Blacks, in a hyper-volatile time. Charles Manson's initial death sentence was commuted to a life sentence in 1971. Manson died at a Bakersfield, California hospital after being transferred from the Corcoran State Prison in November 2017, just days after his 83rd birthday.

Fruit of the Poisonous Tree

IN DIRECT EVIDENCE of how curiosity exercised can lead to solving a mystery, figure in the eventual capture of Unabomber Ted Kaczynski, and the work of FBI criminal profiler and forensic linguist James "Fitz" Fitzgerald. Over almost twenty years, leaving a trail of three dead and twenty-three injured, Kaczynski was finally found holed up in a lone cabin, deep in the Montana woods, in the mid-1990s. Investigators originally assumed he was a former employee of an airline company until Fitz convinced the agency that they were actually dealing with someone who was clearly playing them. But he found himself paddling desperately against the mighty Bureau's current, with only a handful of spelling errors and idiosyncratic language to back his case.

After being forced off the case, with his marriage on the ropes and with just shreds of leads, Fitz gets Kaczynski's brother to come up with some old letters, which, when patched together, prove the Unabomber's identity.

When finally caught, it was found that the Unabomber had an IQ of 167, clearly in the genius territory, attesting to his being able to stay ahead of pursuers for so long. It also accounted for the cat-and-mouse game he challenged the FBI agent in, even with the mountain of evidence against him. These included bomb-making materials, chemicals, and a famed manifesto.

The only hope for law enforcement was to have their man plead guilty; otherwise, he would disappear back into obscurity, free to continue his reign of terror. The process of doing this was all but assured, except for the man they were dealing with. One major setback was when Kaczynski quoted an obscure and pivotal legal manoeuvre, the Fruit of the Poisonous Tree doctrine, based on a case from back in 1920. He claimed that since the FBI agent's warrant for his arrest was based on a new and to-then untested procedure, forensic linguistics, all of the blatantly incriminating evidence to hold him found in his cabin was inadmissible in court!

There is, of course much more to the story of the lone person's drastic position against what he perceived as man's own alienation from the true self. Both he and Fitzgerald, each in their own way, can be seen as artists in thought.

As with Einstein, just the power of the imagination can move mountains. The real story of Kaczynski's reasons for wanting out and striking out so violently at society began much earlier when as a boy-wonder, he was admitted to Harvard at only sixteen.

While there, he was summarily subjected to a federal government psychological experiment, which left him totally against the world. After dropping out of academia he put his entire fibre into warning us about our dependency on technology, to the extent of a kind of unattached violence.

Fair be it to say that he, now so willingly alone in a fast-changing world, could well have seen himself as just another fruit from such a poisonous tree! And, more, this absolved him of all the harm he did.

The rest, of course, is history, such as it is.

One surer reckoning of all of this is that our Navajo Dineh Hataatlii, medicine man, Child of Morning Star, in ceremony clearly sees that life is the many-faceted and ever-changing crystal he uses to scope it all out.

Aunt Mary to the Rescue

There is a good reason many of our Elders never go to the White man doctor.

IN THE YEARS just before I quit drinking, the early 1990s, I was getting very careless in my ways to be sure. Accidents happen in Northern life when an axe in hand is about as common as a cell phone these days.

I cut one of the fingers on my left hand pretty bad out at my brother-in-law Bob's camp. In a few days, I could tell that the poison had set in, feeling a dull and throbbing pain all the way up into my armpit.

I must have mentioned it in time to my Aunt Mary Wilson, though, because she told me that the only way to fix it was to go and get some tse lineh, the soft runny yellow spruce gum, melt it on down, spread it on some type of cloth, and put it on the wound. She said to leave it for a couple of days, which I did.

I was so thankful for her and Dene medicine, because it left not even a scar.

Ye Olde Snowbird Shuffle

"O tell her, Swallow, thou that bravest each,
that bright and fierce and fickle is the South
and dark and true and tender is the North."

—*Alfred Lord Tennyson, The Princess*

I GOT INTO A ROUTINE of going south for the winter months. 'Round about mid-February got to be too hot for me in sunny Arizona, and I headed back north, as far as Yellowknife. Kindly Glenn Wadsworth was the manager at the Northern Images Art Gallery, and I just walked in one day and asked him if I could be an artist-in-residence, to set up and paint. He thought that was a good idea, so this became a pattern over quite a number of years, in the mid-1990s. I would paint on-site into the spring, all summer, and up until the first snowflake drifted down from the Far North.

There was a lady, Sharon Lennox, who had gone to the Spiritual Pilgrimage in Fort Reliance and who had a homemade log home in Bragg Creek, between Calgary and Morley, Alberta.

I would stop at her place there and spend a few days, and we would go on out to the spectacular Kananaskis Country to take some reference photos for future paintings.

She took an interest in the Sundance ways and we would go and visit with the Blackfoot people she knew.

Painted Ski-Doo

Felt good to have the old man taken down a peg or two

I SPENT a number of years going back to paint in Somba K'e, Yellowknife, from my runs south. One of those times, I was setting an easel at my usual spot towards one side of Northern Images when my father came in. The place was also a part of the Western Arctic Co-operatives, and he wanted to send some money home, I would guess. Meanwhile, I was talking with a Mola woman, an art collector, as it turned out, from Ontario.

My dad was always after me to paint him some signs for his hunting lodge at Hume River, about twenty miles (32 km) south of Radelie Koe, Fort Good Hope. Spotting me, he came up behind me, and stood there for a while looking at the work I was just finishing up of a grandmother teaching her granddaughter how to smoke hides.

"What a mess!" says he.

"What are you talking about?" asked the woman. "This here is some fine work of Art, sir!"

"Well, lady, he's my son, so I can talk any way I want to him."

Now offended, the lady goes, "So sir, if you were sitting where your son is, how would you paint it?"

"Paint it all one colour. It'll look better!"

This time, she's about had enough of the ol' gent. "Well, I'll tell you what, sir. Ahhh, Antoine, you're the artist . . . and you are now just about done with this one. What is your price going to be if someone comes along and is interested in buying it?"

I thought I'd just take her up on her little game and answered, "Oh, I think $6,000 would do it."

"Sold! I'll buy it!" she says, without even a moment's hesitation.

"W-W-Wh-attt!" stammers my poor father. "Y'know, lady, that's the price of a brand new Ski-Doo!"

"Well," says she, smooth as peccadillo on ice, "now you know what he does for a living. Go ahead and wrap up my brand new Ski-Doo for me, son."

And best yet, the old man never did talk to me again about wanting a sign painted for his lodge!

Widest Part in Rocky Boy

The old man shook his head, side to side

"BUT NOT when it came to go to that one meeting," storyteller Bobby Murie confided:

That there time, y'know my dad, he used to take me to the prayer meetings of this here Native American Church every once in a while. And this was one of them, held in a Hogan, as I recall. That one had a leaky tin roof, with drops of rain coming in every once in a while, all night long, here and there. Well, we wouldn't stop the prayin' we do for any ol' reason like that . . . so it just went on like that fer us, y'see.

One other thing we did notice, though, was that there was something up there, scampering around all over the place, right above us sitting in there prayin' and singin' away.

Come the morning time, the Water Woman had her bucket of water right in front of her, goin' about her main prayin' business, real humble like they do, y'know.

I could tell my poor ol' pops was really trying to hang in there. He had been on a bender a couple of nights before and was now jes a-sweatin' it out, waitin' for this here meetin' to be over and done with, I guess.

And 'round about then is when I figured out what it was there was up on that tinny roof to make all that noise and fuss all night.

Sure 'nuf it was some kinda tomcat, a real regular lowdown rez-cat, half-wild and all and now jes lookin' for a place to jump down.

Well, it just so happened that the best place this ol' polecat picked was my dad's head! Here, you gotta understand, my dad was really gettin' on in his years by then. He had braids, but not same as you usually see. His were just kind of coming straight down from just above his ears, with his whole head being all bald in the middle, like a big ol' bowlin' ball with right skinny bits-a-braids a-hangin' loose-like.

People 'round there said he had the 'widest part in Rocky Boy's.'

So, that wildcat picked and landed right on top of my pappy's head and jes kinda stayed there, trying to figure on what to do next, I guess.

And all that time that Water Woman is goin' on and on with her prayin' for every one of us and God's each and every creature and livin' thing on earth and beyond. My dad's trying to get that cat loose, shakin' his head all back and forth to make that dern cat git on off!

And I was the only one sittin' right next to him watching the big ol' sweatballs come rollin' on down both sides his cheeks, tryin' to stay real quiet and yet goin' right plumb cat crazy! Every time the old man shook his head that cat would dig in deeper into his bald head and finally jumped off and lit right out the open door!

I noticed my dad didn't once mention wantin' to go to 'nother one of 'em ceremonies for quite a bit after that one."

From The Big E to Joe Blow

I was all-shook-up, Russia Style!

RIGHT FROM when I stepped up, June of 2003, cowboy hat and moosehide jacket on to the lady at Russian customs at the airport in Moscow, I was told that I would be greeted with Horasho and Open Arms in our original homeland. The nice lady said that they had all grown up with me in their storybooks and movies.

What she was probably going on about was some ol' dime store novels set in the American West, by James Fenimore Cooper of *The Last of the Mohicans* fame, with a French actor who I just happened to look like playing some wild Indian name of Chingachgook, would be my most educated guess.

Be that sorta nonsense fiction as it may, our group of cultural ambassadors from Canada's Far North made our way to the grounds of Siberfest, an economic and arts event held every four years somewhere in the circumpolar world.

We were followed and held up wherever it was we were, in the streets, on the subway, and certainly in the venue itself, at Siberian Novosibirsk, fourth largest city in this huge country.

So, I got to be a celebrity of sorts, with the Russian media, radio announcers, and reporters ever eager to ask their 'Antoshka' what he thought of this and that. I couldn't resist having a little fun with it and promptly told them that I usually travelled with a big white horse, but that the airline, shame on them, lost it to someplace in Africa! The big story the following day had to do with helping the Motherland go ahead and find Antoshka's Horse!

Needless to say, all these whirlwind activities got to my head, and upon landing back in Canada, I thought for sure I would be mobbed by my rejoicing countrymen at Lester B. Pearson International in Toronto.

Not so, sadly. In fact, everyone looked at me as if I was just another Joe Blow from Detroit! One security guard even threatened to arrest me for impersonating a movie star.

Such the ignoble trials and tribulations
Of the false Renown

The Bravest Act

Many said later that this was the bravest thing
they had ever seen anyone do

THE LAKOTA under Sitting Bull picked the Battle of Arrow Creek in 1872, several years before the Little Bighorn, to show that they would not sit idly by as the Wasichu, White soldiers did whatever they wanted on their traditional lands.

With both sides at a standstill, Sitting Bull left the Indians' side, unarmed, calmly sat down on the prairie, lit his pipe, and with a pinch of tobacco in hand, called for whomever of the warriors was brave enough to join him in a nice little smoke.

A group of four nervously made their way to where the great man sat, with bullets whizzing overhead and plenty near enough, like angry hornets on fire . . .

His prayer was to *Wakatanka*, the Great Spirit. When the pipe was all puffed out, Sitting Bull, still calmly as if in a peaceful tipi evening, cleaned it and put it away, instructing all that it was now time to go and join their side again.

Once back, he also shouted, "That's enough. We must quit!"

Amid heavy losses the Lakota had also made their point without more bloodshed. Such was this man that he not only gave an example of just what was required of the Lakota in battle but how to be generous in victory . . . often making it a point to spare human life and even adopt an enemy into his own family and lodge.

Over the years, his story also served to prove to us modern-day rebels that it was all well and good to watch this kind of history in a movie or a play, but the times also requires some genuine acts of sacrifice.

"Do Not Go to the *Gray*!"

Many a parched throat has heard these parting words.

You get the keys to the Ford F-150 (*yesss!*) along with these tidings and a stern look. In special cases, these come with furrowed brow and a slow wagging finger, warning signs of danger ahead up the road apiece. The place in mind, like all border towns, is the gas station at Gray Mountain, between Tuba City and Flagstaff, on Arizona, 89 South.

In all of over twenty-five years going to visit our southern Dineh relatives on the Big Navajo Reservation, I have yet to see the number of drunks anywhere else. That is because the Navajo are a moderate, law-abiding People.

However, as everywhere else, there are the odd and persistent requests for a few dollars, usually to tide the person over until some cheque comes through. Another place along the way, Cameron, has a trading post with a number of young First Nations ladies working at the sales counter.

I had one Northern visitor who took a kind regard to these nubile possibles. He would hold us back for quite some time, chatting about his prowess with the bow and arrow or some such . . . All far from God's truth matters this not.

Each and every time we would go sightseeing to the Grand Canyon or to 'Flag', Flagstaff, he would want to make a 'very important' stop at that trading post for a special 'deal' he had in mind. Every single time, again, an extra hour for his swooning ways, Deh Cho Dene eyelashes a-battin' some serious.

So, this one time his wife was with him for his annual run to visit Tuba . . . and she gets to pointing to the huge Trading Post sign, wanting to have a look. "Nawh, honey. *Sweet,* nothing for us to see there. I'm getting tired anyway. Ahhh, yeah, they've got a mean dog too, right by the door! Let's just keeping going."

All being said and so, should the pump at Gray or the counter to Cameron ever be called to bear witness at the famous Gates, some people would be in a World of Hurt, redemption-wise!

Ghosts from Murder Machine

"Death, Death, Death. How could a Human feel?"
—A Soviet survivor

And a Jewish woman:
"There was no God in Auschwitz. . .
God would not go to Auschwitz"

MORE PEOPLE PERISHED, needlessly, in this factory of death than both British and American losses combined in World War II. Unlike Claude Lanzman's earlier and more philosophical *Shoah*, the BBC's Laurence Rees's *Auschwitz: Inside the Nazi State* proves a more visually graphic examination into this one of a number of Nazi death camps. Coupled with the information in his book *Auschwitz: A New History*, it all began relatively innocently, as a labour camp, and even stranger, originally envisioned by Schutzstaffel (SS) Commander Heinrich Himmler and Camp Kommandant Rudolf Hoess, who were both farmers in a former civilian life, as an agricultural research station.

All things considered, there was simply no getting around German dictator Adolf Hitler's searing bigotry for Jews, whom he intentionally conveniently targeted as *the* enemy. When the Final Solution was agreed upon as a way of ridding the entire European continent of these innocent people, there could not be any other reason for places like Auschwitz to exist but to totally exterminate them, once and for all.

To protect itself and individuals in the German army, though, from future reprisals, everything official about it was left purposefully very vague and obtuse; every official communication clouded by inference, although to a military mind there was no doubt that the Jews had to go.

In effect, Auschwitz was a mercurial
Hail of broken mirrors,
A new set of crushing puzzles at every horrific turn
Soul-severing shards, cursed gems splintering.
With every day
Scorching all, one way or another

Orders intentionally vague . . .
Directives, with only the damningly targeted
Jews
a constant

A lasered light Pointed
. . . Fading . . . into . . . Unforgivable Darkness.

The intent of this place was carefully kept secret right from the start, even to the adoption of the erroneous sign at the front gate, taken from the Dachau camp in Germany:

"Arbeit Macht Frei" Work Sets You Free

Especially targeted were Jews. They were even being blamed for Germany losing the First World War, as a part of some international conspiracy.

Birkenau and Beyond

A Soviet survivor:
"Death, Death, Death
. . . How could a Human feel?

You really could not trust anybody
. . . it was a matter of Life and Death."

It does go on, and as a survivor of the residential schools myself, I can most identify with the children who had not a single chance to make it out alive at all. Throughout an extended agony of a hundred years, over 80,000 of us disappeared down the gloomy halls of neglect and outright abuse, many thousands yet unaccounted for, scattered over Great Turtle Island, little mounds to mark the missing . . .

And worse, all written records
Missing
Along with those
Of our Missing
And Murdered
Indigenous Women.

The first in us to die was that precious sense of innocence we all need to become human.

Next went Hope.

In this damning way are the military and religion forever linked, the use of right and wrong, to control and outright kill the innocent, in the name of right, God, using fear, or better yet, politics and police. And of course, closer to home, the worst cut of all, seeing the everyday naked indifference, apathy, especially in the faces of ordinary, educated Canadians, who yet ignore the choice to know.

They, too,
Shadows of the Past
Amongst us

Twenty Dollar Man

"You can have your man,
y'know."

BOBBY MURIE was known all around Montana as the guy with a good story to tell ya. After each and every ceremony of the Native American Church, whether he conducted it or not, he was eagerly sought out for a tale or two. One had to do with his wilder and younger self—outlaw on the range.

"I was some hellraiser at one time, y'know. Would go and do all kinds of crazy stuff jes' to be at it. But one time, I got caught when I was supposed to be gettin' ready for a prayer meeting that very night. Sheriff took and threw me in the county jail over to Havre, jes' outside the Rez here."

Guilty as he was, Bobby couldn't quite convince them police he had something important to do that Friday night and was getting desperate.

"Okay, look here, fellas. You got me fair and square. I will not argue that point one iota ... not one bit I ain't. But I'll tell ya what. You just go right ahead and call my people there at Rocky Boy's, and they will tell you right off I am one big man over there, needed to do this and that— some Big Doin's, let me tell ya that, Jake . . ."

Finally, the Badges there had enough of him, and they called the number he gave them, with this to say: "We've got a man in custody here. Says y'all know him. Bobby Murie ... says he's Big Stuff over to there? If'n that's to be true, you can have your man, y'know . . . but you have to pay the $20 bail . . . no problem."

On the other end all they heard back was "Well, yes, we do know the man you got there. But here's the deal. Over there he might be worth the $20 to you but 'round these parts he ain't worth nothin' at all! You can just keep him there where he's at least worth something!"

The heavy-duty bargaining went on for a bit, Bobby said, but eventually, someone agreed to just come on over and claim him to run that prayer meeting that night.

Some Came Home

First, the Beauty Way

BEFORE A SOLDIER was about to go to battle, they were put through a traditional protection ceremony. Some of these elaborate events would go on for up to nine days, requiring much preparation. The idea was to create a shield all around the combatant, which no weapon would be able to penetrate.

Witnesses said that they saw the bullets go right through the soldier in battle. Navajo veterans returning from tours of duty said that others would often simply sleep close to them . . . knowing they would be going back home safe and sound.

Another and just as important reality is The Enemy Way, to get rid of all the negative impacts of the battlefield from the ones returning. The man of war would be required to strip off all his military uniform on the far side of the hill from his Hogan home, and go through another series of prayers, called The Enemy Way.

This one would ensure *Hozho*, Beauty and Balance, all around the person, below, above, before, after and to all sides.

In order to again Walk in Beauty

In Yo-Yo House

Look for the right footsteps

THAT IS ONE of the first things we were taught in the tipi. Many generations of our First Nations People made and left their tracks around the fireplace, and we want to, at the very least step into a great one and follow it for life.

So, it was really no surprise when I first started with the Native American Church in the early 1990s that I now had a lot of time to really see what was going on. Just then I was also taking my very first baby steps on the road back to sobriety, one I have been on now for a quarter-century.

On an average day, I was often left alone with a houseful of children while everyone else was either at work or busy doing laundry in town or something.

Before he left for work, one of my brothers was being pestered by his young son, just now able to walk and say his first words.

"Daddy, take me to Yo-Yo House!" the little tyke insisted. "Take me there, quick to Yo-Yo House!"

"What's that, son?" his father asked. "What's Yo-Yo House?"

"Hey, Hoi-Hoi, silly! You know, Daddy. Hinana Yoi-Yoi House!"

It took him a while, but he finally figured out that his son was talking about his favourite song, which he'd heard his dad sing a number of times that weekend during a Native American Church ceremony for the family.

The song is of a memory of your grandparents and how your first lessons in Life came from them. Young as he was, the little guy already wanted to walk in the footsteps left by his ancestors.

Invisible Me

Less than a yard from the Security Man . . . GONE!

ONE OF MY very best friends, a famous Navajo artist, gave me some powerful tobacco. All he said when he gave me the pouch was to go ahead and "use it if you really need help."

What worried me at the time I finally smoked it was the fact that I was rather dishevelled, having been standing on a bouncing bus all the way through the State of Utah and then for the long plane ride north.

I thought for sure I would be asked many questions, and maybe even searched, so I just asked the special mixture not to be noted 'in any way'. Simple request, right?

But as I stood there in front of the security officer behind the glass partition, he paid absolutely no attention to me! As it turned out he couldn't even see me, much less ask any questions! It was only when I moved that he noticed and jumped with genuine fright. After a few words of apology about being a little drowsy, he quickly stamped my passport, gave a wan smile, and welcomed me back in-country.

Sometime later I thought to use this same sacred tobacco mixture when my Elder hunting friend Joe Martin mentioned a moose hunt.

The night we were to leave out on the Tu Nedhe, Great Slave Lake, a cow and a calf mysteriously showed up just above where I lived, at the home of Peter Cullen, on School Draw Avenue in Somba K'e, Yellowknife.

It was later said to be the first sighting of moose in the City of Yellowknife in over forty years!

When I told my Navajo buddy about it, he said those were "not really what this tobacco is for."

No complaints from THIS customer!

"I've Been to Hell and Back!"

My Navajo Dineh brother Johnson Tochoney always did know how to make himself understood. There was a time when he was legally dead. His heart had stopped on the operating table for about twenty minutes.

He later said that he was travelling at great speed to a very "bright light at the end of a long, long tunnel" and that he "heard a drum sounding away back there, where I came from. I was given a choice to keep going to where the light was or going back to the drum."

The drum he spoke of was that of a water drum, an old-time cast iron kettle with the handle cut off and half-filled with water, with a hide tied over the top with seven rocks around. This sound came from a teepee in which we, his family members, were holding an 'emergency meeting' for him.

Luckily for us, he chose coming back . . .

Johnson was diagnosed with diabetes a number of years before and was going through weekly sessions of dialysis in Tuba City, waiting for a kidney donor. When one finally came along, he was okay for a while, but his body eventually rejected the organ, and he was rushed off for the operation in Phoenix, to the South.

Ever after that he is fond of telling young people that he'd been to "hell and back!"

The Banality of Evil

"Life itself is neither good nor evil.
It is a place of good and evil.
According to what you make it."
—Michel de Montaigne

IN A SWEEPING INDICTMENT of all things political, social psychologist Hannah Arendt systematically places both mass murderer Adolf Eichmann and officials of the Jewish State as responsible for the deaths of the millions of fellow Jews during the Shoah, the Holocaust.

Hired by the *New Yorker* magazine to cover the trial of the war criminal, she originally found it impossible to come to a starting point for her report. How, she thought, is it possible that such an ordinary-looking person could possibly be responsible for these crimes on such a massive scale?

It wasn't until she hit on and coined the phrase the 'banality of evil', that she could get a handle on what she was dealing with. The fact that the work itself made Eichmann incapable of thought started to take root:

> The longer one listened to him, the more obvious it became that his inability to speak was closely connected with an inability to think, namely, to think from the standpoint of somebody else. No communication was possible with him, not because he lied but because he was surrounded by the most reliable of all safeguards against the words and the presence of others, and hence against reality as such. *(Baehr, p 324, 2000)*

Arendt furthered her argument, in that this same kind of willful 'self- deception, lies and stupidity' was shared by all of German society.

To make matters worse, the Israeli State accused her of making excuses for, even to the point of supporting the Nazi criminal's behaviour, and they thought that blame had to be assigned to deal with the grim matter at hand. What Arendt was really trying to say, now pointed to by Israeli aggression to Pakistan, was that as basic human beings, both faulted and blessed, we each share in the blame for how we invariably behave. She believed that in certain extreme cases there really is not an 'us or them', 'good or evil' and that we have a long way to go before we see the light of true human day.

One other, and more famous Jew, Albert Einstein, no doubt felt this duality of person and work. His work in nuclear fission originally begun as early as 1905 with the Theory of Relativity, $E=mc^2$, eventually resulted in the two nuclear explosions over Japan, to end World War II. He listed his involvement as 'the one mistake of his life', signing a letter to then President Roosevelt, to go ahead with the bomb.

To add existential evocation to ambiguous foreboding, famed French existentialist Simon De Beauvoir outright sets we humans as 'nothing', caught amidst the past and future.

"If you want to make God laugh,
tell him about your plans."
—*Woody Allen*

From Calvary to Ground Zero

"IT MARKED THEIR DEPARTURE from the community of 'civilized' people" Thus Daniel Jonah Goldhagen maps out for us in *Hitler's Willing Executioners*, the way ordinary German citizens were thorough and zealous accomplices, ultimately leading six million Jews to certain death during the Second World War.

There is absolutely no doubt, too, that ordinary German citizens as a body were anti-Semites long before, to make it all possible to simply follow Hitler's directives, to first put Jews outside of German society and then to essentially kill them all off, period.

That the Nazi Party was duly elected indeed helped all of the mass killings along.

Goldhagen's meticulously researched arguments include a study of how prejudice has little or nothing to do with the object. Everything started in the minds of the perpetrators and was certainly helped along by mad leaders and zealous individual groups like the SS.

In this particular case, it should be noted that no matter what the Jews did they were marked and especially targeted for mass extinction right from the start and could never hope for even a show of mercy once the murderous plan was set into motion.

One feature of anti-Semitism, hatred for the Jews, is that although their treatment by the Nazis was a first of its kind in sheer terror, it was just one in a continuing line going all the way back to the very beginnings of history.

As for the reason I have included the four chapters pointing to the Nazi death camps, in particular, we of the First Nations in the Americas share very similar relationships in the hands of those who claim Christianity as their reasons.

Our own fall to Ground Zero began almost half a century before the hapless Christopher Columbus blundered upon our Great Turtle Island, in June of 1492, with Pope Nicholas V's 1452 *Dum Diversas*, the Doctrine of Discovery, a Papal Bull claiming any land of non-Christians in the name of God.

> "The only thing new
> In the World
> Is the history we do not know."
>
> —Harry S. Truman

In truer form, the real date can be traced back another millennium and a half to Mount Calvary, when the Son of God hung stretched, crucified. His apostles set forth to spread the Word, in a worldwide trail of blood and pagan bodies.

From His last utterance of "Into thine hands I commend my Spirit" these teachings also passed from his followers to what became a number of interpretations, bibles for people to swear on, an oh-too-human departure from divine origins.

From the fourth century on, when the Roman Catholic Church assured its control over the Roman world, the poor Jews were charged with the death of one man who lay claim to the Heavens, suffering for it ever since.

Thus from their religious beliefs they somehow committed their own form of an Original Sin, conveniently inherited by future generations for all time, to be continued on by Jews ad infinitum.

Far from any road to Jerusalem, we of the First Nations had no Jesus to settle our scores upon, if that particular story was even true. Wasn't it the Romans who sent Christ to Mount Calvary?

For our part, we of the First Nations did have one thing the Mola, White man craved more than even vengeance . . . LAND, the best of any in the world, seas, oceans of green pastures filled with every kind of hoofed and winged animal and vegetation.

Yet by insisting to this day that we wanted to keep our original love and faith with our Great Turtle Island, we also came head-on with Christian Manifest Destiny, its sword and gun being mightier than any previous rights we claim.

Turn the page to our precarious chapter, we're one of the right mind to ruminate, castigate, and gesticulate at will; there's at least one marked and disturbing parallel between the rise of Nazi anti-Semitism and our modern Canadian apathy for Missing and Murdered Indigenous Women and Children.

In many other ways, we are seeing the same kind of fascist turn away from social order that began in early 1930s Germany. Far from a spur-of-the-war moment as an explanation for Hitler's Final Solution, the fans for anti-Semitism were well-nigh aglow at least a half-century earlier in that one country, only waiting for the right moment to completely burst into reality and beyond.

Even in February of 1933, with the Reichstag Fire, it still took a questionable event, after some decidedly political moves to make the Nazi Party viable and the economy in general, to ignite ordinary citizens to the eventual Holocaust.

One damning feature of this modern hatred for Jews was that it became so identified with the German character as to assume a morphed and all-too-real common sense.

The single most terrifying period of assaults on Jews, their businesses, and places of worship began right after the Nazi takeover of the government, with a boycott of all Jewish businesses in April 1933, and with a brief pause, the imposition of the Nuremberg Laws, September 1935, but again making its final stupendous and definitive statement, *Kristallnacht*, Crystal Night—the utter destruction of 7,500 Jewish stores and businesses—in November 1938.

There was no doubt this was initially the grisly stamp of the SA—the Brownshirt shock troops—but by then ordinary German citizens no longer needed any other reason but soul-numbing hatred for Jews to carry their actions forth.

In matters of religion, the churches faithfully followed official anti-Semitic policy, as did the media. But it was not like everyone blindly followed whatever orders came from authority, military or not. In Bavaria, for instance, a vociferous public outcry followed orders—the Crucifix Decrees—to remove crucifixes from schools, while all around their fellow Jewish neighbours were wantonly brutalized. Foreign Poles found more favour than the targeted Jewry. In a single year, there were almost two hundred labour strikes.

Perhaps the most telling point is that even with the general population brainwashed to the point of outright killing Jewish citizens, the Gestapo was never properly equipped to alone engender the Final Solution on its own.

Whatever the socially calamitous buildup, by 1941, with the deportation of the hapless Jewry to their deaths in the East, there was no longer any question of where all of this would lead.

Countless evidence of the inhumanity to follow included a
"death banquet for the Jews,"
following closure of the Chelmno Death Camp,
April of 1943
Leaving 145,000 Jews in its final wake.

In the West, our 'Jewish Problem' started off with "the only good Indian is a dead Indian." After the Indian Wars were over it was a simple matter, handing over the War Department to the churches, once dismal reservations were allotted, as was done here in Canada, for the advent of residential schools.

Indeed, word had it that Hitler himself was inspired by the reservation system. One can clearly see an eerie resemblance to mass Jewish graves in the one dug for victims of the Wounded Knee Massacre of 1890, where hundreds of unarmed Lakota men, women, and children were mercilessly murdered.

After our surprising survival and for the purposes of these schools the only good Indian became "kill the Indian in the child."

Either way, there was little doubt that cultural genocide was the ultimate goal.

One can only wonder at the reasons for people, civilized or not, to instigate these kinds of fear-based departures from humanity.

Could it be that should an all-powerful being exist to oversee our very human foibles, at work too is this quixotic reasoning for a kind of free will run amok?

> "You cannot wake up
> A person who is
> Pretending to sleep."
> —Navajo proverb

Bully Me, Bully You

THE HORSE CALLED HISTORY wears blinders. And carries us all, including artist, always about Vision, being able to at the very least appreciate what there is right in front of us. The old-time Indians would say that the best Spirits just want to live on the side of an old dirt road, in a little patch of the most ordinary kinds of grasses and weeds, with an odd flower sticking out at an odd angle. It's the first place we pass on a wondrous hike to the top of an exotic mountain or clawing our way to a magical Oasis of Truth in a faraway desert.

Yet even with these kinds of secrets in our kitbags we still see what we want, most times, including our own history . . . and this can be dangerous. To its credit, Kananaskis Country gets you to just stop and think about it some.

One important lesson I learned from people like my old hunting buddy Joe Martin is that these kinds of crossing places, neither at home nor quite where you're going are the best for this kind of bearing.

You take a good look back to know what the place looks like for your return, in terms of thinking you know things by being reminded of what happened in the past with them ol' History blinders off.

It could also be the fields of sage along the Bow River on the Morley Indian Reservation, which held an extra-Memory to help it all along.

Over the number of years, when I kept making my way down to

visit our Navajo Dineh relatives, I began to notice a pattern. Even the poorest people in the farthest, remote corner of those First Nations lands had it in for the poor Arabs on the other side of the world.

The word 'Bully' came to mind. America, for now the biggest on the block, just wants to push its weight around.

It reminded me of the Lakota of South Dakota, stubbornly clinging onto their sacred Black Hills, even when offered hundreds of millions of dollars.

When the matter of claim comes up, words having to do with their ancestors being right there for 'time immemorial,' 'millennium' are used, as if more of it will make it come true. Yet these same people were once horseless and on foot, far to the East, among their Algonquin folk.

Once mounted they rode as far as a horse would carry them, making for greater numbers from better living . . . and an aggressive, bullying way of life. It all came at a cost, too, of people lesser able to defend themselves against this aggression.

On a wider scale, of course, we are back to America wanting it all for itself.It comes to the point where people actually start calling themselves "God's Chosen."

It could just be that every once in a while, whoever is in charge up there or below there, simply chooses to turn a blind eye for a spell . . . , .. just so we know what 'power' we really have.

Old Gourd Box in Big Rock

The row of feathers fair beckoned

I SAT THERE in the Navajo couple's home marvelling. We had been up all the night before in yet another of the ceremonies of the Native American Church I got into the habit of attending with my good friend Leonard Claw.

But there was something bothering me about a new prayer fan set of bald eagle tails, which I wanted to do something with . . . other than keep it for myself. Around noon, after the customary feast, Leonard, who had conducted the prayer meeting, wanted to catch up on some sleep before heading back to Page, Arizona, some hours south, then west. I couldn't sleep, so I went next door to one Dineh couple's home to visit. While there, I broached the subject of the fan, which I eventually just offered to them as a gift. The man said something in Navajo to his wife, and she left to a back room and returned with a sturdy, hardwood gourd box. From within she took and lined up a good number of older prayer fans, including a red-tailed hawk and an ancient waterbird.

The man began, "No one does this for us, y'know. So here you are, you can take whatever one of these or more you want and have them, including the box. It was my father's, from before. He was a roadman, like Leonard over there. Used to take this here box with him on horseback to run them prayer meetings way out there in the boonies."

With that, I went and picked up the oak box with its inlaid silver markings of the USA Eagle Emblem, put the two fans I had noticed in, and thanked them very much.

I had learned that generosity in its way has healing ways.

Search for the Bruges Madonna

"We have Art so that we shall not die of reality."
—Friedrich Nietzsche

For the second time leaving its home in Belgium, the monumental, sculpted Michelangelo statue came to be spirited away, securely wrapped in mattresses, bouncing along aboard a Red Cross truck. The story of German soldiers making off with the Renaissance's priceless "Madonna of the Bruges," only to have it miraculously rescued from Austria by a special team of Allied soldiers, is one to match any of the vast store of mysteries surrounding Michelangelo and his genius in chaotic times.

This loving and stately depiction of Mother Mary and the child Jesus was commissioned by Flemish cloth merchants in Rome, for their family chapel in the Church of Our Lady, Onze Lieve Vrouwekerk, back in Bruges, Belgium. Long have I fervently worshipped at the altar of the divine Italian sculptor and painter.

From the first glimpse of his Renaissance majestic depictions of a truly rare artistic epoch extended forever in his work, I have made it my personal quest to somehow even brush against his pictorial eminence.

My third year of art school in his native Firenze, Italia allowed me as extended a contact as any may enjoy in this day and age.

There in the shadow of his David, at the feet of a tipsy Bacchus, retracing the man's very sandaled tread, the painter in me began to breathe in no small draughts artistic succour to return home with.

I incorporated copies based on some from Michelangelo Buonarroti's Sistine Chapel's ceiling and "The Last Judgement" and thought to draw from his Madonna of Bruges.

What inspired me to render as such also comes from the story of this particular sculpting of the Queen of Heaven, toddler at her knee, not looking directly to Him, certainly already sensing Lord Jesus's first faltering steps into an uncertain future, but having faith nevertheless, that she, too, would one everlasting day serve to intercede on behalf of some of the unworthy come Judgement Day.

What intrigues so about the Bruges Madonna is that the artist Michelangelo displays a singularity of purpose throughout much of his life's work.

For instance, the look of classical, lasting beauty in this Madonna, as in his *Pietà*, shines forth, especially in the way the Queen of Heaven interacts with the Saviour.

If true Redemption is to be found, it would be in this, Mary's pleas to her Prince, on behalf of our lost Souls. In the end, perhaps, this shares somehow in the mystery of the Madonna of Bruges having gone missing twice and yet finding her way home again.

I, too, returned to my beloved Firenze, Italia, in May of 2015, after some six years, just to spend a number of precious weeks, to write, draw, and breathe that rare artistic elixir, Italian air!

All whims aside and associated kudos for the special American recovery mission and team associated with the rescue of this particular artistic gem, it was England's Prime Minister Winston Churchill who said it best, when asked about cutting funding for the Arts in favour of the WWII effort:

"Then what would be we fighting for?"

Upper and Lower:
Search for the Bruges Madonna

Lee's Grand Entry

All the good stuff happens on the road, don't it?

WHEN WE WERE IN JAPAN for the World Expo 2005, everything we saw and did was brand new it seemed. Including the time we were sitting in our fancy hotel lobby and all the staff were especially gussied up for some reason or other.

When we asked them what the occasion was, they just said that they were there to bid farewell to the son of the Japanese Emperor himself, who was just on his way down the elevator to check out. Knowing that was something we had to see, we decided to wait along with everyone else in their tuxedos and evening gowns and such.

Without warning, we heard some whistling, like a Métis reel of some kind . . . an' here comes the great Northern fiddler himself, Lee Mandeville, on the loose and rounding the corner from the side door, into the bright lights. He was really dressed for his time of leisure—baseball hat kinda tipped on the side, gangsta-style, pink earphones on for some loud music, Hawaiian-print shirt with loud and colourful flowers of all kinds (looked to be varieties of hibiscus), cut-off khakis, and hairy legs bare down to floppy sandals just a-prancin' to beat the band!

It sure did not take hotel security long to size him up for some kind of a troublemaker, cultural ambassador from Canada or not . . . and about six of them tiny little guards got a hold of him and hustled all six-foot-two Métis musician of him out back through the side door, to the alleyway, it looked like.

His Highness the Emperor's son need not be bothered by suchlike, after all . . .

Of course, it took us a while to explain that this man they had in back was a very important and vital part of our little international entertainment committee. When we got that all squared away all we ever saw of ol' Lee Mandeville after that little social episode was when he was dressed all neat and tidy, like an important delegate going to a business conference in far-off Ottawa, just keeping himself busy humming the Japanese anthem whenever anyone official came up to him . . . or us . . .

Delegate or not, I do know for a fact they stamped his papers right quick at the airport—leaving Japan

Cree Chiefs
Pihtokahanapiwiyih and Mistahimaskwa

HIS NAME, POUNDMAKER, came from a unique ability to draw the buffalo herds into a pound, a kind of corral, for killing these animals for food. At Poundmaker's Lodge in Edmonton, we were treated to some history of the Cree People.

Both Poundmaker and Big Bear were wrongfully accused of taking part in the Riel Rebellion of 1885 when in fact they actively sought to prevent bloodshed. Charged and found guilty of treason anyway and sentenced to Stony Mountain Penitentiary in Manitoba, both died soon after of failing health; Poundmaker was only forty-four.

Big Bear, especially, resisted all official government lures of presents to have him sign away traditional Cree lands in the numbered Treaty 6. With the buffalo gone and the people starving, there was no recourse but to go along with the drastically changing times.

Like Blackfoot Chief Crowfoot, Big Bear sought a grand alliance of all Indians north of the Medicine Line, in Grandmother's Country, Canada, but also fell short in these attempts.

Poundmaker was an adopted son of Crowfoot. It should be noted that this great Nehiyo, Cree Chief was finally officially fully exonerated by the Canadian federal government in the summer of 2019 after well over a century of misunderstanding.

A Giant Awakens

The colossal figure stands an imposing twenty feet (over six metres), defiantly guarding the city of Florence.

WHEN FRIENDS told Michelangelo, then in his mid-twenties, that he should return to his native Firenze to make rightful claim on a massive block of Carrara marble, abandoned by two separate sculptors and left for almost half a century in a sculpting work yard close to the Duomo, he did. With the thought that "nothing is easy except the difficult," the young talent vowed to save the castoff boulder without even adding another block of marble. There were yet serious doubts.

His only claim to ability so far was his Pietà, magnificent though it may have been. The masterpiece was on display a great distance to the south, in Roma, which at the time, for all intents and artistic purposes, may as well have been a separate universe.

He eventually did receive the city's approval for this prize, even over his archrival, the formidable Leonardo da Vinci, with whom the sculptor shared no modus vivendi—much less even artistic bonhomie—and set to work, in secret, with hammer and chisel, behind an enclosed workshop especially built to keep out the nuisance curiousi.

In the interests of anatomical accuracy, Michelangelo had secretly sought and was given permission to steal in dead of night into various places where bodies were kept to study anatomy, which he in turn rendered in superior quality in his various works of art.

Almost two years later, the *David* was ready for public display. After much debate by a rather large group of fellow artists and civic authorities, the David was initially installed at the front entrance to the Palazzo Vecchio, site of the Florentine Republican government, until 1873, when it was replaced by a copy and moved to its very own gallery, the Accademia.

Along the way, the statue honouring the city of Florence went through a story quite its own, even standing exposed to the weather for a number of years and going so far as to have its left arm knocked off by a chair hurled from an open window in the Palazzo Vecchio in 1527 during a rebellion against the Medici's!

Several others featured are from a set originally planned for Pope Julius's massive tomb, of slaves literally coming out of inert marble, muscles tight with effort— one "The Rebellious Slave" and the other, "The Dying Captive." Two of the set are in the Louvre, in Paris.

One can clearly attest to the genius of a man with the hammer and chisel, expertly hacking off huge chunks of stone with the strength of four. There were other versions too, granted, like Donatello's earlier and decidedly effeminate version, flowered hat and slender arm akimbo . . . so natural looking that other artists assumed it to have been formed over a live human model and one from the magical hands of Bernini, said to be an even finer creator in stone, with its magnificent, contained power . . . but, alas, none with the sheer grandeur of the Florentine's.

As a true Renaissance Man, in addition to all three of the Arts proper—sculpture, painting, and architecture—Michelangelo was also a man of letters, having personally penned over three hundred poems, sonnets, and madrigals. But he fervently believed that his was a language of imagery, and he felt specifically called forth by God Almighty to redeem his creations in renderings of Carrera marble.

In a time when each city-state was more often than not on its own to somehow face invading armies from France and Spain and even other Italian provinces coming south to lay claim to entire areas, this new giant statue of the David, like its biblical hero, now forever rose for Firenze's bravery, defiance, and fortitude.

The Italians invented the concept of sprezzatura, which is an effortless way of doing and making things of superior quality, be it clothing, cars, preparing fine cuisine, or in the case of this Florentine artist, the best art the world has ever seen. Michelangelo took it to another level, though, with a lifelong need to feel a part of some royalty and certainly a sense for his innate divinity, from God's thoughts to his busy hands.

Yet for all of this, and with every stroke of mighty chisel to solid stone, Michelangelo Buonarotti helped define the artist as a mighty force within Creation, with a definitive essence for the epochal.

Wake-up Art of Maria Gabankova

RUSSELL SMITH, *Canadian Arts* columnist said, "Tenderness and fear jostle for the same space on the canvas." Smith also mentions this Czech-born Canadian artist's 'astounding technical prowess', in great evidence in her *Body Broken—Body Redeemed*, a 2007 collection of a large number of Maria Gabankova's drawings and paintings, and how her ultimate "compassion and humanity dominate."

Maria's sense of humour and discipline were also in much evidence in her class I took at the very end of my time at Toronto's Ontario College of Arts and Design University, working towards my eventual Bachelor of Fine Arts Degree in the spring of 2011.What I could not help but notice, too, was her genuine concern for the 'state of our world, the signs of our times'.

Into the very first pages of *Body Broken—Body Redeemed* are renderings of the homeless, many of whom she sketched in New York's subway, huddled for all in intents in their only available shelter for warmth and a bit of rest.

In a few more images, one is confronted with the highly detailed *Forgotten News*, based on the biblical Lazarus from the story of the raising of the dead, but here as a newly resurrected and embalmed human figure, wrapped in tangling sheets, sitting upright in a large cardboard crate, atop a stack of old newspapers casting accusing gauze-shrouded eyes to an indifferent modern world. Even the painting's frame is of yellowing news of the day just gone by.

One direct result of this kind of influence, artistically, was that I began to think in terms of ethics, what rightfully fits where.

It wouldn't be for several more years, though, that I would come face to face with its implications, in an Indigenous PhD Studies program at Trent University.

Trudell on Peltier

"Nations do not die from invasions.
They die from internal rottenness."
—*Abraham Lincoln*

O F ALL MEMBERS of the American Indian Movement (AIM), John Trudell has the thickest dossier in the FBI, making him the most threatening to the USA. On February 12, 1979, after he was involved with some activism in Washington, D.C., a highly suspect house fire at the home of his father-in-law at the Duck Valley Indian Reservation in Nevada killed his mother-in-law, pregnant wife, and three children.

Trudell's involvement as a spokesperson for First Nations rights went all the way back to 1969, the two-year occupation of the site of the former federal prison on Alcatraz Island, across the bay from San Francisco. There, he set up regular radio broadcasting to provide information on the Indians' reasons for being there. He also testified in the trial for the kidnapping and murder of AIM member Anna Mae Aquash, a Canadian from the Mi'kmaq of Nova Scotia.

Throughout all of the worldwide efforts to free AIM political prisoner Leonard Peltier, Trudell has consistently said that Peltier would never be allowed to go free. As of late-2022, he is still in prison. Put in just this blunt way, on the outside, it seems we have little choice as to what we can do. On the other hand, we begin to realize the distance we need to start our first faltering steps towards FREEDOM. Like the cooling wind and peace of mind, it cannot be bought but must be earned and fought for . . . like THIS:

Seventeen-year-old Lepa Radic was a Bosnian Serb who fought with the Yugoslav Partisans during WWII but never got to see the Nazis lose the war.

In February 1943, Lepa was captured. Preparing to publicly execute her, the Nazis tied a rope around her neck but offered her a way out. All she had to do was reveal her comrades and leaders' identities.

Lepa responded: "You will know them when they avenge me."

Catch-22

"You have to be crazy to be drummed out of the Army . . .
But you cannot be crazy to want out . . ."

THIS KIND OF STILTED LOGIC, oddly enough, makes up the theme of the popular sixties satirical must-read by American author Joseph Heller. At its centre is Air Force B-25 bombardier Captain John Yossarian who, along with his fellow airmen, tries to make sense of the Army's impossibly convoluted paradox, *Catch-22*.

The movie version clearly showed the book's various characters desperately trying to hang on to their sanity . . . and all in one way or another failing to stay alive at least to the end of WWII.

Because the book itself remained out of our reach, and for good reason, during our colonialist 'education', it was definitely one everyone of us made it a point to read and still stands as one of the greatest literary works of the twentieth century.

Those just south of the American border could definitely relate to its anti-war stance, and we could relate to the anti-everything-else approach. In a manner, too, Heller's use of the new free association and a unique timeline/plot sequence was one that struck a chord with our search for new artistic expression.

Other entertainment forms picked up on this, including the TV sitcom *M*A*S*H**, following the exploits of an earlier wartime medical unit. One character, in particular, Corporal Max Klinger, spends all his time thinking of ways to just get formally discharged from military duty, most times dolled up as a woman.

Given the basic groundwork of a decidedly anti-establishment era, the public scenario took on a myriad of purposes in reporting events following the turbulent times. Following in the convoluted format of *Catch-22*, an example of this circus of media and rule is given in Herman and Chomsky's *Manufacturing Consent: The Political Economy of the Mass Media*. In the chapter "Free Market Disinformation as News", Mehmet Ali Ağca's attempted assassination of Pope Paul II was initially supposed to have been undertaken on behalf of the KGB and Bulgaria in May of 1981.

Just a smattering of the media's manipulation of the story followed quite a number of changing leads, the main being a Turkish right-wing source but with Soviet bloc origins. For lack of evidence, the story then became one involving weakening Turkish ties to NATO, thence into dissolving Polish Solidarity, even steering into Italian stories and on into further fabrications and leaks. Finally, a U.S. co-conspiracy became the one to follow. Throughout, various mass media, *Readers Digest*, the *Wall Street Journal*, and *CBS*, failed to follow principles of responsible journalism, most often veering towards the most believable paths and into outright propaganda.

In a more pointed and personal take, the chapter "Orwell's World and Ours," from *Understanding Power*, Chomsky gives forth that every single military exercise of power is directly related to the concept of defence, saving oneself or another country, and that our Western preservation of 'democracy' is the norm and ideal, the real aim being "the right people running them; if the right people aren't not running them, then they're not 'democracies.'"

Again, any intention, wanting or, especially, official mention of out of these ideals, in author Joseph Heller's words, makes you 'crazy'.

Catch-22

Just There

It did have its day . . .

After a time,
Too soon,
America was just this place
With the memory
Of something new
You wanted to do

And could,
Like nowhere else.

. . .

Now it became
Bad
Right from the start,
Losing a good part of it,
Before even leaving,
At the exchange.

Trying on
A favourite coat,
Now worn and frayed,
Too tight at the collar.

Or getting used
To the new bully
On the block,
Now turned to relatives.

While just beneath
All that coast-to-coast,
Fields of asphalt shag,
Hidden beauty, old-growth
hardwood

Harkening back.

Surer footed, forests alive,
To the very first
of fires.

. . .

The saddest part, though . . .
Just getting back
From the place,

Another wreck
In the mirror.

Medicine Teachings

"Nothing ever goes away until it has taught us
what we need to know."
—Pema Chödrön

A TEACHING TOOL FOR ALL AGES. When I began the two-year Master of Environmental Studies at York University, we were asked to design a Plan of Study. Having used the Medicine Wheel as a model for my personal prayers for years, I now presented it as a suitable framework for my research. It passed muster with my supervisor of studies, and it worked well enough to come in handy for other purposes.

When it came time for the fourth and final quarter of my studies towards this master's, I met with a teacher at my alma mater, the Ontario College of Arts and Design University (OCADU), the famous Anishinaabe artist Robert Houle. He said they were looking for someone to take over a teaching position he had held there and thought I would be the ideal candidate.

I applied for the position but had a hard time actually connecting with the hiring board, being on a research trip to the American Eastern Seaboard to look into the effect of Hurricane Leslie. But we did manage a phone interview, and a week or so later I was hired. Now given the chance to put all of this into action, I noted that there were four months for the course itself, making it ideal for the use of the Medicine Wheel approach as a teaching tool.

When I was faced with my class for this course, "Rethinking Abstractions in First Nations Arts"," we first rearranged the tables and seats in the teaching studio to make four study groups with five or six students in each. I then outlined the syllabus we would use:

The first of our four months would be taken up by the concept of ideas and concepts in art, along with some detailed history of the roots of modern art, and the various ways in which women have contributed to our visual past.

A good part of this had to do with the link
Between tradition and ethics,
How, for instance, non-interference

With the Natural Order, spiritual laws,
Saves both memory and practise
For the future.

During this time, I was also told that some students were specifically assigned to my course for being a problem of some sort in other
classes. Of course, this would not create any kind of a situation. Our
First Nations world sees these unusual people as being special in the
eyes of the Creator.

For These Lost

A lone woman goes out into a secluded shore . . .

AS IF BEACONING into the wayward early morning mist, she sits.
Before her, vague images from water sprites rise to her pleas
for at least one of the thousands of our Missing and Murdered
Indigenous Women to reappear.

Their ghosts, though, fairly haunt these lone, hallowed places,
near earth and water. All around are reminders of those who walked
and laughed amongst us. Now they can only make vague signs, in
answer.

In autumn bushes, amongst yellowing trees, human figures,
some in mid-Round Dance, grasp for a formal reel.

Drummer to the left salute the lone woman's grim memory.

. . . for These Lost.

Welcome to Hell Street!

When I first moved in, I had to raise an eyebrow
at the sign on my narrow street
—Via dell'Inferno— with Soul Street nearby

ALTHOUGH WITNESS to your usual flashpoints of Italian passion, my art school months in Firenze were, for the most part, a pretty staid and steadfast time. But there surely must have been some queasy ghosts lingering from the hidden past, when wars between city-states— Florence vs. Rome, Spain, or France—were the order of the day. Every narrow cobblestoned street, in fact, has its tale of woe and misbegotten deeds, if you take the time to bend an ear to the whispers of the ages.

Ever-present hammerings and boisterous shouts of builders at their trade bespoke Italian fondness for keeping busy, especially with household renovations and projects. This surely carried on way back from Roman times, when straight roads carried on, to boats used to cross rivers before actual bridges stood their place.

This first week was going by well enough for me, quietly, Andrea Bocelli from my iTunes, studiously tucked into a book, again, one of my favourite subjects, the famed and gifted rascal/artist, Caravaggio, he of sword in hand, given to creating sustained mayhem wherever sandaled feet and flowing cape took him.

Italian apartment courtyards are a little world unto themselves and specifically designed to shut out the busy, noisy world—for a chosen few quiet, peaceful living. What started as a friendly meeting over glasses of *vino blanco*, white wine, three floors below, became rather heated over the second or third course of food. Past washings in the lazy breeze, I spotted a husband and wife—and the lady's boyfriend, over to sort out a nervous situation, little doubt.

In no time, jovial talk and cordial toasts became angry epithets and curses bursting out onto the neighbourhood street, like the famous Arno flood of 1966, drenching all sense of order and decorum! With my limited Italian and from what I could make of it and for reasons of her own, the lady of the house became increasingly irate over her husband's accusations of her seeing this other man, very likely his best friend, given the amiable way it all started.

For this tiny neighbourhood, just off the majestic residential Palazzo Strozzi and the touristy Piazza della Repubblica nearby, all of this flash of emotion must have either been a novelty or the usual for this one couple because it took the police some time to get there. When they did, the husband's police hat on the street must have tipped them off that this was going to be resolved anyway, so they left. The time of year was too hot, and no doubt that had something to do with it all.

Just in that momentary lull in the action, all the nearby church bells began tolling sombrely, from the tiny Santo Apostoli down the way to the famed Santa Maria Novella and, of course, the grand boom from the Duomo itself, only a few blocks northeast, all as if ringing time for Round Two of Battle Matrimonial Bliss-Royale!

There was some hair-pulling involved, judging by the various strands trailing back to our 7 Via dell'Inferno in amongst the bikes and scooters now on their sides, from all the sudden ruckuses. Even the cats fled their alley haunts to seek refuge elsewhere! But to his credit and foresight, the boyfriend had the fortitude to just take and pull the husband back into the courtyard before the woman really got worked up! I had no idea what the angry lady had in her purse, but she left some major damage in her wake—to the wooden doors of buildings along her exit, towards Via degli Strozzi.

As it turned out, this was my welcome to Hell Street, Via dell'Inferno, and I felt right at home!

With the same bells marking the half-hour, all was again quiet, a hinge or two sounding . . . and a furtive procession of straggling church mice, casting beady eyes to reclaim sanctuary in back doorways of the higher-end clothiers and pizzerias.

Later that same day, all three—husband, wife, and boyfriend—were sitting back in the same courtyard, calmly sharing a plate of artichoke hearts and drinking espresso, enjoying yet another pleasant Italian twilight by daintily flickering candlelight.

Whenever I chance to hear church bells in my travels, I always pause to smile about that wild melee on Hell Street!

What *Somba*, Money Can't Buy

ONE OF THE THINGS we got involved with during my several months in Mongolia, in late 2013, had to do with a Buddhist Centre in the capital city of Ulaanbaatar. My hosts, the Canadian ambassador Greg Goldhawk and his wife, Sharon, made it a point to take me to the place, which, for the most part, had classes for a good number of orphans from the area, along with meals for these unfortunates.

The best part, though, was right at the time these youngsters found out through an interpreter that they would be in the company of a bona fide American Indian artist, no less, along with a stockpile of art materials and supplies for their use.

What I also found out is that this here is what money don't buy:

> A crowd of boys and girls dancing for joy
> Having a chance to allow
> The one thing, their artistic talent.
> Be recognized
>
> And maybe even furthered
> From out of nowhere

What really gave this added meaning, was learning that young orphans in this country were already set apart, their ID's having to mention this fact, that they were parentless . . . for life! Something not even the most hardened criminal in America has to deal with.

I also knew that the simple act of volunteering like this does a world of wonders for all concerned.

Bear Paw Dreams

How it got there she hadn't a clue. Just one of those out of the blue'
moments that remain a mystery. Why would a single bear paw stand by
itself beside the stream? Yet there the reminder was when she awoke.

S OME TIME AGO, her Uncle Thomas told Ursula White Bear to go by
'the Mountain Waters' by herself, even overnight, to rid herself of the
person she had become.

Lately, she had to remind herself she had been okay all of her growing years. Just struck hard when her mother passed. She became moody,
to the point of snapping at people, even an Elder or two.

"You don't do that to them," her uncle sternly cautioned her. "They've
earned the right to be any way they want and are probably just trying to
do right by you".

When she found it too hard to just be around anyone, he also told
her that "the best way is to go by yourself, out there." By that he meant
someplace people usually don't go, or if they do, spend as little time as
possible. He also described the way the old timers would often just wander off, to lose themselves 'amongst the Spirits,' to awaken something
missing in there.

So she went to a quiet spot, way upside of the hills, kept going, beside
a fresh brook, one that almost sang, it was so high up! She felt light-
headed but warmed, too, wearing a borrowed sheepskin cloak.

Ursula hadn't brought anything with her, just a light lunch and a few
berries picked along the way. One just went when Uncle told you. She
sat for quite some time trying to get in touch with her feelings. Why was
it she wouldn't choose to be around the People? All the Elders said that
was the only way to get well again, after a close relative dies. Some said
their Spirit went to a place "which lives forever, past the Mountains!"

Others simply spoke of the deceased's favourite place when yet alive.
She relaxed, crouched on the hard flat black rocks, the sun long gone
over the trees above her perch. Even though alone in a strange place it
really did have that 'homey' feel she longed for so, the sounds from above
so soothing.

The lullaby from splashing waters nearby and falling leaves above
was now a soft downy blanket to rest a weary soul . . . so drowsy she

eventually began . . . dropping . . . off, drifted breeze, full of stories . . . stars . . .

What was at first so annoying, too, these intruding elements, now sang Ursula into easy slumber. She had to remind herself she was the visitor here. She had a kind of welcoming sleep, which put all the rest of her waking life to the side as if her softer shadow had somehow gone through a cave into a different Circle.

She walked across a vast, empty horizon, so hungry and lonely, crying, even for a drink of water.

A single cloud above kept her company . . .

When it finally did change, though, the rain brought sweet water to slake her thirst. Just as she started, the small pool simply sucked poor Ursula right in! In the split second a heartbeat caught before reaching for light, Ursula saw not one but two of herself lying there! One was still caught up in the past, her life, and present, always Mom! The other, facing her, strangely mirrored, framed in her story, shone full of the promise of times to come, yet indistinct . . . fogged.

By the time she woke up, the warm sun was already high up above again. After stretching to greet the new day she realized she hadn't even eaten her salmon and egg sandwich. Reaching for it in the packsack, it was gone, simply vanished in this thin magical air!

"Oh well," shrugged Ursula, "must be the Little People, mischievous sprites." She lazily ambled a few steps ahead, to wash her face, in a still pool. Then she saw IT, a single bear paw printed deep into the solid rock! She could tell it was from the left and front, the way the claws cut in so.

When she turned to leave, in case this was some bad omen, she made out the figure of a sleeping animal, encased in rock, just behind where she slept. From the rounded ears and humped back she took it to be what certainly must be her new Spirit Guide and Protector, Bear!

For some reason now lost of all fear, as she went to instinctively pet and maybe get something good from it, she also noticed the full, rounded belly . . . and the left paw, in a small round circle of water, rimmed by fresh moss.She left an offering of tobacco. Certainly this mystery needed a return to when the World was Yet New.

Of course, Uncle Thomas had to know all about all of this. In the family, he was always the one to go to about something from "Outside."

But for now, as in days long gone, she had the high mountain country now with her, full of promise for tomorrow!

He told her that whatever made that bearpaw print was meant for her alone. He told her these places need us just as we need them.

He spoke of a time now long past, when there were no such places like the Indian hospital to just phone and go to.

Bear, in particular was commonly regarded as a 'doctor', one which knew where to go in times of need. When carefully followed, this one was seen digging up certain plants the people came to know to heal the sick.

For the time being, there were still more questions than answers for Ursula White Bear, though. The pawprint of her Bear was clear to be seen, at first look. But why was there only one? Why facing into the land? And claws dug in so! Could it be the careless animal fell into the falls and tried to get back ashore? Maybe it was even somehow saved later, too, like her?

Over the years, she decided this must be so . . . but then again, the one paw mark slowly faded completely out, too quickly for Ursula, leaving the shoreline smooth again. So, too, the now rounded rock behind where she had rested.

There really was no logical reason for it. This place was widely known to be even more sheltered than any in their world.

Whenever she could make it up there, she always brought an extra salmon and egg sandwich to leave, in offering. Ursula even went through a ritual, going right to the shore and suddenly turning, hoping to make out the Bear, as once she did.

Her two children always thought that so funny! They quietly giggled about Mama Bear.

All taken though, the one thing for certain is it didn't much surprise her. It was a very confusing time for her, too.

Now these memories, at first with a face, became teachers . . . and the mother she now was.

Ursula was now at peace with herself.

The Whistles

IT TAKES TWO THINGS to eventually end up with a usable eagle bone whistle. These are the ones used in the Sun Dance and other ceremonials. In equal measure, this demands of you, patience and of course the skill to put one together. Going back, though, you only have the potential for one of these: the time it takes. The younger you are, the less of it you have.

When I first came down to the Big Navajo Reservation over a quarter of a century ago, I got to know a Navajo Dineh man, Leonard Claw, and his family. That was in Page, close to the Utah border. I was new to this part of the land, and we ended up doing a lot of things together.

The Native American Church services, all-night ceremonials, were a good part of it.

One day, he said that he had to put one of these eagle bone whistles together. Leonard formally initiated me into having the skills to put these whistles together. Making the whistle is actually the very last of what needs to be done.

You have to have the bird itself and know which part you need and how to remove it. Cleaning the bone of its internal grease is a different process altogether, requiring a very specific plant and a secluded spot away from your home.

One of the things you learn, which goes with it, is to know that all of it, the church services, the sacred paraphernalia, are actually the property of the Almighty. The Indigenous virtue of generosity also plays into it.

Today, December 15, 2019, I finally got the chance to actually put one together. The ability to do the work itself is a given at this point, but one of the first lessons you learn is that not everyone can even do this.

Just to get a sound at all is a major part of this process. Done right, you can get higher-pitched sounds, on up to maybe four tones. Once you do so, the patience you have and the faith to know that you will eventually end up with a finished whistle simply come with it.

Some tribes only have a selected few people who are entitled to put these together or to even carry them. I prefer to think of the days when people had to make their own.

Now, too, even the eagle feathers are getting hard to find.

Too, you have to figure how life itself is. I was also inducted into being a pipe-carrier, that is, to have the right to use the traditional pipe. But there was a perceived issue, mistaken, as it turned out, with my membership in the Native American Church. So rather than live with the dispute, I simply returned the pipe.

When you add it all up, the skills that make you a true human being—hunting, setting up a teepee, running a Sweat Lodge Ceremony, making a pipe, even learning to bead—are all a part of carrying on our traditions.

As the Elders say, "It's hard to be an Indian. No one's going to do it for you. Pick it up, learn it."

Especially anything to do with the big bird, Eagle. While you are busy going through the motions, in a good way, it's going to take out all the bad stuff—heal you.

In any case, some Sundancer or a Roadman, conductor, of the Native American Church will be thankful that someone like you can still carry on our traditions in this way. Meanwhile, another thing that happens is that you get to know the Spirit behind these whistles.

So, I still have five more to collect

No doubt there will be more.

Aho, Mahsi, thank you.

The Other Side of the Coin

"We learn from history that we do not learn from history."
—*Friedrich Hegel*

FEW SONGS have the prophetic and staying power to have their original meaning passed down to us as initially intended. So too, those like the one popularized by Billie Holiday "Strange Fruit," with its telling and unmistakable reference to Southern Black bodies lynched at the altar of racism.

There could never be any denying the imagery of "Them big bulging eyes and the twisted mouth."

Nor the fact that this drug-addicted Black singer herself paid a price many artists do for their Art.

Timely, too, when Abel Meeropol penned the masterpiece, before the very start of the calamitous World War II. Written as simple as it is, there are deeper, Indigenous, and primordial impacts of the implications here, roots going all the way back to how history sometimes seemingly preordains some events we are taught as such.

People from the very birth of human life unceremoniously kidnapped from deepest Africa to slave for America's brutish beginnings! Only the simplest of racist minds are intent on bending these forces to personal and privileged design.

Fortunately, not all Art carries such portent. Else, where is the room for reality? But in terms of the meaning, what this protest song intended in its messages cannot be denied. On the one side of the Coin of Life, shall we say, is what we go through in our daily doings many humdrum and repetitive, by intent, to carry us forward in time. Turn the coin around though, and you have an oft opposing view, which, too, because it takes a bit of effort to have a look, goes on unknowable.

If imitation be flattery, or, more, interpretation, the simple fact that "Strange Fruit" has been covered by others as diverse as Tim Buckley to Siouxsie and the Banshees points to its purpose.

The Arts, as in no other form of human contact, serve to remind us that we always have something to learn—"Here is a strange and bitter crop"—a way to change back to what the REAL Art—nature—intends.

Homing

An Accident of Birth
Made You White

History,
An Oppressor

Racism
Keeps it alive. . . For now

That same
Fortune cast-a-chance
Made me Dene,

Our History,
An Earthly horizon . . .
Remote,
But for this

Homing instinct.
On the Inside

It's just one of them things
You can't get . . . be

No matter how Big you are,
Or even brave,
Just echoes of the shots called,
On the inside

It's just not there

That simple feeling,
Of the fresh, free breeze,
Sweeping through

Your Being
Going on forward
From the Inside.

All else, the same,
The cares, your worries,
Simple time making even of You

History.
Over the mere passage of time,
Mercifully doomed to end,
That still-foreign feeling,
The wayward breezes,
Over chasms of land,

Always,
Taking you HOME.
. . . yet neither now,
The knowing

Beyond
The inside.

Abineh Goh Toh: Morning Water

OVER THE YEARS, beginning in the early 1990s, I have been to many of these all-night ceremonials. With a total of ten of them done for me, my art, health, and schooling, I got to learn some of the meaning.

When the 'Roadman' of the Native American Church, usually set in a teepee or Hogan, blows his eagle bone whistle, the 'Fire Chief', by the eastern doorway, opens up the flap to let in the Water Woman, carrying her pail of water, fan, and cup. She is usually the wife of the Roadman or a close relative.

This is the most important part of the ceremonial, begun the night before at sundown.

Once settled inside, with the water set before her, the woman rolls her tobacco, and begins her prayers for the well-being of the 'patients' who have sponsored the prayer meeting. This can be for a number of reasons, health-related, to begin a new event in their lives, or even in celebration.

When she gets down to blessing the water, the container goes around, each person partaking of the Holy Water. You can even take some home with you, for your relatives, should you want.

Along with all of the blessing, including travel all over the world with my art to represent Canada, and so far, two university degrees, and my very own teepee, the medicine peyote has done more than its share to turn my life around.

Some of the Roadmen will even share their experiences during the prayer meeting with you. My Navajo brother, Johnson Tochoney, told me of a mountain he saw, when out at midnight, with his eagle bone whistle and fan.

"The mountain, to the north, was actually a volcano, so when I walked up to it, I could even see inside. There were a lot of paintings slowly coming out from inside. And at the very bottom, on the ground, there were all these animals slowly walking around in a circle."

I was very fortunate with this one work; it pretty well having painted itself from memory. Of course, and as usual, I have to call on a few relatives to get the details right.

My Dineh brother, Lawrence Curtis, himself a Roadman, is always helpful with these. Mahsi, Ahehee, thank you.

Upper: *"Abineh Goh Toh"*
Lower: *"Whispers in the Wind"*

Whispers In the Wind

A prayer over a foreboding distance is barely heard.

A ND YET this great bird, the bald eagle, is forever vigilant to the needs of the earnest. An oversized water drum stands ready for use in the Native American Church. In former settler times, these cast-iron pots were used for cooking, on the long trek across the Great Plains. American soldiers posted forts along the way . . .

As in any such harbingers of change, there were clashes with the First Nations.

At the very end of the Indian wars, we found ourselves marooned for all intents and purposes on desolate reservations.

Our ancient and traditional ceremonials were eventually entrenched in the constitutions of both the USA and Canada, paving the way for a modern-day redemption, through our faith, hope, charity, and love.

This painting, like others, is in the collection of Gary and Mary Sandoval of Tuba City, Arizona.

Amongst the Holy

T HEY ARE HERE. Our People say the Holy Ones are in the mists, come visiting, drifting across land or water. Three canoes meet on a seeming floating setting, making ready to offer tobacco to Moment.

The rare time when sky and water meet, none to define a divide 'twixt the Above, to recall HOME.

The two canoes at the bottom are on their way back from an over-land visit to a sacred site. Their hosts, outlined at left, beckon for them to return now. Others in company await in their craft, ready for more adventures. All around are the Spirits of Lake, some long-lost relatives, others animistic. The three main here are, Woman, who calling her man back from pilgrimage and the two brothers at the centre.

One with an eternal mien to Hope.

The other, with inner plans for every moment.

Together, a promise, more measured, assured rhythm in travel, at least. Just above, a watchful Guardian with his Sweep of Light handy stands ready to clear all of even tomorrow's cares into the distant past.

As heat from a splendid dying sun bursts forth, we too are amongst the Holy. As sunset aura plays, we are in amongst the Holy!

Stardust Maiden!

Travelled Afar, has She

There are a good number of Spirits present at our various ceremonials.
They come, bidden by the clean surroundings . . .
soft auras, of pungent mountain tobacco,
Sweetgrass, cedar, and sage.
. . . and the words, in heightened tongue,
Always the words, murmured . . . real.

"Maybe the two-leggeds are talking about us!
Or wanting something special from their home!"

This one, beckoned from eons off, alights,
Hovering just above the smoke flaps,
In folds of wind and driven snow,
Her hair the evening frost.

She carries a translucent bag of stardust, apace of full lunar. . .
gently dropping her precious Magic, first of winter's chill . . .
then, Behold! . . .
Reminding where we were before.
. . . and what we Need,
To Carry On.

The Weight

When falls that evening chill
Fires all but embers
No, not idle, I,
Just adrift.

Before you a dimmed
Thought,
For company.

Another on its way
Veiled in shades,
Pasteled shadows.

This country home
Once so familiar, inviting

Now pressed to
Casted fears.
Weighted twilight,
Always, right about
this time of year,
When the police would come, for
That place,
Home to another
And inner searing heat,
To drive especially family away

High, Even unforeseen
Stars.
Ancient tomorrow

Big Drum Way

In, through the bustle,
bursts West Woman,
The doorway fair alights
a coming storm.

Frightened sprites awaken, sparkling off the Fire,
Their childish echoes expecting

"Why the sitting,
The hiding?"

She gently chides Sitting
Grandfather Drum.

"Hear you not
The coming Wind?

Someone great this way passes!"

Now relaxed of its Presence,
she sits,
With Man and Eagle Bear,
Already there

PART THREE

ARIYONEH SEGOT'INEH

ALL MY RELATIONS

When You Were *Ready!*

It seemed then,
Every glance, every smile,
A spark!
To spring *you* back
Again

For the moment

All was Life
Breathing,
Through you.

Where did this go?
Who stole the Light?

'Outside'

*"There have been no wasted people in my life.
There's no time for waste when you're obsessed."*
—Faith Hubley

Everything that was not Radelie Koe, was 'Outside'

The land we were born into and still used on a regular basis for hunting, trapping, and fishing was huge, and there were yet only several hundred people in our town of Fort Good Hope at any one time.

Other than the presence of the Hudson's Bay Company store and the DOT weather station we didn't have a lot of contact with what was happening in the rest of the '50s World.

There had been some activity in the Esso Oil Company town of Norman Wells just to the south of us, about 100 miles (160 km), and along the Canol Road. The American army was attempting to build a pipeline to the West Coast, but if anything, that had more to do with the tiny fishing village of Fort Franklin on the shores of the Great Bear Lake.

A French prospector Gilbert LaBine was told of the uranium nearby at Port Radium in the mid-1930s, kicking off a concerted mining operation, which eventually resulted in some 260,000 tonnes of the deadly chemical taken out all on the backs of the Dene.

The fifties were more a time of global recovery from the Second World War. Then the onset of the Cold War began to highlight basic differences between American capitalism and Soviet communism. Too, the fifties saw the beginning of the Space Race, with the Russian launching of the Sputnik satellite in 1957.

There was increased testing of nuclear weapons but otherwise a politically conservative climate. Although there were some serious anti-colonialist stirrings on the faraway African continent, we in our far North American slumber had no way of knowing that we were already unwitting pawns as British subjects. In fact, we wouldn't even begin to question our situation until my generation first ventured out from high school in another decade or so.

Yakale Bahbil Morning Swing

CALLED a bahbil, the homemade swing is basically ropes between teepee or tent poles, with a sturdy blanket wrapped in upon itself to form a comfortable bed for the baby. It has two sticks as separators on each end, head, and foot, with an extra string added for Mom to keep the little one in motion with ease.

This little mini world for baby, Awabishdah in Blackfoot, is the most relaxed place to be. As the day carries on, the child's mother will make a blanket wraparound backpack to tote the youngster around camp, leaving her hands free for chores.

I recall being carried in this behbi t'ats'edetl'o way for long distances, travelling in the mountains of my youth. My mom said that she used to really worry about me, because I never made a sound of wanting or needing anything but also called it a 'blessing'.

She was probably at her wits' end to know what to expect, having had me at only sixteen.

Across from Norman Wells

WE HAD ANOTHER HOUSE, farther up the river, at the Imperial Oil company town of Norman Wells. The two-storey log home was built by my grandfather on my dad's side, Michel.

This was so long ago now that, like my memories of being in the mountains with my other relatives on my mom's side, it is a rather scattered affair.

My oldest sister Judy and I did have a lot of fun, though, and really enjoyed the times we had visitors from town.

There was an old pair of overalls we had them put us in and hang us up against the wall.

Years later, Dad had the ol' building taken apart, log by log and put back together at Hume River, closer to Radelie Koe, Fort Good Hope.

Early Hometown Memories

It was always the crystal-clear bells,
marking times to pray and the evening curfews in summer.

T HAT LONELY PEAL from the belfry of Notre-Dame de Bonne-Espérance, Our Lady of Good Hope, across our small frozen northern town in winter carried a long way into spruce forests, echoing along the ramparts cliffs to the south of Radelie Koe, Fort Good Hope.

And to the artist in me, it was just running my hands along the geometric, hand-carved, and colourful works of an early missionary, Émile Petitot, whose artworks went a long way to making this building a Canadian national historic site, much, much later.

At the time of its building, in the late 1800s, there was no linseed oil for an oil base, so he used plain ol' fish oil for these magnificent decorations! There were other large paintings, too, done at the Mission in Aklavik by Bern Will Brown, the Steen boys, and Wilfred Rivet, all self-taught naturals. I would meet the older boys a few years later at the Aklavik residential school.

I also recall doing my share of serving mass in Latin, the language in use for services at the time. Standing there next to the priest, in Roman red cassocks and lacy white surplice tops so prim, we had absolutely no idea what this cultural genocide was really all about, nor would we for a good decade or so.

We knew nothing of this same church's hypocrisy and that in years to come, a park named after the artist Émile Petitot would change its name, after finding out about him as a pedophile, a sexual deviant. But a genuine "National Historic Site" looks good on paper and plaques and there it yet stands, with priestly closets filled with shame, divine or not.

Still, the grandest affair in our northern world was Christmas Midnight Mass, when almost all of the little town would fit in, our collective breaths rising in a steamy ice-fog cloud overhead before the wood stove kicked in, men to the left and women on the other side.

Then there was the church choir, such as it was, with the Kakfwi brothers, Jonas and Noel and their families urging the people on in song, with an organ for backup. In the frosted winter, there was always something of a magical feel to it all.

The Circle Within

"Everything tries to be round."
—Black Elk, Lakota Holy Man

I HAVE MADE MENTION of our Medicine Wheel, here and in my first book, *From Bear Rock Mountain: The Life and Times of a Dene Residential School Survivor*, quite a number of times and for good reason.

The four directions designated by this traditional Indigenous teaching tool serve to outline how each part of the human race is included, making for a holistic approach to life. Further, each of the quadrants is assigned a gift given to the Peoples by Creator.

This third part of *Child of Morning Star* is where the Medicine Wheel really shines, to include how Community, for instance, is at the heart of all our doings. Without this vital aspect of our lives on this fragile planet we tend to think, as at the root of Medieval thought, we the two-legged are the be-all and end-all of Creation.

This section then has to be about how you, as an individual represent the very heart of Community.

"When a man moves away from nature, his heart becomes hard."
—Lakota saying

The circle extends to your immediate family, relatives, hometown, and on to the rest of the world.

In my own case, a good deal of my sense as an artist became early disjointed, first in that northern Dene culture has always been more about survival, leaving little time for creative efforts for their sake alone. Neither was it encouraged in any Canadian residential school, where the inner person was last to see the light of day! I often think of how this affects the Youth. Then you hear of the epidemic of suicides in nearby Nunavut, an especially isolated part of the Indigenous World. In the end, though, One way or another, We have to make THIS our World!

"Begin doing what you want to do now.
We are not living in eternity.
We have only this moment, sparkling like a star in our hand—
and melting like a snowflake." —Francis Bacon

Juliet's Song

OUR ELDERS say that the ones who have passed on have their favourite place where they go to stay. Here, such a young female Spirit roams the Fall woods, hand raised to 'receive the drumstick floating just above.'

> Songs live by the water,
> Melody in gurgling sounds . . .
> Hers, Juliet's, is a winsome, lyrical presence.
> These trees love her.

Somehow named after Shakespeare's maiden, hers now is to forever intone, "Wherefore art thou?" in rankling question to our chanced birth. Another hand both expresses doubt and desperately grabs for a small drum she had her grandfather make for the one child she lost. Even in deepest grief Juliet hopes against hope that this place her son was born will somehow bring at least his Spirit to her, forever.

She needs a song from these waters.

For now whispered amidst rustling Autumn leaves, come it will!

Judy

We had our share of mishaps!

OUR LIVES, from the mid-1950s on, including my oldest sister Judy, took us all the way from the land to the way it was changing for the Dene in general, to town, and beyond. At the time, we only knew the small-town life of Radelie Koe, a tiny northern community of only several hundred northern Dene, with almost every family out for the winter and back in town again come summer, only to return, but to the fish camps along the Duhogah, Mackenzie River.

Our parents being separated by choice, and Mom having contracted tuberculosis, we two were brought up by our grandparents, Michel and Elizabeth. When we were about eight and five our grandfather died, drawing us even closer to Grandma, who cherished us as only a loving grandmother can. Aunt Marie made up the rest of our little family.

Grandma was very strict with us, demanding that we grow up only in the Dene way, while our aunt was probably the most serene person we would ever know.

You have to understand that life in a trapping camp is especially close, with everyone in a single tent, a wood stove keeping you all warm, and the hiss from the hanging gas lamp the only sound, long into the arctic night. Of course, that light had to be turned out early, to save gas, but not before we were treated to a different kind of story each night. The legends from a time When the World was New were especially long, so we usually drifted off to sleep long before Grandma ended each.

We early on learned our own roles, as boy and girl. I recall Judy making me what she said was a pair of moccasins when yet about six. When back in town, I was very popular with the rest of the boys, who hung around outside, waiting for me to eat and go on out and play.

We were so emotionally attached that Judy always wanted to be with me. Given our style of rough-housing fun, she often found herself in a puddle of mud and waited for big brother Antoine to come and pull her out!

In a time when bush planes and barges on the river were the only contact with the Outside, as the world beyond our little town was known, we could simply never imagine the other not being there, nor the merciless Velcro of Separation tearing it all apart so.

Of course, at such a young age we had no way of fighting back, but our little Dene souls clung desperately, as only they could, fighting with every fibre straining against grim . . . determined . . . inevitable . . . merciless forces of Church and State.

Meanwhile, granny, our maternal grandparents, and godparents faded back and away, into arctic night.

Now, as then,
Souls
Exhumed,
Into descent of rebirth,
Only to bear Witness.

O, brilliant
Blinding Light
Why?

When so sweet this resolve
In Paradise.

As a part of our artistic family, my late mom, Judy, and other sisters proved to further the Dene cause to be recognized in our own right as professional artists, yea unto the point of cultural icons.

Being so jealous of ondieh, older brother, they would make me sit between them at the art shows we met at, telling all the curious women to "Move on! Nothing to see here!"

Fiddlesticks and Beyond

*We dreamed of these moments
months before.*

W HILE STILL AT GROLLIER HALL, residential school years, we talked of nothing else, from the beginning of each June on. It was usually about what we would 'do first' upon arrival back in Radelie Koe. No doubt all the other groups of children from as far away as the Eastern Arctic did the same.

When we finally arrived back home, the entire town came to greet us, the old grandmas holding each and very one of us for long moments, up along the Bay Bank, having missed us dearly over a long, cold winter.

Of course, one of the very first places we went was Fiddlesticks, our swimming hole a little ways up the Ohndah Dek'ieh Leline, Jackfish Creek, which ran along the eastern side of Fort Good Hope, to the Duhogah, Mackenzie River. There we dove and splashed the long days away and only came trudging back slowly at 9:00 p.m., when the church bell sounded our curfew.

Another favourite spot was at the Point, on the southern edge of town, where we jumped off the top of McNeely's boat if it was moored there.

Our gangs of boys had some pretty rough games, too, including all out wars against the older guys over the girls, whom we kidnapped and held in forts. There was nothing genteel at all about these contests, which we 'played' with anything we could find or make—sticks, stones, clubs, spears, slingshots, bows and arrows, and even .22 rifles were all fair game—as long as no-one got permanently maimed.

One favourite 'sport' at Fiddlesticks was for everyone to just go and toss a handful of whatever kind of shells, .22s and larger calibre, right into the fire, with everyone ducking and diving every which way to get out of the way of the coming blasts!

Most of us, of course, went out on the land, to the fish camps along the Duhogah, for the summer but these games of chance went on all through the seasons of the Midnight Sun.

"Nobody Home!"

Most people just knew him as Nobody Home,
which is all he had to say in English.

FROM WHAT I WAS TOLD, it was my grandfather, Peter Mountain, Sr., who brought Ole Joe Dillon over the mountains from the Yukon. He was always a cantankerous gentleman and living with a little bitty woman name of Kahbah, Ptarmigan.

Something must have set off the RCMP in Norman Wells to want to jail Ole Joe, because he was made to spend one winter far to the south, at the station in Fort Smith.

Confinement in them earlier times also meant some kind of labour, probably for the police to feel like their prisoner was making himself useful. The man's job was to cut wood for the constabulary, which he got busy doing every single day, all the long, dark winter. Finally, the warmth of spring came along and ole Joe was brought back North.

However, when the police went to check on all the cords of wood Nobody Home was made to cut they also found that each length was slightly longer than the stove!

No doubt, all through the tall pines along Thebacha's Slave River they could almost hear an echo of "NOBODY HOME!" followed by a derisive chortle or two.

"Oooo, Thatah OOOLADAH!"

Some comics don't need a stage.

ONE GENUINE cut-up for sure was our boss on a construction job to build an airport for Kabami Tue, Colville Lake. I and Winston McNeely signed on with the German contractor to do this big job. Being just off of my high school sophomore class and driving a Caterpillar D4 ground-clearing bulldozer, my first-ever summer job was far removed from what I knew back at our preppie Grandin College.

The only thing that guaranteed my sanity, I swear, was this absolutely baboonish boss, whose English wasn't all that good to begin with. He had this habit of ranting and raving for any reason at all. My introduction to this was when he out of the blue asked me to hand him "dose blokes . . ."

I looked around for blocks of wood and gave him a blank look when none were to be had. "Dome!" (he couldn't even say the short Tony for my name). "I said, and me dose blokes!"

Between desperately stifling his giggles, Winston came to my rescue by pointing to a set of spark plugs the man wanted.

Every once in a while though, when we had to wait for parts to come in by plane that boss would get into these moods to let us know all about his lady back in the Olde Country . . . a sweetheart he chose to call "OoooLaDah", for Hilda, I would guess.

He would get so excited he simply couldn't stop himself from stammering, "Oooo, I wouldna mind to get my hands on thata OoooLaDaH!"

He definitely was a pretty rough character and liked to push his weight around the little village down the hill, physically attacking someone for taking something from his tent, or yelling at my poor buddy Charlie Kochon for not bringing him his drinking water from the lake. The poor guy had good reason for not doing so, being paid only five dollars per week.

There was a big rock we were really trying to dig out from the middle of the level ground. We slaved on in the midday heat while the ole boss slept after working on his own all night. And when my partner was busy over in another section, I would think nothing of just taking myself a little snooze in the cool hole, with that shady boulder for a backing pillow.

Of course, the mad boss man was none too pleased with this, either.

What really did set him off was when I stalled the D4 I was on, in the intense Midnight Sun summer heat, and he stormed up screaming that I had "broke his D4!"

I reminded him that he hadn't paid me.

When he finally did, I quit and walked away on the spot.

Elvis in Kabami Tue

He would be literally rolling on the floor with laughter!
Northern life makes for whatever kind of fun you can come up with.

WHEN YOU are at least a hundred miles (160 km) from the nearest town, everything has to be flown in to Colville Lake—where we shared many close relatives—from Radelie Koe and Fort Good Hope, both close to the Arctic Circle.

Summers in this Land of the Midnight Sun, of course, were a time of sunlight all day and all night, for weeks at a time. Were it not for the swarms of mosquitoes like nowhere else we surely would have had us a more relaxing time of it. Yet in a place where a week is like a year anywhere else, there were the moments of little distractions we looked forward to.

There was one Mola, white man, there, Joel Savishinski, a university researcher from somewhere, but he was too much of an oddity for our isolated village, so he just did whatever it was took him there.

I spent most of my days at work driving a Caterpillar with Winston McNeely up on a nearby hill, on what was to become the airstrip. But evenings were free and long.

Kabami Tue was home to my childhood friend, Charlie Kochon, from our days at K'afohun, Willow Point, just up the Duhogah from town, this side of the Ramparts.

The Masuzumi home in town was usually empty, and it had a radio in there. Reception had always been the best right in Colville Lake and all the songs we wanted, especially Elvis Presley, is what we craved and got!

I must have also been wanting for our Grandin College rock band, The Electric Storm, in far-off Fort Smith, so I could put on a personal appearance of the 'Big E' for Charlie right there in that little log cabin.

All of my wild antics must have struck some kind of chord with my pal, for he would begin first kind of giggling a bit . . . followed by outright chuckles and raving belly-laughs. Towards the end, he'd be holding his sides on the floor, reeling with mirth, his legs making little circular running motions! As our years went by, Charlie would often recount the good times we had.

Plumes Adrift

"You give but little when you give of your possessions.
It is when you give of yourself that you truly give."
—*Kahlil Gibran*

IN THE CHAPTER called 'From Six Hundred to Six Million!' of my first book, *From Bear Rock Mountain: The life and times of a Dene residential school survivor,* I mentioned one of the original Woodland School of Artists, Eddy Cobiness.

As it turned out, I was lucky enough to be included, along with John Turo, my boyhood friend and fellow cross-country ski team member from home in Radelie Koe, Fort Good Hope, to be included in a number of shows and exhibitions in the City of Toronto with the rest of the Indian Group of Seven. In the late-70s, with a distinctive Indigenous approach to visuals, the likes of Norval Morriseau and Daphne Ojdig were turning the world of Art to a distinctly Indigenous direction.

Individuals like Cobiness, knowing of my recent residential school background, then made it a point to let me know what I had been missing out on. He showed me how to lay out an entire array of colours to work from, all pre-mixed in their own Styrofoam cups.

More than that were his words, coming from my own father's generation, in fact he, the Anishinabek artist, born the same year as Dad, but without the adopted, brainwashed Roman Catholic approach to life: "Well, believe it or not, this here is what you've been missing out on, the Real Indian stuff! Lucky for you, you haven't had any kind of art training in them places.

But your mind is still in them walls. You have to start thinking for yourself, like our people do. Think Nish! Don't hold yerself back. Jes' forget 'em priests and nuns. They never wanted you to do this." As his kind words sank in, I could feel myself on my way back *home* again. It was the familiar humanity all Indigenous Peoples share, and in this case, to a deeper, creative soul. This early brush with fame also had its own hidden dangers, but for the time being I began to feel like a real human being, and not just another little brown kid brushed into a corner.

Looking back even further, the old Navajo Dineh man, Child of Morning Star, with his corn-pollen offering must have been thinking of his sons maybe off at war, with their own bitter memories of the Bureau of Indian Affairs (BIA) boarding schools.

Set adrift
In a darker Night Air,
Embroiled Miasma,

This soft, downy Plume of the untold Stories
Somehow, Meanders back.

Birthplace of Hockey

Franklin's crew squared off against Deline on October 25, 1825!

IT MUST HAVE BEEN quite a game, on the frozen Hidden Lake, a tad off the Sahtu proper. Here once again, Elder Joe Blondin, Jr. came to my rescue, filling me in on far more than the simple written records, which were, of course, invaluable to pinpoint details such as this exact date.

From what he and others in the fishing village pointed out, this must have been some game, to say the least, given their memories were passed down from relatives from immediate family lines who were actually there at the time. This evidence points to some serious abuses on the Mola, White man side, including outright murder of the Dene.

However, there is no doubt that with the hapless English explorer Sir John Franklin's ship being landlocked in the little safe harbour for the winter and the original Fort Franklin itself serving his crew for housing, the puck, on whatever frozen matter was at hand, was dropped on that October day, to mark this spot on our Dene Nation, and no other, for genuine Canadiana.

As part of my work there, for the Summer of 2010, I helped to produce the mural, with the help of the Youth, who as you can see, in their manner took no little amount of smirk and joy in spoofing lore of yore.

The Four Sacred Plants

IN THE EARLY SEVENTIES, as we survivors attended our initial First Nations ceremonial ways, we began to learn what life in a natural world was all about. One of the basic things we were forced to know and think in the harsh and foreign residential schools was that our culture, being pagan, was evil to the core.

Even, and especially the ones who appointed themselves as our spiritual saviours—the priests and nuns—looked upon and treated us as savages not worthy of knowing their God as is. We were made to accept the fact that we were somehow born with something called 'original sin', and yet "made in the image of God."

That was just the beginning of a vast array of contradictions based on the bible, which has at its primary tenet that the natural world is an evil to be uprooted and changed in every way to suit man's needs.

When we finally learned our own history, not force-fed in the schools, it became apparent that there was absolutely nothing wrong with our land. One would surely assume that the land of savages would be so contaminated as to be avoided and abandoned to all peril and purposes. Definitely not so. In fact, just the opposite. When we learned of the pattern of the oppressor—wherever and whomever—this was what the fuss was all about, for the Mola, Europeans to gain access to our country, no matter what human misery was left in its wake.

In the Sweat Lodge Ceremony, we found out that Tobacco is a sacred currency, to be used whenever we ask Mother Nature for anything, and that this is the first of the four sacred plants the Spirits wanted.

Some believe that the Creator, much like our culture hero, Yamoria, traveled all over the World, making great leaps from one far-off place to another, leaving a bit of Tobacco in each spot, from between his toes.

Next was the Sweetgrass, the hair of Mother Earth. Over time, too, we were instructed to use this whenever we really needed help.

The third of the spiritual, natural herbs is Cedar, which is most often used as an act of kindness, perhaps the greatest of virtues. Along with it came a story of a very kind-hearted man. When he died, a tree grew out of the spot he was buried: Cedar.

The fourth and final of these medicinal plants is Sage. There is Male Sage and Female Sage, with women using the latter.

Relatives Over the Mountains

Mayo, over the mountains beckons like a shining star

GRANDFATHER Peter Mountain Sr. originally came over from the Yukon to the Western NWT. He left behind a sister named Judith, who married a Mola, White man trader. James Mervyn, originally from Scarborough, Ontario.

Over the years, one person in the Canada Council for the Arts whom I stayed in touch with was Louise Profeit-LeBlanc. As it turned out, her mother was best friends with my grandfather's sister.

Judith and James Mervyn had a trading post at a place called Lansing, where a number of our elders in Radelie Koe, Fort Good Hope, were born or travelled to. One interesting fact is that the ill-fated Mad Trapper of Rat River, Albert Johnson, even worked for a winter or two, running one of James Mervyn's traplines. Their trading post got flooded so they opened a hotel in Mayo.

One of the times I was at the Great Northern Arts Festival, I caught a ride with the world-famous knife-maker George Roberts. When we got to Dawson City, he kindly arranged for me to do an artist-in-residency at the Tasty Bytes Internet Café.

An interesting twist revealed itself a few miles down the Yukon

River, where the annual Moosehide Festival was in full swing. I made it be known when I arrived on the visitor ferry that I was a relative of the late James Mervyn from Denendeh. In a while, I was told that one of the chiefs was looking for me. When I met him, he turned out to be a cousin, a lifetime or so removed. Not from office, mind you.

The world of relatives somehow always has its way of coming around for you.

Romance a-la-Strange Range

When love calls, all reason shall be duly forsaken!

THE GOLD RANGE BAR in Yellowknife has seen its share of the bizarre, yet even onto the macabre. One high-ranking staff member from the Indian Brotherhood of the NWT's office and a top eligible bachelor who hailed from Rainbow Valley were both after the pretty young Dene lass from Trout Lake. With the weekend coming, she gave both suitors an ultimatum: whoever came up with a bouquet of nice flowers for her would be shown her favours!

She must have surely fair smitten both more than slightly off the deep rail, and after your usual jockeying for love's favour, the gentleman from the city's far northern end took it upon himself to make and play the definite note for her hand. He thought long and hard, weekend, at work, and when quitting time on Friday rolled around our self-anointed Romeo still had no idea what would take his romantic airs over the top for her hand.

He left her at that landmark bar, kindly asking her to wait for him as he went out for the big surprise. The local flower shop being closed by then, he took a Yk 44-cab to the Yellowknife Lakeshore Cemetery, out on the way to Giant Mines, had the taxi wait while he had a hurried look around and spied just the right bunch to delight his chosen.

On the way back, he explained to the puzzled driver that these flowers for his aunt needed some 're-arranging'. Back at the Strange Range, he grandly presented his magnificent gift to the surprised and delighted young lady. Now for a suitable coup de grâce, he asked her to wait again, this time while he went to fetch them some beers.

This all seemed too odd to be true, thought she and with that, she noted a card stuck in the midst of the slightly damp set of bloomery. Now turning a genuinely suspicious eye she read: With Our Deepest Condolences.

Needless to say, the man from Latham Island had to rework his A-Game . . . and wear the ill-gotten flowers and beer bath as well.

Delta Country Summers

Nothing like the Land of the Midnight Sun

THE NORTHERN TOWN of Inuvik, formerly East 3, has always been the only place for me during the month of July, when the sun has already been up 24/7 for some time and would be so to about the end of August

Sales or not, I have also liked the way the Great Northern Arts Festival was originally set up by Charlene Alexander and Sue Rose, with everything accounted for in the service of visiting artists and guests.

In earlier years, when the ten-day Festival was over I would make it a point to stay on in the Delta, at least for a few days at Bob Mumford and Margaret Nazon's fish camp across the Mackenzie River from the tiny fishing village of Tsiigehtchic, at the mouth of the Arctic Red River.

In town, I would always drop in at the home of Chief Hyacinthe Andre, just to hear his hunting stories, as everyone else wanted do. Some others were my father's old pals, Dale Clark and Billy Cardinal. Times at Bob and Margaret's fish camp would pass slowly, with people sometimes dropping by from the nearby ferry landing. Most were going on, to Fort McPherson and on down the Dempster to the Yukon or the Alaska Highway.

Of a time, Bob would drive us up in his truck, telling of the pre-history of the place and how these would be the haunts the mastodons of Beringa . . . all the way back to our original home in Siberia and Mongolia. Some years later, a young man even found the entire remains of a prehistoric bison, sixteen thousand years frozen in the permafrost, with the meat and hair still intact!

Back at the Festival, as we came to know the event in Inuvik, I often used the photos of Robert Alexie Jr. for my subject matter, if only for his love of the land and people there, which was legend indeed!

One favourite who would come by quite often was the famous fiddler Victor Modeste. As most Delta Country folk, he had his cut-up ways and tales to tell, true or not. One had to do with how he drove his folks crazy trying to learn how to play that fiddle . . . and also driving off all the ducks, muskrat, and beaver at their Spring Camp!

Probably the only regulars would be the bears, coming to hear what all the fuss was about!

I surely did love to take my long daily strolls along the Duhogah, the Mackenzie River, just to feel the warm, earthy breeze off the river bank, ramparts, and sheer cliffs, which dropped down a hundred feet right into the water.

Just the smell of that familiar mud marked me for the life of a small country boy. Back to the taste of Margaret's dry fish, fresh on a grill, with a cup of Red Rose tea.

Faded twilight, golden rays of sunlight shining off a nearby shoreline
Church bells bringing you back home.

Reluctant Heroes

They came upon a scene just short of Dante's Inferno!

AMONG ANY NUMBER of stranger-than-fiction episodes from the seventies was one that boggled the mind of ordinary citizens, near and far. Two valiant truckers to be lauded were found to be less than enthused to receive the annual Commissioner's Award for Bravery. When details of their plight came to light, of news from the road, amazement only led to further bewilderment, bordering on social concern.

They were on the last of a long-legged 18-wheeler run, bringing in supplies from Edmonton, Alberta and upon rounding a long curve were met by a strange scene, between Hub City, Hay River, and the turnoff to Thebacha, Fort Smith.

There on the side of the road in a bright blaze and just visible in evening northern gloom were what appeared to be two ladies and a group of their children, shivering . . . trying to stay warm, all hands, big and small, extended to the hope for warmth. When the two truckers neared to offer help, they were greeted by the story that the housewives had gone all the way to Hay River to do their laundry but broke down on the way back. With no heat in the vehicle, nor axes to cut wood and the light dwindling, for proper heat they saw no choice but to make a fire of their washing, with a spare tire on top for good measure!

One thing this cleared up for the dismayed but discerning public was the real reason the two men were rather shy for any public acclaim and glory for their heroic exploits.

Were it me, though, I would still proudly show the grandchildren the medal of honour and replace the heaps of burning garments and sheets with maybe piles of Top Secret government documents and files, needing immediate and secretive flaming, away from prying eyes!

In the Shedding

ONE ADDED EFFECT of residential schools, closely associated with those traumas mentioned in books like Viktor E. Frankl's *Man's Search for Meaning*, is the lasted stamp, much as the numbers worn on the arms of survivors of the Nazi concentration camps. In fact, along with a standard issue of institutional clothing, we victims of the Canadian attempt at cultural genocide, were given numbers, more often used as forced identity.

When Frankl talks about the "hard fight for existence which raged among the prisoners," these are the ties that bind, long after the years we were forcibly confined in these hated residential schools. To this day, well over a half-century from the empty halls of these places, I still maintain contact with others I first met there.

When you were simply too frightened at the thought of punishment to function as a human being, almost every waking thought was about your relatives at home, and what they might be doing. Even though most of those times were actually physically harder, it still seemed a paradise compared to being confined against your will.

Without any kind of human support all around, I found myself willfully shutting down emotionally, at only twelve, three years into the place. To this day, almost every other survivor puts on a face to show the public, and a different one, private except for family, relatives, and loved ones, who often felt the brutal burden of caring.

One of my very closest friends, who often spoke of wanting to become a pilot, found himself, like Icarus, who flew too close to hope and glory, got permanently scorched and fell back to an earth too suddenly hard. Another, a mentally brilliant cousin, found himself for a long time in a dulled alcoholically induced mental mire, not wanting to even show his former capabilities, confined to this haze.

There is simply no term of reference for the average citizen of a modern Western country, pampered on privilege, to understand the basic inhuman indignity of being cooped up in a foreign culture. In terms of colonial power structure, even the priests and nuns were unwittingly being held captive by this system, serving much the same as the capos, prisoners in the Nazi death camps, they, in turn neglected and cast aside, even by their own religious orders, when their lifelong tasks were done.

They spoke fondly of their home, in their foreign French, exactly fulfilling Frankl's 'delusion of reprieve', a kind of hope-against-hope, that their religious 'calling', would eventually be answered, by at least one convert to their order, which never did come.

We survivors—Dene, Inuit, and Métis, only knew one thing for certain:

> We were not about to,
> Nor ever would, Change

So had no other choice, but to live in pitiful hope that tomorrow would present at the very least, a little change to this endless misery. A sure ingredient of this repeat over the darkened northern winters was the food, or what passed for it—more often than not the usual fare of overcooked, dried out fish or unfamiliar reindeer, with its gamey taste.

The phrase straight 'from the bottom' from Frankl's recollection of concentration camp life comes to mind, how every prisoner hoped for just a few extra peas, scooped from the richer inner pot digs. In our case, there was never much hope of that, what with the huge cauldrons ours came from. Just to give you an idea of these places, when I was in Aklavik, first arrived at just seven, the one taste I most craved all week was a little sugar in my milk.

That's all.

One good thing, though, was the sports, which almost all of us were good at, and excelled in at least one. In the long run, though, very few were eventually recognized enough to turn professional. For the handful who did, the added burden of the intergenerational residential school trauma simply proved to be too much, when the temptation to legally drink eventually came along. Thus, the release from these places happened at the same time as being allowed to drown our accumulated sorrows in alcohol.

The death toll began soon after.

Once sober though, and by divine grace, through it all there is a very real sense of recognition to it all. Over the years of visiting amongst our Navajo Dineh relatives in the American Southwest, almost all of the people I spend any time with are veterans of one war or another. The PTSD, Post Traumatic Stress Disorder, immediately strikes up a bond permanently there from the experience.

Too, the tears of recognition, from books like Victor Frankl's, each opened page, glazed, coming at me, almost verbatim, like ocean waves from a very beginning birth . . .

. . . and certainly from some psychic past.

What makes our Indigenous Peoples so resilient, though, is another kind, an older, cultural memory, if you will, of a spiritual home we yet belong to.Any sign of weakness, at a time of total innocence, was an admission of guilt, for being a nothing but a 'dirty Indian'. Strange, too, in a way, that that kind of subtle and inhuman strength, should some-how lie now—

Within tears
Then stifled into nighttime pillows,
Sixty years
In the shedding.
Into Light.

All Roads Lead to Vegas!

I knew my mom would like that, Bingo at 10:00 a.m.!

MY FIRST TIME EVER to the American Southwest, walking to the bus depot, early 1990s. There was a group of Navajo Dineh, relatives of our northern Dene, who several years before made their way to Desnetche, near Fort Reliance, on the East Arm of the Tu Nedthe, Great Slave Lake, to a place we call T'seku Dawedah, Woman Sitting Up There, where the Spirit of a Holy Person is said to live.

Over the ten-day pilgrimage at the mouth of the Lockhart River, we had a number of Sweat Lodge Ceremonies and even two all-night prayer meetings of the Native American Church. I already knew of the medicine peyote from years before, a trip to Crow Indian Agency in Montana, visiting with two American tourists to the North I had guided all the way up to Inuvik.

This time I was having a lot of problems with my legs, which even the doctors could not explain or figure out. After doing a weeklong art workshop organized by Henry Tobac at home in Radelie Koe, Fort Good Hope, I simply took my pay, bought a ticket to the capital of the North, Yellowknife, walked into a travel agency and asked for "the cheapest ticket anywhere in the American Southwest."

. . . and Vegas it was, the Holy of Holy Gambling Joints!

I knew this to be a games-of-chance kinda town as I passed a woman with all her bags and luggage around her, sobbing her poor eyes out, with no-one even batting an eyelash. This must have been a common enough sight; someone lost all their money, even her bus ticket to get back home.

After a long bus ride, I found myself in the tourist town of Flagstaff, near the Big Navajo Reservation. In a few hours, one of the group who had come North before, Garrison Yazzie, picked me up at the Greyhound station and gave me a grand tour of just a small part of the Western Agency of the reservation, including his home in Ganado, also a historic trading site.

When we got to the tourist town of Page, near the Utah border, I met and moved in with a Belagaana, White man everyone simply knew as Sky, some former hippie type now a member of the Native American Church.

Baby Sees All

All you could see of the little fellow was his curious head, with big round eyes looking everywhere

THE CRADLEBOARD is a child's first home. Like the Plains Indians' kind, this one is made of a sturdy wood backboard and a hide or cloth covering laced up in the middle, often with elaborate bead-work. Very likely the design is so that this holder for the baby can be leaned up against a tree or the traditional home, the Hogan, whilst the mother busies herself with any number of daily household chores. But I also learned that the reason for having the infant's hands firmly by its sides is so that they will grow up not wanting to touch every-thing they see.

This so reminded me of the way we grew up in our northern Dene home, to be mindful of the wants and needs of others, of course, but to also just leave their things alone. Besides the deep-rooted spir-it-filled nature of our Navajo relatives in the American Southwest, I grew to appreciate the sensible lessons embedded in their way of life.

For instance, you will rarely see a Dineh person smoking ciga-rettes. Besides the obvious health hazard, smoking is a continuing expense, and from what I was told, "If you can outrun a rabbit, *then* you can smoke!"

Of course, I eventually found out that like we their relatives to the Far North, the Dineh are very independent and will strive to do well in the modern world, and yet make a point to speak their own lan-guage. I have often sat all night in ceremony next to one of the tribe, who will turn out to be doctor, lawyer, or even a chief of some kind, having only spoken in their language throughout.

From a man pointing at a jet airliner far aloft overhead, I was told that "If you shoot down any airplane anywhere in the world there will be a Navajo on board going somewhere!" Which, too, is true.

A Fine String-o-Decoys

Them still Delta waters run deeeep!

ONE PERSON I got into the habit of dropping in on, of a Great Northern Arts Festival in Inuvik, was CBC Radio announcer Wanda McLeod. I always came in early, to make time for either her, Ruth Carol, or someone else already there to tell a few funny stories.

Before we got to talking about the Festival itself, one story she favoured me with had to do with a small group of muskrat trappers from Silver City, Aklavik: Charlie Furlong and his wife Florence and the Freddy Greenland couple. Them men would spend the long Midnight Sun nights out 'ratting', shooting fat ole muskrats that looked like they had good pelts. They would return to camp in the morning, have something to eat and go to bed, leaving all their catch for the ladies to skin and stretch and dry out in the hot Delta sun.

Things went as well as could be expected, with a typical total being in the hundreds of these jolly rodents when the price was good at the fur trader's. A day came when one of their wives had a bright idea:

"Ya know you guys are missing out on something real good here. If you leave us one of them shotguns we can have some duck or even goose stew for you when you get on back next time. You don't know, but lots of ducks are landing right here in front of us, and we can get a few. How 'bout it, boys?"

Licking their lips and already kind of tasting all that good duck or goose stew they left a shotgun and some shells back with the cooks. The very next morning, the men came back all ready for a tasty meal of duck soup, and one of them asked where this new dish was.

When neither of the ladies said anything, one of the men went over to the lake and had a look. All he could see was a line, tied onto a stick on shore, with the end kind of loose-like, going into the water. When he went and pulled it, it took him awhile, but eventually one of their duck and goose decoys after the other came a-poppin' up in front of him, each one smiling their silly goose looks!

So much for an extra good meal on the ladies, he thought, spittin' a spot of 'bacci snoose' on the shoreline.

Used Car Artist

"Can you come down a bit on the Chevy on yer lot?"

THERE WAS A MAN from one of the motor places in town who figured himself a fine artist. The manager of the Northern Images Gallery, Glenn Wadsworth, must have thought as much too, for they organized for a show of his paintings.

I had been there, set up as an artist-in-residence for a few years by that time, so I got to see all the various and sundry-type shenanigans that went on in the name of Art.

The guy had his paintings up on the far wall, just over my right shoulder.

What with my curious and nosy nature, I took note of the same kind of thing happening each and every time someone came in and asked for him and his show. The guy or lady would step up to our man, have a quick look along his row of images and go, "Well, yes, of course, this is good stuff, man, but are you absolutely sure I can't get a better deal on that Chevy (Ford, Impala, etc.) on your lot over there?

I for one was glad I at least got as far in the door to the World of Art as to be sitting there, so people could actually see me at work, painting!

Ghosts

AS THE MEDICINE MAN SAYS, each and every one has done some deed that we do not ever want another Soul to know about. Perhaps that is why we of the Native American Church are simply told to only look forward in life, and to leave the past behind, where it belongs.

Yet again, life itself has its own fail-safes—safeguards—which stand as firmly as bastions daily pounded by seas of regret and remorse.

Memory is funny like that, too . . .

We spend a lot of our youthful energies picking out those people we want to have as enemies, to someday pay back for real or imagined slights. Yet just when we are most able to exact our revenge, there comes a time when we fail to even remember what we are in the next room for, much less the exact person, or reason for our payback ire.

This is also why I wanted to dedicate these stories for the Youth of tomorrow, for they in their inborn store of generations and millennial memory as balm from All, have the only chance to redeem.

Moose at the Point!

There isn't much doubt that our town,
Radelie Koe, Fort Good Hope,
is the Moose-hunting
Capital of the North!

IT WAS YOUR USUAL lazy summer weekday, with people at work and some, like me, just picking out a few items at The Bay, the Hudson's Bay company store. Right out of the blue, between the frozen foods section and the checkout counter someone stuck their head in the front door and shouted, "Moose! Moose! At the Point!"

This meaning food, everyone just left their carts where they were, grabbed a bunch of empty plastic bags and raced out the door.

Some people were just on their way out upriver on a hunt, and one of them must have spotted a moose, of all things, just behind them, swimming right to town and the Point, where people tied up their boats and leave their stash of logs to be cut up for firewood. They simply turned around, shot the animal, dragged it ashore and started skinning it right there. Amid your usual banter and happy faces, the women and elders were given first pick of whatever they wanted.

Within an hour there was nothing left to mark the place where people saw a moose at the Point!

Another story, just as strange, and written in a local newsletter as "Manna from Heaven," told of Dolphus Shae coming upon a caribou that had run clear off the cliffs, falling straight down more than a hundred feet (35 m) to a solid rocky shore.

Fresh meat for the taking!

Taking Turns Marooned

There I was, with a bad case-a-gas from the black caribou lichen!

YOU HEAR a lot of talk just a-sitting around talking about the land, in leisure with other hunters. Given the company, some of it might be true, and either way there is never enough time nor notion to get all the details, minus the actual experience.

But one thing for real and certain is that we all, All, take turns being wind bound or stuck way out there on the land at some time or other or can very well expect to be again, before the year is out. We all have heard our share of these forlorn tales.

One about the poor guy who made it to a small rock island in the middle of the roaring Ramparts Rapids upriver from home to Radelie Koe, Fort Good Hope, and had to spend a week there, with only a diet of bugs to keep himself alive!

Or the American fisherman who chose to throw his anchor overboard and was there in a real Tu Nedhe, Great Slave Lake, storm for an entire two days before he was rescued. He complained of being mighty thirsty for all that time. When asked why he didn't just drink out of one of Canada's biggest bodies of freshwater he said that he thought it might be polluted! And when asked why he didn't just go to shore and make himself a fire and shelter he replied that he was afraid of bears! As if these animals thought of nothing better to do than gamboling around in the rain, looking for a touristy bite to eat.

Granted some such exceptions, it is just the nature of traveling any distance, if you depend on anything else but your own two legs you will break down at some point, often when you least expect it.

Which is what happened when I hit one of them countless hard rock reefs that just seem to grow right out of the channels you've been through so many times before, going either way out of Somba K'e, Yellowknife Bay. This time was towards the Simpson Islands which, wrecked or not, is a maze of tiny places to land, yes, but coming and going, full of dangerous spots with your name on them.

This time, it was a clear and sunny day, which is actually more treacherous than a cloudy one. Reason being, the shimmering reflection just off the surface of the water means you really cannot see what you are heading right into, as opposed to when it's rather dull out and you can at least make out what is there.

So, going at a fairly good clip with my 25-horse Yamaha I banged smack into a rock sticking up at least to my prop's level. I hit it hard enough to take the entire prop right off its shoe.

When I paddled back, I could easily reach right in and get my prop unit back out, but by then the shaft may have been bent a bit and it looked like the blades were too damaged to move me forward anyway.

Without a lot of other options, I just paddled to a nearby island, pitched up my handy tent and spent the night under a roof of stars, Rayuka, Northern Lights and duck calls in night flight.

In the morning, I just rigged up the same tent for a sail and started on my way back to the city, probably a good twenty miles (32 km) back through the main Wool Bay Channel everyone uses in there. I was making pretty good time and I even thought for awhile that I could do this all the way back. Until I ran into a dogleg in there, a backward curve. With no more wind behind I had to go back to shore.

There is no more lonesome feeling on this earth, I am sure, than to be so close to home and yet not be able to go that extra. I hadn't planned on being out there for more than a few hours, so didn't even pack a lunch or anything.

But I did recall different ones talking about the black lichen the caribou eat, so seeing some, I just thought I would try it. Not even being sure if it should be prepared I went and ate some. It was bitter to the taste but did give me enough of a boost of energy to set up my camp again for another night.

And, of course, the added feature of a bit of the runs, probably because this was more like deer food, not indented for two-legged and stranded. I did spot some cranberries, but they were either too small or some shriveled up.

So, again, I slept under the light of a chandelier of other and impossible worlds for the nonce.

I did hear a symphonic rhapsody, though, the following morning, in the person of one David Giroux, a Dettah fisherman on his way back to town from checking his early morning nets. Thankfully, and probably from having this same experience a time or two, he didn't ask a lot of questions, not that I was in a very talkative mood.

Yah Dek'o Tue

Burning Snow Lake, a Very Special Place

S OME TIME AGO, four of us, with my brother-in-law Frank T'Seleie, his
younger brother Jimmy and one of my best friends, Charlie Kochon,
left Radelie Koe, Fort Good Hope, on the winter road to Kabami Tue,
Colville Lake, on a hunting trip. We were on two Skidoos, hauling sleds for
the caribou we hoped to get.

On the way, Jimmy's Ski-Doo broke down, so we stopped at a nearby
tent to check on the problem. We made fire in the stove and were in a
hurry, because that far North, at the Arctic Circle, daylight only gives you
a few hours. Frankie said it was probably something in the gas tank. In the
rush we were in he started looking right into its mouth, a candle for light.

Ker-Whoosh—a huge, long flame from the gas fumes still in there shot
right into his face! He fell back against the tent, dropping the tank. At first,
he thought for sure he had singed his eyes and probably did, but not seriously damaged. It was a long night for him, as it was too late to go on
anyway. We camped there, with the poor guy moaning all night in pain.

We now had more time to figure out the situation with Jimmy's
machine and we did. Whatever might have been stopping the gas was now
out of the way, so we just continued on, eventually making it all the way to
Kabami Tue following day. Frankie went to the nursing station there and
got his face all bandaged up. With these repairs he now could only see out
of one eye. In Dene fashion we started calling him the Caribou Bandit!

On our way back, we got to a good-sized lake Frankie said was called
Yah Dek'o Tue, Burning Snow Lake. He said that there was something 'different' about some of these places on our land and that this one played
tricks on your eyes, with mirages and such.

We could plainly see a large herd of caribou on the other side, but
Frankie said that they might be there, or not. The best way would be for us
to go around, along the shore and to the other, land side, and have a look.
From there, we could see quite a few animals, so we just took out the ones
from one end to the other, until we got them all.

Caribou get confused and besides, that early in the morning their legs
are still stiff from a night sleeping in the snow. After skinning them, about
thirty, we loaded up about half and stashed the rest under a pile of snow.

Yah Dek'o Tue

Frankie could arrange for an airplane to pick them up.

On the way back, the hitch from Jimmy's Ski-Doo got loose, leaving poor Charlie behind, as flag man. This person, hanging on at the very back of the sled is probably called this because of the way you bounce and wave around as you go.

Traveling fast, it sometimes takes awhile for the driver to find out he's lost the sled. When we did get to Charlie he had decided to try to pull the heavy load of caribou meat, eight of them! He got quite a ways, too, even some uphill pulling. Strong man!

The painting that goes with this story features a lot of imagery, of a caribou head, antlers intertwined in the large ice-glazed willow tree. A herd of the animals stretch all the way across, where the land should be.

> Scenes effortlessly morph of themselves into others.
> The Place asking you,
> 'What are you Really Doing Here?'

Hands, one from Michelangelo's David and the other, female, protect the animals, mysteriously descend.

These places also harbour a kind of forward-looking memory, a portent of what will be.

When Cooks the Chief

All we saw was black!

U SUALLY when we went out hunting, he would go scouting on land and I would tend to the vittles. One of the times, mid-2000s, my good friend Fred Sangris called me to go out on the Tu Nedhe, he had one other crew member with him, a film-maker from Toronto, Manfred Becker, who was doing a documentary for TV Ontario called *Diamond Road*, about mining for the precious stones around the world.

This was quite early in the spring, June, with the Big Ice still on Great Slave Lake, so we left by skidoo from his place in Ndilo. The sun was out and so quite warm when we got to his cabin past Wool Bay.

The plan was for the two of them, Fred and the film-maker, to just sit outside to do a rather lengthy interview, so the Chief told me to "Go on out and look for some ducks around the island," which I and another man were glad to do. When we got back about an hour later, they were about done with their recorded talk and as only a chief could, Fred grandly announced that the food, too, should be done to "Dene Perfection!"

What should have been sizzlin' to the discerning nose was an assortment of fresh fish, caribou ribs, and some nice cuts of steak, along with a kettle of tea. What actually met our eager eyes on the grill was all the blackened remains of that fine collection of foodstuffs, almost completely turned to charcoal!

Even the usual whisky-jacks perched expectantly on nearby trees at every northern outdoor cookout were instead holding their beaks a good distance away!

. . . not even a raven or seagull in sight . . .

One thing to consider is that like hunting buddies the world over, we like to tease. So, when the film-maker asked if this was the way we Dene usually ate, just this once I could not help but point out, "This is what happens when the Chief cooks!"

When Manfred permitted me a pre-screening version of the documentary sometime later in Toronto, I was glad to note that the camera work was conveniently averted from the disaster in the cooking area.

For his part, right from the start, Fred Sangris proved to be an invaluable source of historical information about the Samba K'e, Yellowknife area, all the way to the Barren Lands.

There is also always a certain theatre
To the telling of tales,
And no doubt he is a Master!

Shetah Gareh, Up Mountain Road

"I just like to dance"
was all she said,
This Dene woman.

In a dream she was
in one of those places

My Grandpa Peter's recent Spirit
had just passed through

Splendid Log homes
And bush tents set

All along a wintry way

Into freshly frosted

High Country

Everywhere
Winter, yes,
But like just stepping in
From out in freezing cold . . .

Familiar

Through these female
fogged mists
. . . and everywhere I stopped

"Hindugoh, jonhraweyah
. . . He was just here"

But always one step ahead
As the dream drifts on

Just out of mind

Like a warm blanket

Of Memory

Waving on
Into future
Mothers' arms

First Centre of Learning, Bologna, Italy

*It is also ironic to learn
that the first-ever students
were lawyers!*

THE FIRST TWO PLACES where students went to be formally educated were in Italy. One that combined the knowledge gleaned from Greek, Arabian, and Jewish medical traditions was farther to the south, southeast of the Eternal City, Roma, in Solermo.

The other began in 1088 at Bologna, just north of where I now came to study, as guilds, by ordinary citizens—lawyers, as it turns out—non-citizens who also just wanted to protect themselves from the high costs being charged for the basics: food, shelter, and books, such as they were.

At the first of our classes, we were gleefully introduced to the reputed humour spouted by our Art History professor, the venerable Peter Porcal: "There were no classes such as we have here, with loving students sitting at desks in chairs, listening to the teacher at the front, writing on a board.

"No, if they could afford it, the poor pupil would carry a clay or stone tablet and write with whatever they could find to use—a piece of chalk or crayon—what the great man knew or chose to tell them as they walked past other citizens going about their daily chores.

"If it was not too busy with the ladies at the local fountain, they would sit there and have their daily lesson. Going on, walking, for the rest of the time. And maybe stop to have an espresso and slice of pizza or to count the ten dogs, four cats, twelve chickens, and three and a half scooter bikes the place was known to have."

Case in point, books proper, would not see the light of print for another four centuries or so.

Far from being any kind of basic learning, though, it would take a total of ten years for a doctor to actually begin his own professional career. A student of law was expected to become familiar with and on working terms with an exhausting set of almost four thousand texts, just in canon law, in codification the *Decretum* (c. 1140), a science apart from theology.

One scholar's daughter, Joannes Andrea, there to occasionally fill in for her learned father, was so *bellissimo*, beautiful, she had to wear a veil, so as not to distract her eager pupils!

With no classrooms as we know them, students gathered in either the master's place of residence or in convent hallways, for long-drawn-out lectures in the language of instruction, Latin.

Three centuries later, by 1404, ten of Europe's twenty-nine universities were in Italy.

Room Service, Russian Style

THE FIRST OF THE TWO TIMES we went to Siberian Russia was certainly a novelty. After we got our presentation booths for the combo Arts and government event all set up for the visitors to Siberfest, we were instructed to show up for business at the conference, part of the ten-day event. So, there we all sat on a stage top panel, amongst other dignitaries, including the cultural director for the Russian Federation.

One by one, the speakers to my right made their talks to the eager audience, mainly reading from prepared notes. The businessman to my immediate right went in on his, about the bright future for diamonds in Canada's North, making his point by dramatically folding up his shirt-sleeves, elbow high.

When it got to my turn, I let everyone know that it is First Nations protocol to begin with a story. I said that I must comply with this traditional directive and would do so by relating a tale about ordering my breakfast in Russian, from my hotel room the night before. There was a noticeable stir and relaxed shimmer both, in the formal gathering as is very likely intended by this way of addressing serious matters. I began,

So here I am alone in my room, late last night, very much wanting to show my ancient Russian relatives here, both for them and for the wholesome food I had a taste of on the airplane coming over. With that in mind I dialed the front desk's number and let them know right off not to interrupt me with a word in English, nor to change any of the order I wanted to make, all in the Russian language.

I included all that I thought I could possibly eat, thinking this might be the only food I would have all today, stuck in a booth showing off my art and talking to hundreds of curious people. I had da bacon and eggs, potatoes and onions, a pile or two of pancakes, flap-jacks, a good variety of fruits and wholesome berries, a pot or two of good, strong coffee, and of course, some of that rich black bread toast.

When I ran out of things my stomach would appreciate, I just gave my room number and the exact time for this great meal to be brought on up. So, friends and relatives, 0615 hours, 6:15 a.m. rolls around mighty quick, and I heard that inviting knock on my door, right on time. I got on up, walked over to the door and opened it, and there was a pretty middle-aged lady just a-standing there, in a spritely uniform, holding aloft a silver tray, with the dome top on it, to keep my food warm.

When she opened it up to show me, all there was on the tray was a blow-dryer!

I guess out of all I said, this is what I had ordered in Russian! She even kindly asked me if I wanted it plugged in!" When he heard this, the Russian Cultural Director about fell off his chair, some ways down to the start of the panel!

Well, I never did go hungry that first time to Russia but neither did I go and order any more meals in Russian.

Littlest Indian

Round about this time, when the City of Yellowknife took notice of my change of ways, I began to be invited to give presentations and art classes to various schools, including Saints Joseph, Patrick (the one in Ndilo), and others.

At one, Mildred Hall School, Shirley Desjarlais and Diane Blesse were doing a lot of work for Dene curriculum in a teepee-shaped addition in back. They had some very young elementary students and one group happened to be a Kindergarten class.

In traditional First Nations manner, I always like to include the pupils in what I have to say, also explaining that education is all about them, not the staff nor the books. This one opened with a *Time* magazine story on the question of life on other planets. I asked the class what they thought of this idea. I could see there was a bit of confusion about the issue, but right away one tiny hand shot up and the little Mola, white tyke it came from stood up proudly and began in on a group of people on Mars, what they did, what they had to eat, and all the rest of his thoroughly interesting story.

I could tell he was making some of this up for the benefit of some little girl a few children away, but when he was done I told him to just keep standing there while I said my piece.

With that I let the rest of the class know that there "stands one true to life little Indian boy . . . because he believes that there IS Life everywhere, even in places where there is no air." That the real question magazines like *Time* were asking is if 'there's something there we can use?' I have yet to see a prouder fellow as this little guy took his seat with a flourish, his sweetheart beaming in recognition of his vast knowledge!

The Kiss

Both rough-hewn and tender,
A moment forever caught

ALTHOUGH French sculptor Auguste Rodin (1840–1917) is commonly regarded as the father of modern works in stone he did not consider himself as such. He received the traditional training of his time, yet far from playing the rebel, wanted for academic recognition. Even though his highly personal style veered from the decorative one favoured, he refused to change and was thus professionally shunned.

His works clearly show the kind of realism he sought to bring forth, with real human character. Some, like his famous *Thinker*, makes a powerful statement for all time.

Rodin was eventually widely commissioned, as with *The Burghers of Calais*, based on an episode from the Hundred Years' War, when a group of six townspeople volunteered their lives so that their fellow citizens might live.

Even for his deep impression within the artistic community, Auguste Rodin remains a relative unknown to the outside world.

A. Mountain Arts

ONE OF THE ADVANTAGES of being an artist is that you can bargain and barter for what you need. This happened when the president of one of the local diamond companies in Somba K'e, Yellowknife, expressed an interest in my art.

I let him know that I was in need of some sweet 'ice' and even mentioned that as an artist I could go one step further and give him a design for this ring. We struck up a deal and a few weeks later we were both happy campers—he with a prized painting and I a finger a-sparkle!

The next, with much longer-range potential, was when I asked John Simpson of the Genesis Group about a website of my own. When he quoted the rather princely price tag, again, one of my works of art caught his attention, to the point that since then I have been able to reference this E-gallery, no less, complete with a resume, for more work-related needs.

One other person who has always come to the fore was Kirby Marshall, a kindly soul, who simply hosted my website, as a supporter. This totally portable art gallery, www.amountainarts.com, has saved my dry meat more than a time or two.

The Missing Sasquatch!

Bigfoot himself came a-calling!

FROM an oral tradition and a storytelling culture, it is not at all surprising that we have these kinds of tales. This one happened in a place in north-central Montana, the Chippewa Cree reservation of Rocky Boy's. This is where Cree Chief Big Bear's people ended up, after wandering around for decades, following the Riel Rebellion.

Seems a white prisoner escaped a state mental institution and was on the loose, with state patrol cars running up and down the highway, and an all-points bulletin on the missing fugitive from justice. Meanwhile, the desperate man in question spotted a teepee set up in a meadow, under full moonlight, and wisely thought to find out what the place was all about and maybe a chance at freedom. When he got up right next to the teepee, he could hear a series of four songs, followed by happy voices smacking their lips in approval, going, "Mmm-good . . . good un' . . . Yeah, *aho,* thank you."

Figuring these were cannibal Indians for sure, he still had to get away from the sirens on the road, so thinking quickly he smeared himself with some mud from a puddle and bravely scratched at the canvas doorway. When bade entry, he stood just at the eastern entrance, waiting on official permission to go into the teepee proper.

"Ah, Sasquatch!" said the man to sitting to the west, "We were just talking about you! You are a big man, a Chief no less, amongst our Chippewa Cree here in Rocky Boy's. Come in, Man of Legend, sit with us and pray to the morning light. Then, we feast!"

What the man thought of as people eating some poor fool was actually an all-night prayer ceremonial, which he was glad took him out of harm's way. He hadn't counted on the hot fire though, which he ended up sitting right next to. Eventually, the heat melted the mud on the poor guy's face and arms, revealing him to be the madman on the loose!

When the dust settled and word got around that there was a reward for this one missing Sasquatch's head, the Indians made the best of it and turned him in for the reward money!

Listen with Intent

"A leader's job is to remind people of their responsibilities."

WHENEVER I go back home, I always try to spend some time with my cousin George Barnaby, a great Dene statesman in his own right. Just one of the many things I learned from him is to be willing and able to take constructive criticism like a True Human Being, especially if it is not worded exactly the way you want to hear it.

One of these times came up when I was having one of my eventual ten all-night ceremonials of the Native American Church, this one near Shiprock, Arizona, on the Navajo Nation reservation. I was waiting on a payment from a court decision in my favour from the Canadian federal government and when it didn't come in when some bills had to be paid for the event, my adopted sister stepped in and assumed all of the expenses required.

The prayer meeting went through and at the time of the Morning Water, the Fire Chief, who had tended to the central heat source all night, was given the chance to speak. Without knowing all the details, he laced right into me for not seeing to doing things in the way he would've liked to have them done.

We Dene/Dineh are not allowed to interrupt a person, especially during holy doings such as this, and I had no choice but to just take his stern advice in the way he intended. The purpose is to prevent you right away from looking for and voicing an excuse, rather than a reason, and to get you used to—as Cousin George would say it—your responsibilities.

Eventually, you become enough of a true human being to be able to pass along these ways, as an elder. My grandparents, parents, and other close relatives were exactly this way with me while I was growing up. For life's best lessons, this is the way we have to listen, with the intent of doing something about it.

In fact, this way of listening often came at great cost to a First Nations leader in times past. A Chief was expected to suffer a great deal of abuse, with even horses slain and personal property abused and even taken, without saying anything in return, to prove stalwart fortitude.

Fashion Designer RANNVA!

It felt so light and warm!

ONE OF THE NEW ARTISTS to the Great Northern Arts Festival in 2012 was Rannva Simonsen of Iqaluit. Every single person who walked into the showroom at the Midnight Sun Recreation Centre in Inuvik were at some point drawn to her fine collection of furs, just off the central stage, at the annual event.

Many could not help but request to at least try on a hat, a vest, or even a jacket, as I did. Seeing that it fit me so well, her generous response was that I just keep the expensive item, and we would figure on a suitable gift trade later.

Which is exactly what happened!

In turn, she wanted a First Nations hand-drum, which I found at a Pow-Wow at York University sometime later.

Later, when I found a dyed sealskin, she even took the time to make a hat out of it for me.

Big George and His Letter L

There were a lot of good stories shared that night

ONE, by master-tale smith Lawrence Manuel brought us back, at the baseball field where we had gathered for some fun, to a time when his generation were spending most of their time right on the land.

"Erwin MacDonald from Norman Wells was cutting line and asked me for some dry meat, through this other person. I thought I would play a little trick on him and got some bark from a tree and added fat to it, to make it look like a bag of the good stuff. That sure caught him by surprise when he took a big bite out of it!"

Quite a number of tales followed in there—some real gems—which kept the people of Radelie Koe, Fort Good Hope, laughing in a whale of a good-time passing evening. Then the unwitting Master of Ceremonies Big George called the next contestant forth, Gene Rabisca, who started right in about the man himself.

"Well, you all know my good friend George here. This is about the time we went to hunt caribou over to Kabami Tue, Colville that one winter. The other George—George Barnaby and his wife Florence—they were running the Co-op that time. We were out there all day getting our caribou and cutting it up and decided to spend the night with them at the Co-op and then take off for town here the next day.

"I guess my good friend George here had it in his mind to do that couple a good turn and went outside to cut up some wood for them. He was out there for quite a while and we got worried about him, so I stepped out to see what had become of our George. And there he was, all stretched out like some kinda broken toy, or a mummy, right on the pile of firewood!

"When I looked closer there was this little spot of blood on his overalls. He must have cut himself a bit and passed right out from the sight of his own blood! Well, I just couldn't leave him there to catch a cold or anything, so I kinda heaved him up and started making my way to the house.

"I got the door open okay, but there was one more corner to turn before I could get ol' George into the house and safety, y'know. They say, 'Safety Comes First.' Well, that's what I wanted for the man George, to be on the safe side! So, I had to kind of scrunch his big, long body around my hips a bit to make the letter 'L,' so I could get him safely around that one tricky spot.

"But I must have bumped his head against the doorway or something because he woke up right then, took one look at his little spot of blood and passed right back out again! Whatta guy!"

(Here and behind Gene, is Big George, no longer the tall, imposing Master of Ceremonies with the booming voice, but all but gone sliding under his seat at a picnic table.)

Y'know, people, this man could have at least really gotten right up there and helped me get himself inside the house, but no, guess our ole George really couldn't stand the sight of his own blood. Whatever his story was, I still had to carry him the rest of the way in, kinda rushing the last bit of way in, short, choppy steps, to a safe spot on the couch. And that's all I recall of my good friend Big George there in Kabami Tue.

The Real Door

Strange that words on paper, from jumbled thoughts would be a freedom, a refuge, and a place to go

CHOICES, by definition are a kind of prison, holding you in a revolving door, and often just that. A way to a clue takes you right back where you started.

A pair of beaded moosehide moccasins my late mom made me, still new, unworn, reminds me each morning of a bygone age. I was a part of that time, too.

Before being abruptly taken off to residential school, our Dene lives were on the land. I just like to have these memories as a start to my day. Riding her on back all the way, walking, from the Duhogah, Big River, to Loon Lake, in winter. The smell of a spruce-bough floor in a bush camp tent. The smell of fresh bannock each morning. Never in a Mola, White man world.

Another and not so different memory is from a Lakota-style pair, more cactus boot, a little tight, but bring to life another time. Our southern plains relatives tried, too, to hold on to Mother.

The choices that tie both together, like a modern pair of sneakers, is that I am now of a time when we begin to give it all out, to begin a different journey. Because the newer pair are a little binding, I was planning on passing them along to a lifelong Cree brother.

The kind of footwear I've worn all my life are now under repairs. Because the uppers will take more work to do, I have to wait for my oldest sister to put in a bit longer.

Leaving me to the revolving door . . . Should I continue to wear the ones I want to give, hold on to my mother's memory, and not wear the last ones she made? Fine to keep an artist's dream alive, but the way she and my sister think, in the present, best for me to take the simplest path

.

Either way it would be so comforting to just wear hers.
Meanwhile, under cover of cherished firelight,
And Time as present,
I will just wear the new,
Waiting on whatever outcome,

And a traditional smile,
Through my People holding me, like a choker,
Often binding,
But still close
to Mother.

And anyway, no such turn-around door in a teepee.
Yet, and for it all, the page you are now turning,

. . . a fresh breeze,

of its turning,

The Real Door.

Soul of a Woman

Born a Jew in Tuscany, Italy, Amedeo Modigliani's earliest days were marked by abject poverty and a series of illnesses, beginning with pleurisy, typhoid fever, and eventually to tuberculosis, which at just thirty-eight claimed his life. It was said that he could paint the very Soul of a Woman

Modigliani made it a point to study the works of antiquity and the Renaissance but abandoned these artistic roots soon after moving to Paris at twenty-two. Influenced by Henri de Toulouse-Lautrec, he also became enamored of the works of Paul Cezanne, thought to be the father of Modern Art. The Italian painter, who also dabbled in sculpture, took up with the likes of Picasso.

In a sudden turn away from what he considered his bourgeois past, Modigliani adopted a more modern bohemian lifestyle, complete with the life-draining heavy use of absinthe and hashish. Many believe that this was to mask his worsening TB condition.

Little matter, artistically, though, because he achieved little recognition in his living career and only in death was recognized for his superior vision, with his works then commanding high prices.

Today, Amedeo Modigliani continues to be part of a handful of artists I use as references for my daily sketching exercises.

Little Chicago Honeymoon

"Well, here we are, folks! Little Chicago!"

THE NORTH IS chock-full of stories going all the way back to the times of the 1900 Yukon Gold Rush and all the people who busied themselves trying to make their way up there to get rich or die trying.

One of the places these kinds of folk got together at gained quite a reputation for itself, and ended up with the name Little Chicago, after the American version, for its rough and rowdy ways.

Whilst busy in the south with my Indigenous PhD studies, I would make it a point to call home every once in awhile, just to stay in touch, and to ask questions about parts of my study that related to my home in Radelie Koe, Fort Good Hope.

Such a chat was with one of our Elders and close relative, Lucy Jackson, herself a font of information about all things Dene.

The elders, though, like to take you back to a time long before your own birth, with a touch of history and such.

One had to do with a couple from somewhere south of Canada, to the USA. The newlyweds had heard all kinds of stories about this famed Little Chicago and got Lucy's husband Wilfred to take them down the river by boat to visit the place, to celebrate their newfound marital bliss.

Their plan was to have a nice dinner at a fancy restaurant there, maybe share a bottle of fine wine, and maybe even soak in some of that gangster Al Capone lore they craved with such passion!

At one of their stops, somewhere down from Loon River, they mentioned to their Dene guide, Wilfred, that they were in a hurry to get to this famous place, and by the way, how much longer would it take?

"Not much," the outboard motor driver replied. Pointing to a bank of willows above them, he loudly proclaimed, "Well, here we are, folks! Little Chicago! Feast yer eyes!"

After all those years, all that was left were overgrown patches of willows and other nondescript shrubs above the shore of the Duhogan, Mackenzie River! As these special visitors stepped on shore to have a look, Wilfred also had this advice for them, "You'd better bring a chain-saw if you wanna find Main Street!"

What they had especially promised themselves—fancy dining hall, crystal chandeliers with matching wine glasses, scurrying waiters holding aloft silvery platters piled with assorted *fins mets,* tableside guests twittering with comments sprinkled with the latest turn in the foibles of the law vs. Ole-Scarface Capone and an inexplicable guffaw—from somewhere far off to a sudden PRESENT and a somewhat teasing call to crow served . . . past hungered reverie . . . this turned out to be a fine can of fried Spork, with a side of some cold beans and Red Rose tea, as shore-lunch!

Of such, Northern lore.

The Footsteps of Legend Jim Thorpe

His memorial outside of Pennsylvania, PA
surrounds you with the sheer Power of
The Human Spirit

THINKING BACK to my own, his humble beginning on the Sac and Fox Reservation in Oklahoma, and on to residential school at Carlisle, fairly matched mine.

I was glad to have made it a point to go and visit with writer Beth Ansari, also working on a project do with these programs of assimilation and downright cultural genocide.

Jim Thorpe went on to win a gold medal in the 1912 Olympics, in the pentathlon and decathlon track and field events. He was eventually voted as one of the fifteen greatest athletes of the twentieth century, sharing it with the likes of Muhammad Ali.

One of the reason I could identify so much with this First Nations man was that I won the Tom Longboat Award for 1968, given to the Top First Nations Athlete in Canada, the equivalent of an Olympic gold.

Given the physical and social odds, it takes no less than a superhuman effort to attain this kind of recognition.

A Bear Nation is Coming!

"They've been calling you!"

T HE ONE THING that brought me to the Dineh, Navajo Nation, a good quarter of a century ago was an excruciating pain in my hips, which the Mola doctors couldn't figure out, period. Over all the time, from having the first of their medicine men draw the link to a bear's spirit I had injured, it got so that I could at least move around without any pain.

This was all linked to my grandfather,
Peter Mountain Sr.
Who told me to always
"Just walk, use your legs, every day.
Your Mother, the Earth
wants to know you."

Of course as a Dene I had always done just this and worn moccasins out of preference, but over these post-residential school years of the real healing I got to know my own story from the inside. Experiences in the American Southwest in particular brought me to the narrative for this second book, beginning with the Navajo Elder and his early morning offerings of the corn pollen.

Too, it came to me that all prayer essential is a plea to the stars above to come on down and help us get beyond whatever ways we tend to separate ourselves from a living universe.

When all is done and considered, my mind always goes back to a visit I had with my adopted father, Charlie Peshlakai, in Indian Wells. He was so pleased with an extra-long silvery white eagle tailfeather I'd brought for him, all the way back from distant Russian Siberia.

After dancing around his home there with his new gift, he asked me how I was doing. I told him that all was well, except for feeling "cold in my legs, chills, from the knees on down."

He put some hot coals on a sheet of plastic on the floor and did a Hand-Trembling, that is, he scoped out the situation between his hands and the hot ashes.

After some time, he said that these feelings had to do with a "bear standing in water," a polar bear, whom I wasn't supposed to have anything to do with. I told him a tourist had found a tooth of this animal out in an Arctic island, which I traded for . . . I asked a jeweller to make the ivory tooth into a pendant, but that it somehow got lost in his home.

"Well, son, you are lucky, for that tooth could have brought you great harm." He then described my experiences in residential schools as being the same as his service in the Armed Forces, that we both survived a similar ordeal, and that he could do a Beauty Way Ceremony as a cure.

He began at first, slowly, with a few words in Dineh, which I was to repeat.

I did my best, and he speeded it up some and made the chants longer.

After a good twenty minutes or so of complicated ritual he declared, "My son here is a real Navajo!"

The ritual itself took some time longer, but at the end he told me that all my fears of Bear Spirit were actually not real, and that the Bear Nation itself had to get my attention as a puny human being, at first with some kind of an injury, which would lead me to people like him, to Dineh Medicine.

"This Bear Nation is nothing to be feared, son. They were just calling you to join them, to become one of them . . . But once you get there you have to be careful. A bear can take just about anything without getting excited, but once awakened has a very short and powerful temper. So you have to be careful what you say and do around people."

He ended by reciting a prayer, requesting of Beauty, Hozho, a balance restored, before and behind me, above and all around.

What really strikes me when I think in terms of residential schools and Nazi Germany, is that in a very real way our fates are intertwined, and even related, to destiny itself.

We tend to see it in a bad light, with grim consequences
But when we begin to realize that there are lessons to be learned
We can even appreciate their beck and call . . .
Meanwhile, just a certain kind of speckled compassion
Shines through these pains, a special Dantean shaft
Illumed under passing clouds
Unrequited dreams . . .

As Angels Weep

You hear it sometimes,
In a slow deep cello from Mozart or Bach

Chopin's aural confidences

(Even in the pauses
between some breaths
. . . those little catches . . .)

. . . That sound
Which just now reclaims a memory
In Heart and Soul
From some far-off dream

The faltering echo of a dear one's
Brush through Life

. . .

Time, they say
Heals all wounds

Were it not, rather
The tuning

Of Your Life's chords

. . . as angels weep

What SPIRITS Wish

THE PHONE conversation actually went back a number of years, from when I gave away another brand new bald-eagle tail fan, to a Navajo Dineh couple, way out on the Navajo Rez, some ways out of rock Point, near K-Town.

Now the same feeling came over, that this here generation was in no hurry to have any children, leaving, again the question of what to do with this fan.

On the other end of the phone was a friend from way back, a good four decades. "Y'know, bro, you are supposed to be a grandfather to hold such a fan in prayer . . . and here I am, not about to expect anything like grandchildren any time soon. So, for the time being, I will just pass along this here fan to your wife, and she will make sure you get it."

My close Sun Dance friend of some forty years said that in the Cree way it is good to part with something that will "hurt you deep inside," and that this was the way to know it was the real feeling.

Now, only a few days later, a call from my oldest son, Luke, saying that my Grandpa Days were coming up, in half a year.

Amidst the happiness is this feeling that them ol' Cree ways really do work out, that you learn to just give what you know you are going to miss the most.

Meanwhile the Spirits have a life of their own,
And we simple humans ride the waves,

To another
And more Real

FUTURE

In Heaven's Debt

And when my sons, my daughters
Run astray
To even suicide, murder

All say of an 'act', the Will of God!

Somewhere in page of bible,
Word of more than supposed counsel,
To Maintain that FEAR!

What of divine intervention?

All I've ever known,
Your Original Sin
You're Dene *sauvage*, savage,
Forever in Heaven's Debt
Paid Up in FEAR,
of Some ready Hell,
Every Waking Moment

Where, Lord, thy guiding light
YOUR once human hand?

What, O Lord,

of MY Light?

Now that she had seen the movies, times like these put the young
Dene mother, now actually grown old at only thirty, of the servant ladies
in the Middle Ages, how they must surely have felt to be their prison,
away from all but the light shone in from out and above.

Living in a heaven of sorts, true, amongst royalty, but held against
her will, nevertheless.

Just something in the way a stray curl
of the young girl's hair fell loose,
. . . a weary tear from high above.

Seven Tribes of Trout

DELINE ELDER Charlie Neyelly would be sitting by his bay window on the shores of the Sahtu, Great Bear Lake, singing a Dene song, warm early morning sunlight streaming in.

One of these mornings he was also in a talkative mood, pointing out two landmarks farther towards the center of town.

Them two spots remind me of one of our Elders who's gone now to his resting place up in the graveyard. There was talk at the time, quite a while ago now, about a dam for the Bear River.

A whole bunch of Mola, White men, government experts came to Deline for a meeting about something new for the Bear River. Said they wanted to put a dam in there to make power, so we could have it cheaper, I guess. Well, we talked back and forth for the whole week, just to find out how it could be done.

They didn't even ask us if we wanted it or not.

Towards the last day of that week an old man finally started to really speak to them. He said, 'You see that place over there where there is that one dock for the boats to come in and tie up? Well, you come over this way about a hundred yards (100m) or so. There are seven different tribes of trout living right in there.'

You government people, you come in here and even if you do go fishing you probably think there's only one kind of trout here. You don't live here like we do, so there is no way for you to know these things. Yet you are supposed to be the experts.

When the dark clouds come over from around Bear Rock Mountain in Tulita, it makes rain for us here, so the life can grow. That's where the water and snow comes from.

Already we are talking about two different kinds of water. Then there is the steam comes up early in the morning and the ice in winter.

Each one of you White guys, you might know about one of those things . . . Maybe.

But we live here in Deline, and we know everything about our Mother the Earth here. Long after you leave here, we will still be living here with our seven tribes of trout right in front of us that you can't see even today.I want you to think about that when you go on back home . . . how it's not just about a dam we are talking about here . . .

It's all about our Mother the Earth we live on

And it's All written on the Land, right in front of you.

Pahaku, Animal Lodge Under

And, always, this return to the Great Mystery!

Of all legends, just something about this one really hit home with me. At a time in the seventies, when we were all searching for some truths, this one book, *The Lost Universe*, by Gene Weltfish struck me like a bolt of *eedih koneh*, fire from above.

The novel itself is simple enough. An anthologist spends some time with the Pawnee Indians of central Nebraska and northern Kansas and describes a year in their lives, in great detail. From her studies of their language and close relations with the stars, she connects these Pawnee with their Aztec ancestors.

In fact, this one single tribe struck terror in even the most fearsome and warlike Lakota Sioux and Apache, for the Pawnee's traditional practice of capturing a young enemy maiden, feeding her, and treating her well all winter until she was sacrificed as part of an annual sacrificial ritual.

Because of the efforts of Knife Chief and his son, Man Chief the Skidi Band of the Pawnee, on speaking tours to the eastern cities of Washington and New York the last human sacrifice of a Lakota girl of fifteen, to the Morning Star happened on April 22, 1838.

. . . and this one

One tribe camped near present-day Fremont, Nebraska, around 1850, in pre-reservation days. There was a poor young boy, Small, a servant in the household of an influential man, who went out hunting ducks and rather met a "bluish one with a striped neck."

Sitting on the bank of a river with bow and arrow with his friend, Old Bull, Small had a Vision and went missing, falling into the water below. As he sank, he was saved by the two birds he was after.

Small now stood at the opened doorway of a large tcepee, Pahaku, Animal Lodge Under, marvelling at all of the Animal Relations in a Grand Council, with a Scalped Man, Kitsahuruksu, as boss, near the western altar.

When they saw him standing there, some, like bear wanted to eat this choice morsel right away, crying, "He looks so delicious. We need to eat him up right away."

Others, weasel and snake, agreed and were about to make a move to kill the young boy when other animals that didn't eat meat—moose, beaver, and reindeer—spoke up in his defence, that he wasn't enough of a meal for them all and that he was just looking for a duck or two anyway

For four nights the argument became quite heated until duck and the bluish bird who had first found and brought him there were made to decide what to do with the lad.

Given the final word, bluish bird now said that each animal in turn would teach the boy a special skill, and especially about the practice of sorcery and how to cure illnesses: "Let us each teach him our secrets and pass them along to him, so that he will be successful in Life and remind his people later how we have helped him today."

Which is exactly what they all agreed to do.

Meanwhile, back in his village, the little boy's relatives and people grew quite concerned when he didn't show up again for several days, but found him where he had been sitting, back on the high south bank of the Platte River and after scolding him for being missing, things went on as before.

Eventually, the teachings Small had been given were passed along to his friend, Old Bull, who in turn became a great warrior and leader for his people.

SHE

With the natural grace of a dancer she moved.

AND JUST THE THOUGHT that I would be like a magnet for her, a pleasant warmth.

One of those times,
Done for the day
And the Masks come off

She said she was selling tickets for an event in Kayenta, Arizona, as
cowboy as you are going to get on the Great Navajo Rez.
For some reason she hinted at more West Coast, maybe BC.
Her face was almost plain, but pretty, to a slender, athletic body.
Long black hair accented her every move.

Reaching,
Seeking,
Your Secret Heart.

Knowing I would be in support of whatever that was about, we just
picked up on a lot of things, as old and dear friends just do.

Her look was that of leaving off from the many you've known,
and yet something 'new' to your life.

In the crowded, busy eatery of an artsy type place, with people like
her, and probably me, keeping busy doing what the creative ones get
busy at. She said she was sitting over on the other side and would wait
for me to join her and a friend.
In all the dreamlike goings-on, I was up on a somewhat raised dais,
pondering some kind of huge bone structure, which I sensed from
Eagle. In a central spot for all to see but focused on a private life anyway.
With the curiosity of an artist/hunter, I took hammer to it, striking it with a blow, sending big pieces flying. Trying to piece to especial
pieces back to fit, she came along and said it was more from maybe a
moose.

The magical encounter made a magical ending with a long hug, she with just a hint of womanly modesty. Her light cotton dress moved like a summer breeze.

> . . . and the richest, her parting blessing,
> 'You are Beautiful!'

> Like all the best left unsaid, one of those chance encounters
> you just know will bring us back together, somehow.

Friends to the Rescue

Assumptions can lead to a sudden drop, which is exactly what happened to my stomach as I was getting to the end of my studies for a Bachelor of Fine Arts, in Tranna, Toronto. It could very well have been, too, that the Ontario College of Arts and Design was now and newly a part of the university system of studies.

At any rate in late April of 2011, I found out that I had missed the deadline to apply for a Master's Program of studies. For some reason, not realizing the difference between undergrad and grad school, I just assumed you get done and then apply, as before. There followed a period of intense mental wincing and nail-biting, but a few key people, my good friend Nely Atefi, the ever-supportive Diane Pugen and Bonnie Devine, stepped up to the plate with their A-Game!

Through her contacts at York University, Ms. Atefi secured a special application extension as long we got the paperwork in by the end of the month. The four of us went through the mountains of required information and managed to make that deadline, with a day or two to spare. We also had had an interview with a key staff member at York U, Debbie Barndt, to present my application in person, which went quite well.

A couple of months later, I received a Letter of Acceptance to begin with a Master of Environmental Studies there. Well and good to have grand schemes and plans, but key, caring people at the right time will always save the day!

Dear Nely Joon succumbed to cancer during these studies for a master's degree, but as it turned out both Diane Pugen and Bonnie Devine figured in my eventual career as a writer.

Coffee with the Masters

OVER THE YEARS, I have taken to the practice of doing at least one sketch per day, in the manner of Peter Mah, one of our Ontario College of Art's teachers, who himself had been doing this for some forty years, before I graduated in 2011.

Whatever I've found myself doing at the time, a master's at York U after, travel for a couple of years, and now working towards a PhD, these daily drawings have kept me in constant touch with the Arts.

Like reading something from a book every morning, this is a good way to keep your artistic skills sharpened. Any skill, in fact, is nothing but a tool, which has to be kept in shape by use.

For the most part, I draw from images from either the Italian Renaissance, like the immortal Michelangelo, the artist as thug, Caravaggio, an exquisite Bernini, or the Impressionist era, say Edgar Degas or the French sculptor Auguste Rodin.

To add a more realistic touch I will use archival photos of old-time Indians. I have also added a free-style portrait by a former classmate, John Bailey, at Art's Sake, an alternative art institute, which got me going in Toronto, early seventies.

One interesting note is that I actually began my own drawing career when living in our mountain camps, as a young boy. There were no such things as paper or pencil, so I simply sketched on blocks of firewood, using charcoal. Needless to say, many of these of my earliest renderings soon found their way up in smoke!

Upper and lower, Paintings in the style of the masters,
Caravaggio, Michelangelo,Bernini, Rodin, Degas, with a realistic touch.

*Upper and lower, Paintings in the style of the masters,
Van Gogh, Rodin with a realistic touch.*

One Constant

Over the years
The simple act of drawing
Is a Must . . .

As OTHERS have from our time at the Ontario College of Arts and Design did, I picked up the habit and discipline of just doing a single drawing every day, eventually filling up a number of sketchpads.

Peter Mah especially said that he had being doing this himself then, on a larger-than-usual scale, for forty years, very likely beginning in the late-sixties!

I have found this to be a good way just to do a creative act at the start of a new day, and like painting, to eventually find out how your style changes. The why of it is in there somewhere, not that it matters a lot. The idea is to find out first what inspires you and then to do your best to follow up. Mine has always been from the time of the Impressionists on back, say from the Frenchmen Pierre Auguste-Renoir, colourist supreme Edgar Degas, and Italian Amadeo Modigliani. Of course not all artists lend themselves to drawing, but there are a few I've made it a point to render attempts from . . .

Caravaggio's dramatic play of light and superb emotional effect . . .

One can never go wrong with anything from Bernini, in whose hands stone cold marble was "as butter".

Others have to do with my interest in First Nations history, trying to capture the way our People once looked, when we were still truly free of today's commercial pull. The one of the Lakota man, Hump, and two favoured wives, tells of the height of the Indian Wars. Fate would have this man, the famed warrior Crazy Horse's uncle and mentor to the ways of hunter and warrior. Someone else taught him of the mystics.

The date marks only two years since the Oglala legend was jealously deceived by his own people and murdered outside the prison

Judith's Ole D7 Grill

*Home cooking never
got any better*

AFTER SO MANY YEARS of just dropping in with my Shetao, Mountain Dene, relatives in Tulita it was good to be there for an entire summer.

That summer of 2011, I spent most of my time with the Youth there, just painting one mural after another, but did have time to go and visit, most times with my grandfather's brother Maurice Mendo. He told me many old-time stories, and especially one that ended up as the theme for the new swimming pool, based as it was on 'How Muskrat Created the World'.

The community itself spent just about the entire month of July just having a cookout for everyone every weekend at the central arbour, between the Band Office and the Northern Store, overlooking the Duhogah, Mackenzie River. Often it was the chief, Frank Andrew himself, who did the cooking.

One couple who always made it a point to invite me over for a bite to eat was my cousin Judith Wright-Bird and her husband, Fabian. They were especially really smiling around every time I came over, as if they were hiding some kind of a secret right there out in the open.

It took me a bit to figure it out, because the lettering was faded, but when I took a real good, close look at their strange grill it somehow reminded me of my high school summer school days, working summers in Kabami Tue, Colville Lake. But why there, way out in the middle of nowhere?

Then I finally got it. Their cooking grill was a seat and gas tank from one of the two kinds of Cats—Caterpillars, ground clearing heavy machines—we used to build that new airport that time! Some kind of pure Northern Mountain Dene humour to be sure!

In Genghis Khan's 'Hood

As a 12th-century conqueror,
he bestrode Asia, even into Europe.

IT ONLY TOOK this Mongolian mogul twenty-five years to take over all of Asia, including the neighbouring giant China, part of Russia, and all the way to Hungary, which is said to be the only country with a related language.

From Siberian Russia, I went to meet the Canadian Ambassador Greg Whitehawk and his wife Sharon, whom I already knew from my first art school days in Toronto, a number of decades before.

Along with a number of other events, including one to do with the traditional ones of horse-racing, wrestling, and archery, I took in ones like this one, a gathering related to a revolution.

The reason for the Mongolian army's rise to world dominance was their highly mobile light cavalry. These highly disciplined soldiers were sternly instructed to not light any fires on the field at all and would put the carcass of whatever kill they had to eat at the time, under their saddles to tenderize and hungrily eat at nightfall.

A little-known fact is that these fearsome warriors sent fair warning ahead, for those who wanted to join to be spared a gruesome death. Thus, they recruited the best craftspeople, engineers, and tradespeople for the advancement of civilization as a whole.

I was often mistaken for one these ancestral ancestors and even here for the captain of the guard, with my Siberian hat and normal stern visage!

Far from your usual clichés of the Mongol Hordes, Genghis Khan's leadership included a first in so many cultural areas, forging ahead with trade routes and even in matters of women in positions of power.

Jonestown: The High Cost of Faith

"White Night! White Night!"

THESE WERE the simple words announced over loudspeakers, in Jim Jones' Peoples Temple, Jonestown, Guyana, November 1978, to call the faithful to regular macabre drills for mass suicide.

Just at a time when I went down to the big city of Toronto, Ontario for a possible artistic future, ominous tidings grabbed the headlines . . . from Guyana in South America, almost a thousand followers of American religious leader and community organizer, now mass murderer, Jim Jones.

Also dead were five members of a congressional investigative team, led by Leo Ryan of California.

Before some rather startling controversy about human rights violations in that state, the Peoples Temple moved lock, stock, and barrel south, to carry on a mish-mash religious and communist idyll of sorts, liberally mixed in with apocalyptic warnings of impending doom.

At the helm, a drug-addicted leader, the charismatic Jim Jones, who at one point had some high level state, federal, and media supporters, including First Lady Rosalynn Carter, right out of the White House itself.

In Guyana, Jones exercised complete and utter control over the minds of his many followers, who towards the end were living on rice three times a day, half-crazed from a steady barrage of mind control.

A delegation of 'Concerned Relatives' had made their way to Washington, DC, a year before, to try to get some support in aid of people who could be saved from this lethal cult.

On the fact-finding mission to Guyana, Congressman Ryan did manage to spirit out some fifteen dissenters from the Peoples Temple, but the two planes about to take the group out was attacked by Jones' Red Brigade, brutally gunning down the congressman and four others from the media and the temple.

In an ultimate bid for infamy Jim Jones then had almost all members of the Peoples Temple, over nine hundred, drink a deadly mixture of cyanide and Kool-Aid, over three hundred children murdered first.

As one witness stated:

"It wasn't mass suicide.
It was mass murder, plain and simple."

What brings all of this so to mind for me is that we residential school survivors went through exactly this kind of mind-control. In a documented case of bona fide cultural genocide, we of the First Nations, Métis, and Inuit were forcibly removed from our homes, tortured for speaking our own language, and only years after leaving these places given a public apology, only to have us officially blamed for our missing and murdered women!

I see this as the ultimate price one has to pay for putting one's blind faith in a cause supposedly for the best: letting other people have access to our eternal souls.

Jim Jones preached a transition, all of his followers were to die together and somehow live blissfully on another planet.

Many of my closest friends and relatives still go along with this colonialist control, effectively brainwashed, proving its power over future generations. Looking back, I can clearly see that many of my failed relationships at the time were directly because of the Post-Traumatic Stress Disorder I was a victim of.

One saving grace, though, was that for some reason or other, which only Life can take the credit for, we survivors tend to meet, share our experiences, and eventually even set upon the road to recovery.

The Circle, too, tended to be wider than I expected.
I first met Diane Pugen, whose Jewish people
Had their own baptism of Nazi fire.

Other than all the grieving relatives, this, too, may be the ultimate legacy of lost souls.

Like Jim Jones.

For His Sah Bah Sho

Times like this, always felt like a mist

A T TIMES like this, the old Dene granny had to really watch what she was doing. Sharp skinning knife in hand, she busied herself before the real cold set in. She sat to the late fall, fleshing the heavy, dark brown, almost black, beaver hide her man brought in.

Tired from being close to the cold water he now lay resting in back of their bush tent, sound asleep, making low, growling noises now and again, her hungry animal and protector.

She was practically sitting right outside on her entrance log. The wall tent kept the inside warm and cozy, but here only a thin blue tarp on supporting poles kept the winds from breezing right on in. Though she could plainly see frost on the poles, its plastic did help to reflect some good heat.

Agnes's real company was the woodstove right behind her, almost touching, throwing its steady spruce heat into her aching back. She never complained about it, but all the wood hauling just like a man, before she was married, made that part of her ache, even in rest.

In its way, this was the best part of her day, alone, the grandchildren just out of muffled earshot, out there in the trees somewhere, probably chasing squirrels.

The more of this bush tea she drank, a mix of brittle ledi mahgih, Labrador tea and Red Rose, the more it brought back memories of a lost daughter, Yah Sileh. When just a teen she was lost to them, to these high country streams they always returned to.

"Even a dream is better than nothing," the old man always grumpily said.

But leaving it at that was not enough for the aging matriarch. Sometimes the rest of their clan came along, but lately more to just help set up camp and leave some of the dogs for protection. There were any number of bears still roaming around for a good last bite of fish or whatever else left unattended.

The days were getting shorter, in a few months to only a few hours to do all of the day's work. This world then turned to all black and white.

Now ol' Agnes's uncertain thoughts turned to her own mother and grandmother. She had seen them countless times, doing exactly as she now did and showing her all the parts she really had to watch out for, to get the darkest of hides from what she got.

"I want his busy hands, even tired, to do all the things needing doing around here. Wood has to be cut for every day we are here, for the entire winter this time."

She thought of the way he got up so early she hadn't even settled down to her sewing yet. The only sign of her man having been there was a half-empty tin cup of his strong tea. He even liked it cold, too, like the coming winters.

"All *this* really brings him to life, and here I am feeling so sad!"

Over the hours she now spent simply working steadily towards his sah bah sho, winter beaver mitts, the old Dene woman found herself kind of caught between the generations.

True, her granddaughter would pick up these skills, in a few years, which was heartening. For now, the two youngsters came back to warm their hands by the fire and have some frozen bannock and a sip of her tea.

As an Elder, Agnes was set in her ways and liked to just keep to the basics. Another knife stood ready, stuck right into the wood. This she thought of her anger with God, over her daughter's untimely passing. An old lard-can spittoon caught whatever snuff she was fond of chewing, spitting out some unpleasant thoughts, now crowding in. On the far end of her log her favoured small axe, wedged, for use later, for the stretching frame.

"I'll have to ask the old man to do that when he gets up," she nodded. "But better take the axe in first, warm it up."

Brusque though her manner, the aging woman had been taught to keep her 'visitors' in mind. Spirits of the past and those 'other' presences always around these favoured of Place, found ways to make themselves felt, known. These ancestors wanted to make sure this was a camp with no idlers, ones who kept them in mind by tidying around.

This one now, was not far, practically to foot. Yah Sileh, her lost daughter's insistent self, first as fresh-fallen snow, then attached to camp support poles . . . ever nearing . . . even resting.

Now back to the last of this fleshing, Agnes moodily thought, "Even though you try your best, Life has its way of cutting you short, taking something else away, leaving you like this. Yah Sileh would've been right here, sitting beside me on this entrance log, joking about who knows what! Then again, there's these mitts to do. That old man is getting on in years, like me, but we still have to think ahead, what we need." With that she reached for her tea, putting her knife, file, hide and her petty worries away, to stretch later, on its sapling spruce beaver hide frame.

If a bear can do it, wander off with a full stomach
and just sleep this weather away,
so can I let the freezing mists put 'em away someplace safe.

"Soon I'll be to the fun part," she thought. "Put some colours around the trim, fringes and a long-woven yarn strings. Better use the brightest colours, so he won't lose 'em in the snow."

Visiting

AN AGE-OLD TRADITION has to do with just leaving everything on the side and go and see the relatives. Catching up on the latest news, some gossip and eating familiar dishes. Always the stories . . . the words.

My Esieh, Grandfather Peter Mountain, Sr. once told me that "It's not good, grandson, to say you are strong . . . Life is very short, and then you are gone, to a different home. It's no use saying you're strong now. One day you will find out how strong you really are, when no-one comes to visit . . ."

These visits become more like memories, after a time. Even an echo you sound. You are walking forward, mind you. And expecting the good news!

Grandpa also told me that "All of your life you will make tracks, grandson, wherever you go. Your trail is there. One day you will come upon a set of tracks you've never seen before. We have all seen so many. These are the same footprints you made as a child, seeing the World for the first time, running to it, around in *it!*

"And these are the ones that will take you home."

Dene stories are often just like that. They seem to just hang in air.

What my grandfather was really talking about is the way it starts with visiting. Then the memory.

And, at last, how you are always awake to see what's next.

And this moving forward into the past is a kind of memory of its own. A Life it has. And you, finally understanding!

Home to Sleepy Falls

EACH TIME WE DESCEND to a new low, someone comes along, one way or another, to make it all better with a kiss.

In the wind, as time, passing, sometimes at rest, healing . . .
Yet, looking back, as a hunter will, for future use, it stays with you,
this imprinted dream.
Marked as beginning, in high mountain stream.
Water sprites, Tricksters in our borrowed hats,
Rooted to such folly,
Tied, 'tween grinned purpose.

Pools along the way, feelings, lasting memories. Even those deepest, devastation then, with time and Life, defined of face, go to misting,

Joining
The Holy Ones.

This, to truly mark any sojourn, its presence awakened. Others, even to the smallest of brooks, to the tea in your hands, of song and calm relate.

As you sit to ponder, the tale goes on, this moving spectacle, gathered of such depths..

Yearning,

Slowly ebbing on . . .

To Mother Ocean.

Ever mindful

To Thee
Growing,

. . . for these stories

In the telling.

Teepee of Light

His teepee glowed, yes, but . . .

THE AGING MAN chose to spend most of his time in the tattered shelter. A nearby stream kept him in song. He was always trying to make up a love song, one for his wife, gone to the winds.

She had passed a good decade or so ago, when he drew into himself, hoping, maybe to absorb the memories, like a plant with no name and little sun.

Just when his large family needed him most, all he would talk about was the life he had with their mom. They lived in the well-appointed tent next door, when visiting from town. She, Celeste, was a college grad then, with the best of grades when they first met. Yet he impressed her with his rugged ways, especially with animals. Over the years, many came to get his Medicine for their ailing friends, both animal and human.

When she went, it was as if the old-style clock in his heart stopped ticking. Them kinds need winding, which seemed too much of an effort now. Every twist of the dial wanted for an answer none could give, like an echo in space.

Now it sat in bedding, back of the teepee, someplace, muted, along with a few small worn collection of pictures of her. The love songs he tried to make were not really all that good either, carried over to concerned family nearby. If they were on writing paper there would be scraps all around camp.

Well, he was Dad, but never much of a singer. They knew these were traditional love plaints, right, but honed to fine melodies. What came through the two sets of canvas and cool northern air was an awkward conversation, meandering and run to sudden stumbles, dead ends.

When done, he sat long, puffing his worn pipe, carefully hoping even the bothersome wind had at least this song for them.

Time was there, yes and plenty of it, but . . .

As it ran out anyway, he himself went to join the Elders in Council.

Above, the Rayuka, northern lights danced their giddy show. Only here the young and unfortunate went back from whence they came, retracing their steps, above all concern and caution.

Theirs, a majestic chanced dance.
Sparking down from this, father,
Searching in the shallow water,
Asking trembling reefs . . .
Finally, *there* she is, his long-lost love, rising out of the shore!
They hugged long and true,
Made new to enter, their
Teepee of Light.

A Thought Back

*Somehow it seemed so strange to be sitting here in the home my close
relative Adeline Tobac once lived in . . .
putting the finishing touches to a draft of my memoirs.*

With memories, too, of Grandpa Peter Mountain Sr.

"Ehsieh, grandson, this Life is not long . . .
A short time, and the end is near."

It also seems ironic that in 2014, I qualified for the old age pension.
And yet, too, through it all, from the early winter mornings, decades
past, sitting on the cold wooden floor of our log cabin, lacing up my
mukluks for the day . . .to now in this warm modern house . . .
After a lifetime of adventures so far from our Radelie Koe, Fort
Good Hope,
From Addy teaching me how to draw a can of beans.
The perspectives now granted this Elder.
Are as in the dream my grandfather spoke of . . .

"One day, Ehsieh, grandson, you will come upon a set of tracks
You do not recognize . . .

Those are the same ones you yourself made as a child . . .

They will show you the Rest of the Way Home."

BACK! from the Missing!

Some, from the start,
are indelible

USUALLY THE STEPS involved in a work of Art begin with the most basic of lines and go on to be refined. But in a few cases, like this one to do with over 1,200 of our Indigenous Women Missing and Murdered, it serves it all best to just keep it as powerful as possible.

The artistic tendency, too, is to start thinking, even subconsciously, of a better 'look', or simpler yet, how far we are willing to go. The duty to Art, to Self, then becomes secondary, even superficial.

Luckily, there is a way to have your say, give it free rein and to refine it, deepen its impact. As with most of what is best, you have to learn how to do it, how it works. It just depends how far off the beaten path you've dared to go and what you've picked up along the way. The Indigenous mind is ideally suited for this, having at its root a direct connection with nature.

The most furious of winds happens when a great person passes on, as if to clean the slate and bring That Spirit BACK!

Meanwhile, and as with the case of all the Missing and Murdered, we want to hope for a better future, somehow without a realistic look at what is right before our eyes.

A primordial look of defiance comes back from the grave, recovered or not, to haunt and challenge our male-dominated world. Its lesser, male and earthbound energy, even as test, is enough to waken the sleeping.

She is dressed as royalty, the way the ole tyme prairie tribes identified members of a high-caste family, in a garment fair festooned with elk teeth. Her fan of macaw feathers, too, is chosen for the way in life our women, and women in general, are expected to do their duty and fade quickly into the background, until the next menial job needs doing. At the top of the fan and along under her forearm are figures of her missing sisters, dancing the Round Dance, with more ancient Spirits in between, to keep them company.

"Back from the Missing"

From Lloyd Wright to Douglas Cardinal

"I'll remember Frank Lloyd Wright
All of the nights we'd harmonize 'til dawn
I never laughed so long, so long, so long."

—*Simon and Garfunkel, Bridge Over Troubled Waters*

ONE WOULDN'T USUALLY associate song with the highly technical discipline of architecture,

But it would take a Paul Simon to do so,
Expertly blending whimsical memory
Of the American 'organic' architect
With that of his chosen field

Then again, what better than the building of shelter as an art form? Some centuries, when the study of art was much more of an appreciation, it was included with all of the Arts, along with those we've taken for granted like painting, sculpture, literature, and even music.

Indeed, when you follow the natural harmonics of Frank Lloyd Wright's lines with those of its surrounding natural landscapes, you cannot help but to at the very least see that all visuals, from drawing to photography and on to dance, share a mirroring of nature in all of her splendour.

One can also see a continuation of where someone of Lloyd Wright's talents with the Prairie School movement could carry on in the works of say, Métis/Blackfoot architect Douglas Cardinal, with an added European Expressionist influence.

Born in Alberta, to later settle in our nation's capital, Cardinal was commissioned by the Canadian Museum of History (1989) and went on to contribute his ideas for the National Museum of the American Indian in Washington, DC (1998).

Of course, his work is now everywhere to be seen, even in the Big Cheese, what we called the building that housed our Indigenous PhD Studies, at Trent U, in Peterborough, Ontario.

Mongolian Roots

Her 'eyes', like claws,
Grabbing you!

M Y LATE GRANDFATHER, Peter Mountain, Sr. always told me, "You have to go a long way from home to do any good for your People." In the way our ol' timers speak, the meaning is not always clear, nor an explanation forthcoming. The idea is that your life itself will show you, in its way and time, what the meaning is.

Which is one of the main lessons of any kind of travel, especially overseas.

In mid-October of 2013, one place I found myself was in Mongolia, about as far on the other side of the world as you can get from our Dene Nation here, or anywhere else for that matter.

At the invitation of Sharon Goldhawk, an artist friend from back in my seventies Arts Sake days in Toronto, I extended my trip to Russia by making a land run there. One thing led to another, and I ended up volunteering at a Buddhist orphanage to teach the children some art.

Of course, in a foreign land, and especially in the Mongolian capital of Ulaanbaatar, you find yourself at just about anything that goes on. In the case of going to the Canadian Consulate, where Sharon's husband Greg was the Canadian ambassador, you can expect even more, mainly public events, most culturally based.

I must say that from asking around and actually meeting someone who could also speak English, the rarest of these was to go and witness a thoroughly Mongolian ShaWoman in action.

After making the necessary arrangements, we went to the Ongon Spirit House, in the healing room, which was arrayed in the most primordial of fashions. The medicine woman herself had four different regalia, which she donned, one after the other, just to show me what her inner life was all about.

Of course, whatever spirits she was to summon were, as the Inuit would say, be her 'Familiars'. One of the more curious items she had to offer them were candies, along with milk and water. These candies were neither any ordinary. Like their Russian counterparts, they were no less than, da, sweet of tooth and, more, upon closer inspection, *Fruit du Monde Vivant*, now bound for the ethers of rare taste.

Her drumming and singing eventually led her to a deep trance, her only contact with this world being the young lady who also served as my interpreter.

Having been allowed to take some photos, I was later astounded to see that an image had superimposed itself on the most impressive of her gowns, this one dedicated to the Spirit of Sa, Bear!

Looking deep, it fair impressed me that with the two perfect claws where her eyes should be, she had the *power* to look deeply into whatever my life held in store!

She also ended up by revealing that mine is a 'very old, old soul', and that it had to do with the Spirit of a White Wolf, from some distant cave dwelling nearby.

When I showed her my business card, which she had no way of knowing about, we having just met, she nodded sagely, that it featured the same White Wolf.

Our ol' time Indians used to don the hide of this animal, to get close to the animals, buffalo and others, because they were used to seeing them. In those times the scouts for raiding parties were even called 'wolves', for this practice.

I see all artists as scouts, more or less, for our way to extend the human reach.

One more interesting turn of events is that I am working on a plan to look into one particular tribe in Siberian Russia, with Dene filmmaker, Raymond Yakeleya. As a part of its Dene Reunion effort, the Dene Nation is backing these plans.

The Mongolian ShaWoman also had no way of divining I had designed this card, almost forty year before, at the very start of my art career!

What amazes me is that true of Grandpa's words, the farther you go from home, too, the more it has to do with who you really are.

All else casually falls away,
Leaving you,
At the whims of the Winds.

PART FOUR

A HOME BEYOND,

CALLING

A Different Fare-Thee-Well

"Solitude gives birth to the original in us,
To beauty, unfamiliar and perilous."

—*Thomas Mann*

I ALWAYS WANTED TO LEAVE. And in a way, I always did. My favourite place was on the south side of my hometown of Radelie Koe. Commonly known as the Point, it stood at the southern end of Fort Good Hope, the first spot you'd come to.

I would just sit there, imagining the big ol' world and all that could be going on right at the moment I tried to look beyond the ramparts, where the Big Eddy was, just upriver on the Duhogah, Mackenzie.

One person who got to hear more than all about it was my cousin Barney. I would pester him mercilessly about what people on the other side of the world—what we called The Outside—were doing right then, what they ate, did, all of it. For his part, he took it all in, in good humour, and I am sure, made up half the answers I got for my questions.

One other person who saw me early on as an artist was Cousin Addy Tobac, who gave me my very first lessons in art, letting me know that some surfaces on tin cans were round.

Another was Barney's older brother, Walter.

Wishing Moon Shawl

And a butterfly flitters by
How aerial, her movements,
Such a wondrous delight to behold!

THE MOVEMENTS of this one Pow-Wow dancer, the Fancy Shawl, are those of the fleeting butterfly. Unlike the herky-jerky Chicken Dance, hers are fluid, given to a lyrical work of art. She fair twirls effortlessly across space!

Afloat before a Wishing Moon,
crescent, new and inviting of what one might want
the future to be . . .

Yet to be in such control of Powers of Moon, to tide, to sea, caught in mid-step, beaded footwear about to pounce.

Her hands extend to draw in all of whom wish under her protective shawl, its fringes to all corners of the Earth.

Deep within, just the head
Of Michelangelo's David,
Already spent of taking down
Our gigantic reservoirs
Of demonic blocks

. . . to whisper in butterfly's ear,

Let these Heavens themselves

Serve our tired fortune.

Ama Le'teh Hadih

"There are many things that can only be seen
Through eyes that have cried."
—Oscar Romero

A POOR START always shows up later. This was quite a regular occurrence. One of the children from poorer relatives would show up just as we were about to have our morning meal, fresh bannock ready, with:

"Mom wants bread."

No matter how little else we had, you could always count on Mom to simply cut the pan-sized bread in half, wrap it, and send it on over. This kind of upbringing is sure to find its way to a future in the Arts, coming from such simple folk.

Today, I can well identify with the likes of the famed Dutch painter Van Gogh who had a lifelong identity with the common people, those who had to scrimp and save their way just to survive.

Even after our father had been Chief of Radelie Koe for a good quarter-century, our house was more or less a community drop-in place and we could always be counted on to keep an eye out for people in need.

"This is Not for You!"

There are some things we were not to touch at all

IN OUR FAMILY, we were brought up in a very traditional way, so we learned early that our Elders are very special people. Besides being involved in a more personal way, like breathing in your mom's cooking and hunting trips out on the land with my dad were a real experience.

There are things about the older First Nations traditions that sometimes make you wonder. But the practice itself brings it all to light with more personal meaning and for what it is we are to do.

One of the first things I noticed right away was how much easier it was out there with Dad. The ducks would just sit right where they were as we went by when normally the entire flock would take off from even a great distance. Same with anything else—muskrats, beaver . . .

"The idea," he said, "is that as a human being you are a stranger out there, where every other creature is right at home."

To make up for this, "They know who you are and what you are doing in their country. So you have to keep in mind what you are doing this for: who is going to eat from your kill, which Elders, which children."

When we got done with skinning moose or caribou, he would take and put all of the special treats—heart, liver, and kidneys—away in a separate packsack saying, "This is not for you, son . . . This is for the Elders. Old as they are, they earned it the hard way."

More than a few times, I was also told, "We don't have to go very far for what we need."

Yet, hungry as we were for the special Dene delicacies, we had to put away the baby caribou, even the moose and caribou heads especially, for the older people waiting at home.

One part we were allowed, though, upon penalty of discovery was the *akahdefellih*, the thin layer of fat, the stomach lining, which when sizzled over the fire sure made all the tough travel through deep winter snow or summer's infernal masses of mosquitoes worthwhile!

Van Gogh, God's Tortured Soul!

When I attempted in this artist's style,
Almost too late, and
To my horror I began to realize,
There is no return!

A T THE YOUNG AGE of thirty-seven, after yet another in a lifetime of disabling bouts of utter despair and outright mental illness, Vincent Van Gogh (1853–1890) went out into the fields of his beloved Southern France and shot himself, leaving behind thousands of sublime artworks, virtually all unsold and for the most part done in his last years of a difficult life.

He, still, God's missing piece
of an eternal, living puzzle.

This Dutch Post-Impressionist artist started out in the home of a pastor, but, most puzzling, did not actually paint until almost thirty, when others like Michelangelo had long reached their prime. He worked his earlier years as an art dealer but found that with some concerted effort, discovered a talent enough to produce his own sketches and paintings.

The young man did have his share of religious zeal and worked for a time as a lay missionary in rural Belgium. Yet he could not fulfil a desire to be ordained as a preacher proper, lacking the education to pass the rigorous theological exams.

Along with travels in the Hague and London, he arrived in Paris in 1886, and was drawn to the Impressionists, in particular, Paul Gauguin, who followed Vincent to the warm light of Southern France. After the two had a falling out, Van Gogh descended into the final unforgiving chasms of darkest despair, which mercifully claimed his life.

Some say it was his schizophrenia, clashing demons within, which caused him to see the severe and incandescently brilliant colours he used.

Others at the time, Renoir and Monet, though a part of the dawning Impressionist movement, fared better than the hapless, decidedly eccentric Dutchman. But then again, every artist goes through these polarities of intense devotion to craft and a seemingly uncaring public.

Even with sharing something of a kindred spirit, there surely must have been some forsaken corner of an early Dutch evangelical cistern Vincent gulped deeply from.

In my own attempts to paint in Van Gogh's style, I can say for sure that his is a one-way street.

You look Deep into the canvas
Past increasingly blank, negative spaces . . .
and just begin
to make out
Inviting mirages

When eyes just closing,
Springs forth

The Near Room,
a parallel universe

An oasis in softest hues.

Once these secrets of form and style are finally unlocked, though,
you suddenly find there is no way back to our comfy, fetid,
banal reality.

When There,
You can just feel it,
Brush in hand,
Wanting to somehow stretch the most choking colours
Back, to that elastic breaking point
of Existence,
Return it harmless, rewarded.

Too easy it is, to cast judging eyes
Rather, the truth is closer to a beguiling identity
an ancient familiar push from an unknowable world,
somehow too safely inviting . . .

Wolf standing, in alien waters,
Willingly
at hungry guard.

Either fallen
Already placed,
Pawned, out of moves, or
Soaked, Rising . . .

Golden wispy moonlight

(. . . yet a strain, always timely . . .)

For his part, philosopher and historian Hippolyte Taine caught an impression very likely that of Van Gogh . . . "a suffering and triumphant cry from the heart."

Through it all, though, what shines forth as a shaft of hearted mercy, was his love for the common people, as in one of his earliest works, "The Potato Eaters." An oil, done in April of 1885, in Nuenen, Netherlands. In it we are presented with a grim vision, cast in a lowly lit peasant hovel/home, a humble family sitting to their simple fare, accustomed to this daily scene.

And somewhere, far off, through distant times and fields of crows, a beckoning plaint.

His song, like he . . . haunting
Returns
Through stellar ages,
Impassioned,
Compassionate eons ago.

Plain Ol' Robe of Gunnysack Cloth

His lonely home was way up high in the humid Italian mountains.

ON THE WAY to the Tuscany provincial town of Assisi, our Art History teacher Peter Porcal, showed us one painting that featured an army of soldiers at the head of which was a man holding forth a tiny cross. This traced the story of the True Cross all the way back to the days of Adam and his two sons.

From the time of the Queen of Sheba originally having recognized the wood of the abandoned timber from the Tree of Knowledge to the use of any fragment of this religious relic, we came to the story of Saint Francis.

The Franciscan Order began with this 'Alter Christus,' second Christ, humble monk's insistence that all they needed was the simple sackcloth robes and maybe, a bible and to emulate the life of Jesus Christ in replicated meditation. Thus, this humble man's targeting of the Roman Catholic Church's bent towards earthly treasure predated Martin Luther's by several centuries.

There were two kinds of orders for monks to follow: one, like Francis, emulating the life of the Saviour himself. The other sought to live by the principles of Christian belief. As we carried on to a modern-day monastery built at the site of the original Saint Francis of Assisi's, we all became curious about how anyone could survive these lofty climes, much less one sainted.

What we found was a damp cave with no fireplace and only a flat slab of hard rock about the size of a smaller table, where the man slept, when not meditating on the divine mystery of his Lord and Saviour.

Although the high country where now sits the Papal Basilica of Saint Francis dedicated to him is subject to the cruelest of damp Italian winters, there is a pocket of serenity right where he spent most of his days, when not leading his disciples to beg and preach The Word.

A set of his monk's robes made of the roughest and patched-up gunnysack cloth also told of this man's humility in the service of heaven.

Saint Francis received his stigmata, the wounds of Christ on his hands and feet.

The real ones do not heal, the live wounds needing to be covered, so he did not even wear sandals but for the last few years of his life.

How this simple kind of clothing can relate to the Second Christ, as Francis was also known, was pointed out to me when I saw the exact same kind of material, ordinary gunnysack, used by various Siberian Russian painters a few years later, especially by the hand of one Vladimir Rasputin, from whom I bought four. He somehow transformed this coarsest of materials into a surface a-shine, like glass.

Far from the simple lover of the birds and all animals we have been taught to know, Francis the holy man was rather petite in stature, yes, but a terror to any and all who got in the way of his vision for a better life. He even had pet vultures, which he would gleefully sic on any of the church clergy he despised for their marked preference for costly robes and gay and ungodly manner.

In our travels to his native Assisi, we also bore witness to the very barred dungeon where Francis's father had him jailed for not wanting any part of the family merchant business future.

His mother freed him to go forth and do the good Lord's bidding.

Sleepless at Haden Gates

With Moon a grim witness

IN THE STILL of the colder Arctic you tried to sleep, always restless. In a tippy canoe, headed for the falls, cold waters lapping in. Often just barely awake, sleep-walking the steep rampart cliffs back home in Radelie Koe, Fort Good Hope. Under flickering autumn leaves, your mind tries to recall other, more comforting nights.

Home, in a warm tent,
wood stove humming its lullaby,
Relatives all around.
Familial scents of Dene Life.
In lifeless freefall, totally naked.
That sudden, brutal, foreign violation.
A waking nightmare, every move futile,
bound in clean Christian sheets,
all love washed out.

This kind of shame was something new to us, as Dene, and in fact a slap to the inner person. At home, we were expected to learn to do things right the first time but never humiliated for trying.

You may as well have been shot to that barren moon.
But at least there,
You could still see *Negot'ine*,
Love of relatives
Distant, yes,
But of the same world.
All this and more, and at only twelve,
you shut off a vital,
pumping valve from your Dene heart.
That Godless innocence . . . foam on a sacred stream,
Just afloat . . . aimless,
Until such a day as will come,
to be Human again.

Artists of Radelie Koe

He could take you
all the way back to
When the World Was New

THIS WAS AT A TIME when all our Animal Relations and People spoke a common language. With the passing of generations, we have lost some of that spiritual attachment we once had in Denendeh, the Dene Nation.

Yet this feeling lives on in the words of my cousin Alfred Masuzumi, who could easily hold you spellbound for hours with stories and legends of how life was at that time when dinosaurs lumbered across the land, odd and fearsome flying reptiles above, our ramparts homeland a part of a humid tropics.

This was also the realm of our cultural hero, Yamoria, who went around making the World safe for our People.

A few others who shared a Dene historian's mastery of pencil and brush were John Turo, who made quite a name for himself, as the second Benjamin Chee in the Toronto area at a time when First Nations Art was sweeping the country back to its roots. Fred Edgi, too, had a fine hand for drawing and some painting. All three shared a fated life, the two younger ones ending in misadventures on the mean streets of southern cities.

Poor Alfred met his end in as dramatic a fashion as any of his tales of derring-do.

He accepted an invitation for an arts event somewhere, and the bush plane he was in crashed right into the landmark, *Yamoga Fieh*, featured in one of the legends he related. To this day, I always think of him every time I am flying over the spot, thinking of what more of a mark we all could have made together in the Northern art world.

There are others, of course, who are gifted today, but for the most part, they have been too influenced by a lifeless digital world to contribute much.

Saving the Dene in Us

He was always there, as Chief, hunter or friend.

ONE OF THE UNMISTAKABLE FALLOUTS of our years in residential school was that we lost the Dene within us, our way of contributing to our community. Worse yet, because no one could yet see through the devastating colonialist plan to entirely wipe out our Dene selves, we as survivors were even blamed for this.

Having lost out in the eyes of the world itself and our own peoples, we were left to fend for ourselves. Luckily for many, we had a major fighting chance to still give something, on a human level.

During the original McKenzie Pipeline debate, in the early to mid-seventies, we fought tooth and nail to save our Dene lands, originally promised by Treaties 8 and 11 to be preserved.

History always has its own plans.

Little did we know that we had yet to save what we did know of our Dene way of life.

Leaders like Frank T'Seleie, François Paulette, Johnny "JC" Catholique, and John Louison knew early on that the real battle was a personal one, to do with our assumed lifestyles.

As a part of the revived sixties, most of us had picked up the use of drugs and now alcohol.

Some fell by the wayside early.

It would take a concerted personal effort from the likes of Frank T'Seleie to bravely take on these damaging changes on several fronts, both political, as Chief of Radelie Koe and as hunter for the community of Fort Good Hope and family man.

My sister Bella knew right from the start of their marriage that her husband not only wanted to carry on our traditional Dene ways but to stand out among the best we had as a hunter. This was going some, for we live in the best of the North's moose-hunting country.

He and my lifelong friend, John T'Seleie, Frank's young brother, had firm familial roots though. Their grandfather was the one who signed Treaty 11 for our Dene tribe.

Out on the land, you always noted the methodical expertise they did everything with.

Frank himself would've succeeded in any world, being a fine engineer in his own right.

One saving fact is that most of our activities to do on the land are not possibly done alone unless you want to live as a hermit. The Dene have never chosen to survive alone as such, so we residential school survivors ended up being asked to come along on the hunts.

The lessons on the land are first, to respect all that you see and not to kill just for the thrill of it. Then comes the practical part of it, to eventually have your own equipment, in our case, a boat and motor. Though some still clung on to their own dog teams, the new way to get around became the Ski-Doo.

Frank and others like him also taught us to start thinking of others, the needy ones at home. One way to ensure this was whatever kill we did make became public property. Once skinned and cleaned, people would simply come and take what they wanted of the meat.

Of course, this all became part of a Dene revival,
With the drum dances
And handgames coming back.

Over time, we learned to do for ourselves and once again re-joined the Dene community. Of course, in these times of change, many of us chose to live elsewhere where the work and a marketable future was.
Wherever you are though,
An Indigenous Circle, once reclaimed,
Even expands.

Home being home, though, there are still the many returns.

There was a time before I started on this protracted time of post-secondary education that I thought for sure all I ever would do was cut wood on the land for the Elders.

The best memories,
Standing out from my tent,
Nights ablaze with distant stars,
And Rayuka, northern lights,
Snow falling straight into me,
. . . into Eternity!

Especially as an artist, these times out with people like Frank T'Seleie and later, Joe Martin and Fred Sangris of the Yellowknives and Dettah Band were a godsend. I got to learn not only the country away from the towns but also a good many of the stories behind the landmarks and history of the place. These even ended up figuring in the murals I did.

Of course, individual expressions of the PTSD remain, as in anxiety, formulating the future into present situations. For the time being, though, at the very least we were on our feet.

In fact, some built-in features for traditions, the reliance on relatives for psychic stability, kept things on an even keel.

John T'Seleie went on to high government office, representing our Sahtu, Great Bear Lake Region, in the Government of the NWT. As it turned out, leaders like Frank T'Seleie served, as in the old Navajo Dineh grandfather with his corn pollen, in this book's intro, to remind us of our responsibilities to our cultural traditions.

Over the years, farther away from the soul-stifling residential schools, we began to learn that the Dene hunt far more than just going out to get food, prepared you to target, seek, and get what you needed to keep mind, body, and spirit in place. This often came to life when thinking of what my grandfather, Peter Mountain, Sr. meant when he often told my oldest son, Luke, that they two would go hunting together. Both my sons, Luke and Lorne, turned out to be fine young men.

Without all of these key elements in place, we would surely be like the proverbial rudderless boat, asail, yes, but with no direction. Whatever the situation, it would take me another couple of decades of misdirection and frustration to be drug- and alcohol-free.

For its part, the hypocritical Roman Catholic Church has yet to seriously address the problems of pedophiles within its clerical ranks, instead hopelessly clinging to whatever religious authority it once had.

All this, even after a recent pope, Benedict XVI, resigned over this very issue in February of 2013.

Montessori

"Humanity shows itself in all its intellectual splendor during this tender age as the sun shows itself at dawn, and the flower in the first unfolding of its petals; and we must respect religiously, reverently, these first indications of individuality." —Dr. Maria Montessori

LONG ADMIRED by the likes of Sigmund Freud, Jean Piaget, Thomas Edison, Alexander Graham Bell and even dictator Benito Mussolini for her innovation in early childhood education, Maria Montessori was born in Chiaravalle, Italy, in August of 1870.

With the official backing of no less than Pope Pius XIII, she was the first woman in Italy to receive a medical degree in 1896. Montessori soon began work with disabled children, believing that some suffered more from a lack of training and sensory stimulation than any serious innate abilities.

One strong forebear Maria learned from was Friedrich Froebel, the German social reformer who founded the first kindergarten and a Swiss pioneer who helped young ones think for themselves.

Through her work worldwide, Montessori became a specialist in special education and was asked to work at a special school in a Roman slum to teach retarded children. First were lessons in a garden and physical skills to improve the pupil's sensory abilities before the formal lessons. Most of these had to do with visuals, for the eyes to learn to grade difference. Children handled varicoloured blocks and went on to the chalkboard. Officials found a marked rise in skills, even within months of the school's opening, bringing its students' education up to normal levels.

Montessori returned to the University of Rome, expanding her involvement with the betterment of women's everyday lives. She began Casa dei Bambini, a child-care centre for working-class families. With the teacher as an observant guide, children would teach themselves what became known as the didactic method, learning by experience.

Again, within months, her four- and five-year-olds could read and write, with the right approach, fully a year or two before any others. These students also responded better with more freedom and personal choice.

Montessori schools spread to Europe, the Netherlands, and to New York in 1912.

In the 1920s, Maria Montessori was made government inspector of schools under Benito Mussolini, who wanted to be associated with such a successful venture.

Although foundering over much of the world for some basic business issues, the Montessori Method had a major resurgence in the 1950s in America and yet remains a major reference in worldwide education.

With even its own branch in far northern Yellowknife, these Montessori schools were the kinds of educational options we were denied in the residential schools.

Although I was involved with some good work in the early days of the Indian Brotherhood, in setting up for what became community radio in the North, my own artistic skills were never given any freedom of expression during my youth school years.

I would have to see to that a few years later.

Moonhead

He was shown the grave of Christ, now empty,
"Where Christ had rolled away the rocks at the door of the cave and had
risen to the sky." He was shown always under guidance of Peyote, the
'Road,' which led from the grave of Christ to the Moon in the Sky, which
Christ had taken in his ascent. He was told by Peyote to walk in this
path or 'Road' for the rest of his life." —Omer C. Stewart

FAR FROM SIMPLY a pagan belief, the earliest of those who took to what eventually became the Native American Church had their Christian influences. One, John Wilson, a Caddo medicine man born in 1859 in Oklahoma, was of mixed blood, half Delaware, a quarter Caddo, and another quarter French.

Having an inborn flair for religion, he first took to the Ghost Dance, an ill-fated belief begun far to northwestern Nevada by a Paiute ranch hand named Wovoka or Jack Wilson. The Caddo Wilson had a much more famous neighbour there on the Kiowa–Comanche Reservation, Chief Quanah Parker, of Indian Wars fame, also a staunch supporter of the new faith. Although they lived less than fifty miles (80 km) apart, they seldom even mentioned one another.

Sometime after the Caddo medicine man heard of the peyote, he gathered a supply of it and enough provisions to last him and his wife a few weeks, and just camped out, taking a bit more of the traditional medicine from northern Mexico each day, until it pitied him with its various wisdom. He thus became an early leader in his own right of the Native American Church.

There are actually quite a number of variations on the way individual all-night ceremonies are conducted, depending on where and how they were originally envisioned, tribal belief and customs. In the Caddo John Wilson's case, his variation became known as the Moonhead Ceremony, a name this man also had.

The nearby Comanche use the Half-Moon Ceremony, mainly based on the shape of the altar, and mostly used today with Chief Peyote accorded its place at the very apex, where a person reaches their midpoint in life. There is no doubt that spiritual leaders, with their undying quest for the divine, serve as living cultural parameters for mankind.

Of Echoes and Dreams

"You neither sow, nor reap, yet God provides you the most delicious morsels, streams, and lakes to quench your thirst, hill and dale for your home, tall trees to build your nests, and the most beautiful clothing, a change of feathers with every season."
—*Saint Francis of Assisi (1182–1226) Sermon for the Birds*

LIKE OUR FIRST NATIONS PEOPLE, the earliest missionaries often went out into the desert and other far-off, lonely places to receive a Vision for their life's work. Some, like Saint Francis, were especially fond of birds, perhaps for their way of being closest to the Creator Above.

In the dreamy manner of Chagall, a bird sits perched in the dead of winter, storing its song for the coming spring.

Just outside camp, a dreamcatcher hangs, collecting memories and strength of land taken back later when warmth yet visits.

Mother Nature, like people, needs a time of rest to awaken to a renewed world.

"He Was Dene Then!"

Out of the mouths of babes and spouses

ANOTHER COUPLE I visited quite often in Deline, was my residential schoolmate John Tutcho and his wife Helena. They made everyone feel right at home in their big log home close to the lake and church.

John was one of those fishermen who simply took great pride in carrying on this Dene tradition of checking the nets every day, so you could always count on having at least a good meal of trout whenever you arrived.

Whenever she was not too busy from cooking and baking, Helena would add to a steady string of dried fish strips on the rack above.

As at most homes there, summer evenings were a time of cooking right outside on a grill, with all kinds of fish fresh out of the water. We also enjoyed the delicacies of fish guts, all cleaned and roasted to perfection.

Helena was originally from overseas in Scotland, and the two would get to talking about their next holiday to visit relatives on over there.

I shared an avid interest in crossword puzzles with her.

She may have had one of her own before, but she shared a decidedly Dene sense of humour, not pulling any punches when she wanted to make her point.

When I asked her if John had changed from the time she first met him, she quickly answered, "Yes, he used to be Dene then!"

The poor guy visibly winced, his shoulders all but disappearing into his favourite armchair. His soaked-to-inking look also spoke of a man who knew that if he so much as dared a word back at his wife, his next meal, if served at all, wouldn't be quite a hot one.

Mad Prince Hamlet

"Something is rotten in the state of Denmark"
—*Wm. Shakespeare, Hamlet, Act I, Scene IV (67)*

IN THIS DRAMATIC EPISODE of the English bard's play, Hamlet and Horatio encounter the ghost of the dead king, Hamlet's father, poisoned by the hand of his brother Claudius who now sits on the throne in the Danish republic.

Marcellus, deeply troubled by it all, comments about dastardly skullduggery afoot in-country.

In all the confusion, the Prince goes mad, largely feigned, to help his plans for revenge along.

After staging a play with the exact theme of a poisoned monarch, Hamlet is banned, along with an order to be murdered by his fellow travellers. The two accomplices instead meet with their end.

The banished prince returns to Elsinore, only to find his ladylove Ophelia dead.

These twists and turns of plot cruel and sublime were penned by England's William Shakespeare (1564–1616), along with almost forty other plays, around the time of the Italian Renaissance; so long ago that at the time it was rare for them to see the printed page, for fear of being stolen to a foreign stage.

Poet, playwright, and actor, William Shakespeare is widely regarded as the greatest writer of the English language and certainly the world's pre-eminent dramatist.

Once you get past the antiquated language you soon realize that words and turn of phrase are like soft and delicious condiments—rare of taste from a rarer still literary chef's fervent imagination.

Although his body of work stands for all time as a hallmark of the craft, it is a mistake to start thinking of this writer, William Shakespeare, as the end and be-all of writing.

In fact, many hold that over three centuries before, Dante made *the* literary classic of all time with his *Divine Comedy*, inventing his own poetic form just for it, and presenting the vast collection of cantos in Italian, just to have it recognized as a viable language to compose in, which the French deigned to honour him with.

Too, others, like the Roman poet Ovid, even before Dante Alighieri, greatly influenced our man Shaky Will, with frequent mythological references.

But in his then-modern pen:

Hamlet— | Now might I do it pat, now he is praying;
And now I'll do't; and so he goes to heaven;
And so am I avenged. That would be scann'd
A villain kills my father; and for that,
I, his sole son, do this villain send | To heaven.
O, this is hire and salary, not revenge.
He took my father grossly, full of bread,
With all his crimes broad blown, as flush as May;
And how his audit stands who knows save heaven?
But in our circumstance and course of thought,
'Tis heavy with him; and I am then avenged,
To take him the purging of his soul,
When he is fit and season'd for his passage? | No.
—*Hamlet*, Act III, Scene IV

Throughout my years of presentations and teaching, I always strove to have young people just pick up a book and read rather than walk around like a robot with their noses stuck to a little screen in hand.

Perchance e'en to come across an Edmund, from *King Lear*:

This is the excellent foppery of the world, that when we are sick in fortune, often the surfeits of our own behaviour, we make guilty of our disasters the sun, the moon, and stars; as if we were villains on necessity; fools by heavenly compulsion, knaves, thieves and treachers, by spherical predominance; drunkards, liars and adulterers by an enforced obedience of planetary influence; and all that we are evil in, by a divine thrusting on. An admirable evasion of whoremaster man, to lay his goatish disposition on the charge of a star. (Act 1, Scene II, 130)

As our mad Hamlet, Shakespeare spares no rein in the way of even counsel timbered of solid oak, cloven to wizened breast, in Polonius's sage advice to his son Laertes, about to embark to faraway Paris:

Beware
Of entrance to a quarrel; but being in,
Bear't that th' opposed may beware of thee.
Give every man thine ear, but few thy voice;
Take each man's censure, but reserve thy judgment.
Costly thy habit as thy purse can buy,
But not express'd in fancy; rich, not gaudy;
For the apparel oft proclaims the man,
And they in France of the best rank and station
Are most select and generous, chief in that. 560
Neither a borrower nor a lender be;
For loan oft loses both itself and friend,
And borrowing dulls the edge of husbandry.
This above all- to thine own self be true,
And it must follow, as the night the day, 565
Thou canst not then be false to any man.
Farewell. My blessing season this in thee!

—Hamlet, Act I, Scene III

My Brother's Wife

I calmly sat there, taking it all in.

I HAD FIRST MET my adopted brother Johnson Tochoney at a Christmas teepee meeting about ten years before. In our world, when you take a person for a relative, that is it, for life, no matter what happens.

I could barely see this man behind the huge fire he was tending to. It was so colourful, like a huge, decorated Christmas tree, sparkling and even tinkling a bit in the night air. I just knew I wanted to know any person who could control a natural element like fire in this way.

From then, near Page, Arizona, and over the years, we went to a lot of ceremonies of the Native American Church together, from his home, first in the Navajo Western Agency town of Tuba City, and then by the Old Airport, where I lived with him and his family.

So it came as no surprise that once again we were sitting in some prayer meeting, this time way over by the Navajo Nation capital of

Window Rock. I did not recognize the Elder running this particular event in a teepee . . . but he knew who Johnson Tochoney was, the way Roadmen knew each other from over the years.

In a break whilst the Fire Chief cleaned up around inside the circle, this man wanted to recognize my brother, and he began thus, and all in Navajo, so I didn't know what was being said:

"Brother . . . over there, by the doorway in. I know who you are. Johnson Tochoney . . . and I just want to say a word of welcome to you and your lovely wife (meaning moi!).

"Everybody talks about the good meetings that you run and how you've helped a good number of people out on our Navajo Reservation here over the years.

"And they also say you have a very pretty wife, but I haven't had the pleasure of meeting her in person."

(Johnson now playfully nudging me with his elbow)

"Now I know for a fact they have been telling the truth."

(Nudge, nudge . . . and an audible but stifled chortle)

"So, brother Johnson, I just want to thank you and your wife for coming all the way over here to the Eastern Agency for this occasion."

When asked if he wanted to say anything, my brother Johnson had to explain that his supposed "wife" was actually a Canadian Dene visitor to the Navajo Nation!

In typical taciturn Navajo fashion, this revelation from the Book of Jestic Foibles raised not a single eyebrow nor any other response. (Probably not until people were in their own vehicles the following day on their way home!)

I know we had our laughs on the way back to Tuba City about how he could have two wives, one by his side in a meeting and the other entirely unawares, way across the country, by the Old Airport!

Cowboy Ron

Over the years, some came on down

IT WAS ALWAYS GOOD to see a familiar face or two from the North to Arizona way. One of them was Ronald Antoine of Fort Simpson, who was having some kind of a problem and wanted to maybe get help.

My "twin" Dineh brother Lawrence and I met him in Albuquerque, New Mexico, and followed this with a grand tour of the Big Navajo Reservation.

Not quite getting what we were after for Ron at one of my adopted parents' places at Indian Wells, we just continued on to our intended Tuba City. Ron got along famously with my brother Johnson Tochoney, who marvelled at his way of walking around barefoot in the December sand dunes without any shoes on every morning.

Of course, our northern visitor also loved the familiar and comforting woodstove heat and his new sister Sarah's wonderful way with country food.

One day, it was decided that we would all go for a tour of the Grand Canyon. Before we set off, Johnson gave Ron a nice cowboy hat, which he proudly wore for the daylong event. As the rest of us were busy getting ready for the daylong drive, Cowboy Ron spent some time listening to some acting stories our neighbour, Sarah's brother Tsosie, had to tell him, about being in the movie *Pale Rider* with Clint Eastwood and showing our guest a genuine pair of spurs, he got as a gift from the ol' cowpoke.

On the tour itself, all was going well, and I took a lot of pictures of our little group way up on the edge of this natural wonder of the world. When we looked at some of them, we sure got a good chuckle, because Cowboy Ron couldn't quite get the hang of his new hat yet. He had the tassels hanging straight down in front of his eyes, and they were meant to be in the back!

This hat was not the only thing Ron had to get used to either.

As part of his healing journey, he sat right next to me for the all-night Native American Church ceremony, which Johnson conducted for me in a teepee.

Left to right: Antoine Mountain, Johnson Tochoney,
Sarah Tochoney, Cowboy Ron Antoine

When we finished the following day, we were in a hurry to get our visitor onto a bus he had to catch from the Greyhound bus and train station in Flagstaff, about an hour south. We got to the place in time and our northern traveller proudly stood right at the front of the line, all ready to go, across two states and back by airplane to Edmonton, Alberta, Canada.

Poor Ron was in such a rush to pack that he had misplaced his ticket we got some time before. It didn't help one bit that he had like a thousand pockets on him, on his shirt, jacket, and even up and down them pants he was a-sportin'! The whole truck was rocking back and forth as the desperate and heavyset guy dug through all his bags in the back, finally finding the missing important item.

When he finally found the missing fare, he was the last in line to board that Greyhound, with the driver all run out of "All Aboards" to say! I'm sure I had me some of these kinds of moments myself when I first arrived amongst our southern Dineh relatives some twenty years before Cowboy Ron came to make his grand debut.

The Fires Within

Silent, unseen, the flames burn on

O NE OF THE WAYS to envision intergenerational school trauma is to think of a moss fire. A normal forest fire is one which, while able to blaze quickly over a vast area, in time burns itself out usually for the simple lack of fuel.

The moss fire, on the other hand, after its initial signs of danger, goes largely undetected. Even the smoke smoulders low and out of sight. Moss is not really burnable material as we know it. When out on the Barren Lands, for instance, our Dene ancestors went to great lengths to dry out any of it they could find, to use it to make tea or for cooking.

So can we associate the moss fire with intergenerational residential school trauma. Once lit, it becomes, for the most part, hidden signs of trouble, undetected, even from the most experienced of trained help.

Over many months and years, it can keep burning, deep within the residential school survivor, to eventually erupt at the least likely and inopportune moment.

Like post-traumatic stress disorder, there is no cure.

Only a change of seasons or two can eventually deal with it.

A Whimsical Twin, in Chopin

S O MUCH OF WHAT I HAD, even the apartment with the astounding view of the CN tower miles away and our favourite little pond below, I owed to dear Nely Joon, an Iranian staff member I'd gotten to know.

My mentally demanding studies for a Master of Environmental Studies, beginning in 2011, required a non-lyrical musical source, for I could never go through any day without some kind of tune playing along. When the first notes of classical music began to make sense to me, it was no less than Beethoven's Fifth, on the flight over to Germany almost five years before.

Now with a good bulk of my research tending towards a decid-edly less bombastic turn for my memories of residential schools, those

"Some notes fall into utter melancholy"

stiff-armed Germanic blasts simply did not slice my more delicate aural pastry, shall we say.

Just going through the classical fare in iTunes, I came across Chopin's piano virtuoso, at times dropping off into an absolute freefall of some kind of "missing" I was all too familiar with.

> Like an eagle's plume
> Each tiny fluffy tine a tale
> In a thousand chapters . . . aloft
> Simply . . . and forever

Besides an incomparable virtuosity, there is clear evidence of a wide range of musical scope, with even decided hints of your jolly-jazzy barrelhouse piano flits and runs.

Frederic Francois Chopin came to represent his Romantic era as no other single pianist ever would. It could very well be that he was unceremoniously plucked out of his native Poland for health problems, never to return, lending these notes their real-life majors. Whenever I go back to his invented "instrumental ballads," I, too, like many, hear these musical conversations, which give solace to a life of solitude.

In a very real way, too, these lend company to one kidnapped at an early age, to a life of a separate and, for the most part, emptied reality.

Still Sketching, Always Sketching

Practice makes perfect

THE ONLY REAL WAY to tell how your drawing is going is to do at least one every day for as long as you can. Over time, you can easily see how you are improving and thus gain more confidence as a visual artist.

What could be the reason for this is in memory of them earliest of times, drawing on blocks of wood with charcoal from the fire, and eventually having my works of art unceremoniously cast into the stove, way up the mountains, with neither pencil nor paper to be had.

Others would be to have gotten the professional skill at all, after having completed two different art schools and being involved in a good number of shows and events all over the world representing the North and Canada.

Or just for the sake of staying in shape artistically.

The simplest way to think about it, as in most athletics, is to learn hand-eye coordination. The eye as a guide, in terms of an end result, a gauge if you will, of reaching for an ideal. The hand holding a pencil or colour, serves to apply what it is you know and can do.

Between the two is what you have to work with.

It does take some time, too. In my case, a number of years of doing these daily sketches just to get to a starting point I was satisfied with.

In Art, as with Life, it's all about how serious you want to take it.

Finding the SUN

My road be lo-o-o-ng!

This the old crone would suddenly stop to exclaim, on her way to the Dawn. This one practice was a part of her Dineh tradition, that of going outside to greet the earliest of the day. But it was meant more for the young, to run towards the rising sun, to somehow gain its strength.

In memory, she could still hear the echoes of the men who made it a point to yell out to the Holy People, showing that they were a part of the LIFE! ("My Road, my lot in life, every day to raise a family, now grown and gone . . . working the wood to fire . . . food for the table.")

Her adopted version of the *Kinaalda,* Coming Out Ceremony for young girls, was slower of pace, yes, having now passed her eightieth winter.

This was always the same "Checkerboard," southeastern part of the Great Navajo Reservation near Gallup, New Mexico. Yet every passing year added an extra passing fleet of new cars.

Hers was the day
of rutted roads,
Horse-drawn wagons
And shorter miles, it seemed.

The elderly lady took to adding the extra mile or so it seemed, or at least just to the lowest horizon to still make out the distant mountains.

She always wanted to actually see Mount Taylor, Tsoodzil to her, which also figured in her People's creation story as the Place of Emergence.

> At the same time, she grimly thought,
> "When the Holy Mountain actually appears,
> In all its heaven-sent splendour,
> I will see no more."

("Be lo-o-o-ng," she gasped the rest, taking in the coolest of the day's air, a welcome drink for a growing thirst. This well of mine, soon be dry!")

She thought to in her way, slow down the hands of time to enter the inner heat of this shining Father to the heavens.

> . . . With failing eyes, too,
> She wanted to see for herself
> The gleaming *yas*, snow,
> Off distant peaks,

> Which in her youth
> She could,
> With little effort,
> At least reach.

Sun now past its rising, her slowed walk back to the distant warm *hogan,* seemed more, and less, than just distant,

> Monsters daily slain,

> . . . Towards an inner need.

Upper: "Finding the Sun"
Lower: "Voice in Stone"

Upper: "A Dream So Far"
Lower: "The Banality of Evil"

Becoming

In the end, every bit of any story,
Has its HUMAN side . . .
. . . that distant sound,
. . . a voice in the fog . . .

When she told me there was a very good chance she would not
make it, there was also this real sense of no term of reference, of being
adrift in her thought . . . meandering.

She, on the other hand, knew from the daily cruel reminders that
the cancer was steadily eroding every healthy part of her being she had
any control over—becoming a stranger. Her only choice, it seemed, was
to keep in mind a constant thought for the good and from every con-
ceivable direction.

Raising an infant for a while. And sent off to school.

Directing rush hour, in an alley, blindfolded. Through this.
Especially this.

Any meaning
Will not reveal itself
Unless pressed.

The LIGHT, too,
Then, of its very nature,
Will Probe every crevice,
To find its companion.

I, on the other hand, was, for some odd reason, reminded of the
time I was to deliver some requested, treasured feathers, meeting the
Sun Dance man and wife at an airport in Alberta first.

Over the next several days, the man's wife confessed her helpless
affections, right from first sight. "You really looked like someone I used
to know many years ago. All I thought was that this was like a bright
flash of sunlight, through a summer storm, bringing us back together."

Again, that sense, of acting the past
. . . Always somehow just within reach.

And, too, a life-giving pipe became involved, along with all of the minute details of its purpose and use.

"I know it sounds cruel," she said, "but I was really hoping my husband would just drop dead of a heart attack, just before you showed up, back at the airport. So here, I will just give you this here tobacco, as an offering to whatever this all means."

As it turned out, there was a problem with the pipe; the Sun Dance man was not seeing things the way they really should be.

The wife of the Holy Man knew her husband was wrong, telling me as much.

During its short relations with me, a mature meaning played along its shadows, like the waves slowing lapping a canoe's frame, a song, floating.

Yet the experience did not sit well for being a pipe carrier. With all due respect, the instrument of worship was returned.

There is no perfection, really.
Only the Moment.

With it all and from a lifetime of being a hunter, with the only reality eight months apart looming, the Dene in me could only grab at a seemingly final answer: that there could be no being together at all.

It seems, for all of the big ones, the number of factors just add up, just for spite.

Years later,
Each thought
Like a visitor,
. . . Memories
Yet play
At Life.

The days do go on, of course, but oddly enough, as a succession of snapshots, many of her.

And far off, in dreams, that one mournful sound . . .
In an extended sea,
. . . Becoming

Your Memory Enjoined

This far North,
Breathing air
Like handfuls of fresh water.

Lo . . . linger,
. . . Harken

Farthest shores
of arctic Barrenlands
Comes on in
Indecipherable cadences

Faint waves,
Ancient Drums
Sacred spaces within

That sound,
Time

Rippled
Over Land,
Over You and back
Infinity

Lake Woman

It is you

With a dress

of water waves

Who breathes

Upon my canoe

Floating on this glass

Of timelessness

You hold me,

A part

Of Your hands

Full

Of dreams

"I'm Still Talking!"

"I tell you; one must still have chaos in oneself,
To give birth to a dancing star."
—*Friedrich Nietzsche*

He sat there railing about this and that.

ALTHOUGH IT becomes easier as an adult, it is considered impolite to interrupt an Elder. As a part of needing some help with his finances, my father wanted to talk about things that were going on around town.

He knew that as a writer for the North's weekly paper, *News/North*, out of Yellowknife, far to the south, that I had some influence for change.

But this rare visit was also personal. He wanted to apologize for having been so headstrong about every single thing in the past, I would suppose.

Our Dene Elders are often hard to read, and probably for their own reasons. Out on the land, for instance, a firm hand can ensure survival.

But here in town and as full-grown men, if there was peril, we had learned to at least put it off as, well, life.

He had been our Chief for twenty-five years, several lifetimes, as that one position went so was used to having people hang on his every word.

Except for the fact that them days were now far in the past . . . and at his age, he was now needier than in any command.

So, for the time being, he would just have to be satisfied that someone was willing to listen to him going on about some meaningless paper problem . . .

. . . And be content to affirm that yes, "I'm still talking here!"

And, as for myself, after a lifetime of heartbreak at his hand, I just had to take whatever I could, as a family member, of his being just too proud even in the face of growing old alone. Besides, that kind of hurting can only be met by compassion, a willingness to admit that we can only do so much at a time as true human beings.

. . . And sadly, just too much of it should have happened decades ago now. When it mattered.

And, blessed too, for his words of saving grace, is one of my favoured all-time writers, Kurt Vonnegut, Jr. His works, *Slaughterhouse 5, Cat's Cradle, Breakfast of Champions,* and a score of others, were pretty well required reading in the sixties and seventies. Of these hard times, his advice:

> Be soft. Do not let the world make you hard.
> Do not let pain make you hate.
> Do not let the bitterness
> Steal your sweetness.

I have always made it a point to let my two sons, Luke and Lorne, know that within reason, I will always be proud of whatever they choose to do with their lives.

So, without even knowing it, they have already succeeded . . .

. . . Life

DOOR by the Sea

Somehow, it always felt a little different.

WITH A THOUGHT BACK, centuries it now seemed, every time the shrouded lady approached the strange door things slowed to so laborious. Especially time and events brought it all back to her thoughts.

Her steps weighted this same walk. Yet her resolve always remained the same.

"I need to find this . . ."

The one constant, the shadowy and faded two figures, mother and child, flickered, more often as wavering candles, always just over her right shoulder, saying:

"Listen there . . . just there."

This she ached to do, making the last furtive approach with exaggerated effort, now bowing in perceived reverence, smiling at her affected posture.

A few years ago, she had heard that there was a place by this sea where bereaved young mothers could go for comfort. She wouldn't have guessed this long-abandoned building to be such a place. She had only come to this doorstep to rest whilst she carried on with her search but felt such a presence at just this spot that she came to think of it as connected in some way.

The flowing robes she always wore made listening a little difficult, although through muffled sounds she could always make out a bell tolling, far . . . off . . . or at least the echo of one, a call to service, she thought.

In her childish notion, she often thought of herself as the mother, Madonna, of the two.

> Too, the odd realization, "When I Find them,
> I will be just as forever frozen,
> A waxed, vexed mould."

But for now, the why. "Why am I really here? Where is the direction really coming from? Have I come so far, though you, you, are so near?"

> The mysterious door itself never did open,
> As she stood, immobile,
> Attentive to its purpose.

A part of the beachside stone villa, it always stood, close, massively impassive, by the living Mother Ocean, a witness to eternal waves come like steady mumbling thunder.

Yet every time the now elderly lady came to its last step, a comforting light shone through from the bottom, gleaming off the solid marble front, warming even the oaken door.

Her ankles too, lately, seemed to warm to the growing glow, taking long-forgotten pains away from weary legs. She did as told, often leaning in as the wind that brought her.

She more often found herself both pushing and trying to draw the structure closer, feeling herself pulled to and a separate self, enclosed, near, but barred.

> The pattern drew the sounded waves closer.

Too, lately, she found herself to be holding a hoop of sorts, made of intertwined sage and sweetgrass. When she relaxed her grip, the band seemed to reach, too, with a will of its own, swaying up and just ahead.

What had always been a door so solid now dissolved, with no walls to house. A lightened breeze unruffled her grave garment, once as caked to her as tears. The carved figures she so long sought drifted off as sands over nearby hills, leaving her search too real.

When the entire door slowly dissolved and opened in sunlight, she could see that her twin, younger, Shining . . . from a parallel present stood, waiting, arms out in greeting, bowing for her living laurels, a-whisper:

"You, MY You,
Come Back to Me!

In Fading Light

She met herself,
It seemed,
Through many other guises.

The more she read
From her small library.

Even from ones
She'd return to
Gave forth
Of Other Selves.

Too, penned love letters
Returned,

Clothed

This Newer Her
Deep into Night,
Through flickering light
She whispers,

"*Where* is the Real Me?"

Judy's Holocaust

A Light to shine

THERE IS LITTLE DOUBT that an artist has an innate gift to hold up a mirror for society to have a good long look at itself. Few in modern times have used those skills in quite the same way, or with such social impact, as Judy Chicago.

Best known is her controversial *Dinner Party*, with its lasting statement on women in history now permanently on display at the Elizabeth A. Sackler Center for Feminist Art, Brooklyn Museum, New York.

She also took the time to explore more personal meanings, with a searing exploration of her Jewish peoples' experiences in the 1985–1993 *Holocaust Project: From Darkness Into Light*.

As an artist myself, having just finished four years of study in one of two art schools in Toronto, it would take me another quarter of a century to make the direct connection between the dreaded Nazi gas chambers and our residential schools, attesting to Ms. Chicago's impact on the world in general.

Of course, the daily reminders are always there, for each in our own way . . . some yet and forever doomed to denial of Dante's fourteenth-century inferno awaiting all.

Others like me, still then desperately trying to survive an unknowable past.

> We each in our time
> Waken to our
> Own reality.
>
> . . . Many simply
> Sleepwalking,
> Protected by
> Bestial ignorance
> At the gates.

'Twas courage like Judy Chicago's at the ramparts, the times to wait for a paradigmatic change of heart that would beat some faster.

MY Darkness

This Coming Night,
Its grasp,

Knows the contours
Of my borrowed Soul.
Melted away, Waxing . . .

Candlelight,
Almost blinded,
a-Glimmer
With Hope,

I pause . . . and step,

Floating

Amidst veils . . .
to Great Mystery,

Yet intrigued

For its

Twins of Light.

Why We Don't Want All the Fuss

She simply spoke our heart's yearnings
Achievement is its own reward, really.

MY SISTER Lucy-Ann Yakeleya had her share of people coming to the door, many in the town of Yellowknife, for a few days and just wanted a friendly person to spend some time with. Others, more personal would take the time away from an otherwise heavy work schedule just to unwind and maybe tell their side of the story.

One such person, Velma Illasiak, was in town to receive some major recognition for special projects she had initiated as principal of the Moose Kerr School in Aklavik, farther north, close to the Arctic Coast.

My own memories of the place went all the way back to 1957, as the first of the residential schools I was sent to.

Velma mentioned that she had never really thought much of all that went with getting any kind of an award, for the simple reason that it was never there when she really needed one, on her way to where she eventually got to on her own.

This brought to mind a way of thinking that is all too often familiar to any survivor of these kinds of traumatic places and experiences.

My own parents and close relatives never did say a word of encouragement for what I was doing at any one time and, in fact, made me feel like an outsider from my home and family.

They were not really to blame, either, having been part of the overtly manipulative colonialist and zealous Roman Catholic experience themselves. Their generation was never taught to be supportive of the future generation, or even to expect any good in their own lives. Instead, the promise of a heavenly "reward" could only be expected sometime later.

Partly, too, to draw attention to oneself in the Dene world is seen to be a sign of poor character.

For my part, I am more in support of the Muhammad Ali "I AM the Greatest" school of thought, that is, we should try in every way to rebuild the glory of our First Nations past.

It was very much part of some tribal approach to doing your best in that warriors would perform these Kill Talks, intentionally boasting of their prowess in battle and even outsmarting the enemy for horses.

When I was yet a lad, it was very much a part of our hunting culture for the man who came back with a major kill to tell in glowing terms every step of his great accomplishments on behalf of a People waiting for someone to do so. Overall, our northern First Nations world did not allow for a lot of self-expression until quite lately.

Our Dene way of life, at least, was based on simple survival for at least thirty thousand years. An artist has always been the last to get any recognition, and certainly less any say-so about life.

Even our official organizations like the Dene Nation have been made to struggle just to stay afloat, leaving people like myself out in the cold professionally.

There have been changes, though, with the governments, both territorial and federal lending support when they can. I still very much believe that we are starving for our own heroes today.

It was not until much later, when our dreams became a reality, in most part by our own efforts with the Indian Brotherhood and the Dene Nation that we came to realize our own worth and to pass it along to the youth of the future.

Somehow, between we Northern Dene and the southern hippie youth, we found ways to come to know in reality what George Bernard Shaw had to say about our real destiny:

"Beware of false knowledge.
It is more dangerous than ignorance."

We had also worked to develop a good work ethic. In the meantime, we never saw much use in wanting all the fuss that went along with doing things well, as is expected in Dene culture.

I even found this to be so amongst our southern relatives, the Navajo Dineh.

A soldier, returned from foreign duty,
Never talked much about even medals earned,
Seeing it more as Duty to Nation,
Protecting the helpless.

Shell Woman's Dream

She always "knew" distance as a friend.

EVEN NOW, as she sat staring off into the yonder, she felt completely at home. Out on the prairie, there never had ever been much to look at. You could see a stranger coming up for miles, making it a certain kind of peace.

Yet she, Shell Woman, could always feel this sense of being out of place, as if there was more just over the horizon. Sometimes, like now, it even got closer, easier for her to kind of make out what she needed to do.

After several days of just sitting amongst her scattered cut smaller willow branches, she didn't see it as odd in any way. Her dreams only pointed to this spot, and something needed building, but not how or why.

But the way she was doing certainly raised an eyebrow or to a little way back, at the homestead. Her people had pretty well gotten used to some of Shell Woman's odd behaviour, taking it as a sign of "medicine."

It started several winters ago when she asked a wandering trader for a seashell, of all things. Among other valuables, the Frenchman had the rare cut dentalium beads her People loved so, for the way they could be strung into handsome necklaces or even long earrings.

She had recently gotten the curved seashell, with the warm colour within, like a baby's bottom. Shell Woman grew fond of walking out on the grassland, the odd object to her ear, trying to make out its own way of "talking."

It could be that under the full moon it would tell her something else!

In keeping with the times, her people had moved out of the freedom they once knew.

As nomadic buffalo hunters, all they ever knew was following the herd on their annual migrations.

For now she knew was what her dreams had been telling her: to go on "out there" and do something. The "what" hadn't been made completely clear, or better, she always woke up just when the old man was about to open up his mouth to explain the mysterious mission.

As she grew fond of the flesh-coloured shell, she also found that its pull to her was strongest at the time of the full moon. Then she could almost make out human voices, holding it to her ear as she wandered out, nights. These came in waves, the messages insistent over time.

What did happen was that her aunt, Willow, passed away late that fall. Because she was brave enough to have been to battle a number of times, she was accorded the honour of wearing the eagle feather bonnet.

Too, the spot that she had often sat at, upon her whims, was chosen as the site of her aunt's funeral teepee, set up on the rare occasion.

She took the messages from her seashell to mean that the Other World wanted this to be so, too.

Porcelain at Rest

She had that look,
Of snowy depths,
. . . Treasures embered deep within,

Waiting for the warming brush
Of promised melt,
Over misted eyes forever askance,

. . . Distanced from uttered wishes.
Still these chance, wayward breezes
Preyed upon
Every nagging hope within,

Marked forever
As Time
Before its passing.

Into Your NEW

When your arms
Reach close,
. . . Gently

Within near angel in me,
My heart fails not

. . . Ascending
This life braced

Your earthen tyme,
Your glance a blessing
Brushing away
All tarnish
Off weary flight

Your last breaths
Still teasing
My boyish hair.

. . . With just
enough strength
We, both,
Homeward

Past jealous stars,

Fragrant sage,

Turquoise twilight,
Into Your NEW

Olde-Time Indian MAGIC!

Eyes are useless when the mind is blind. —Unknown

A FEW YEARS AGO, I was looking across our Ohdah Dek'ieh Leline, Jackfish Creek, at Radelie Koe, Fort Good Hope, on the shores of the Duhogah, Big River, for some eagle feathers. These we call 'live' feathers, having come right off the bird and not shot or anything, making them very powerful.

There is always a paddling canoe parked right there at the Point, the southern end of town, for anyone to use. People sometimes just want to take a walk along the shore of the Mackenzie River right there. Others have nets set, there being an eddy where fish gather.

Too, the big birds, eagles, mingle and fight with the seagulls and ravens for whatever dead fish are thrown to shore for them.

From having done this over the years, I got to know where the big birds like to be, usually, on some kind of high spot, a bare tree or, in this case, the base end of a large driftwood, come all the way from the Liard River, in the Deh Cho Region.

At one, I found this very curious eagle bone-like object. My thought was that it was so old and was in the process of changing from bone to wood and someday in the future, the stone our Mother Earth is made of. Having already offered up some tobacco for several loose feathers I found I took it home.

Fast forward to my annual visits amongst our southern Dineh, the Navajo, in December 2019. I had made this eagle bone whistle, the kind used in the Sun Dance and other ceremonials.

One evening, my long-time brother Johnson Tochoney and his wife Sarah came by to do a Cedar Ceremony for me to look into a curious situation to do with my skin. As a medicine man, Johnson said that my problem had to do with all of the worldwide travel I do, this one involving the different kinds of air overseas, especially in places where battles are being fought. Something from it 'caught' onto me. He suggested a tea made from the same plant used to clean this big bird's feathers, Atsa' Azee, Eagle Medicine.

After that got done, I thought to ask him to update a Native

American Church membership card, he being the president of the local
Tuba City chapter. When I went to get the card, I impulsively came back
with a new eagle fan I wanted him to have.

The feathers were passed along to me by my brother-in-law Michel
Lafferty the same summer. This was the second of the birds he and my
sister Judy found in their fishnets.

Of course, Johnson and Sarah were overjoyed with such generosity,
and they left. Right after they were gone, I went back to my room to find
the same object there, somehow having transported itself from wherever it was I stored it at home.

Our Elders say that these big birds like to 'get together.'

All of my life I've never really lost anything. The missing article will
always come on back to me, usually the evening of the same day. In the
same way, the Powers that Be cannot help but reward a fine deed!

The Power of Generosity showed itself
in our Ol' Time Indian Magic!

Dreams of Holyan

Some visions come early . . .

In the times that I took to going all the way down to Navajo Country
in Arizona, a few people really stand out and continue to do so. One
very special couple, Gary and Mary Sandoval, always made me feel welcome, to the point of allowing me to house-sit their home while they
worked elsewhere. They also took to buying my paintings and prints
and ended up with quite a number of them.

One started out as a dream Mary had of her youngest son, Holyan,
when he was still in her womb.

There were two groups making up her Navajo Nation:
On one side the Traditionalists, still kept to their older ways of dress
The younger and more wayward generation
Clad all in black, having wandered away
From Hozhon, the Beauty Way

Her son Holyan was in between . . . with a curious path in going off to one of the Four Sacred Mountains,

Doko'oosliid, at present-day Flagstaff
On both sides stood curved arrow-pointed fencing

These pointed rails were what really puzzled her until I told her years later about seeing these kinds in my travels to faraway Siberian Russia. Over time, she took this to mean that her dreams of Holyan meant that her son, as a marine, was defending the Navajo Dene Nation overseas, where he served his country.

Our Better Angels

FIRST UTTERED by American President Abraham Lincoln on the occasion of his Inaugural Address, March of 1861, just before the Civil War, he appealed for friendship, of a remembered past.

The powerful use of the "better angels of our nature" brings to mind one of the premises of my first book, *From Bear Rock Mountain: The Life and Times of a Dene Residential School Survivor.* With philosopher and political theorist Hannah Arendt's 'banality of evil', even the most ordinary amongst us can bore into our limited human psyche to delve into the bad.

Lincoln's take is for us to reach deeper still, to a collective subconscious, to spout forth the good! As Lakota Holy Man, Black Elk, would have it, we all eventually end up at that vantage point of the 'high hill of old age', to at the very least get a broader view of what our lives once were.

Yet, too, he spoke of the Centre of the Universe being 'everywhere'. Bearing this out is the Navajo Dineh belief that the universe begins in each person's eyes. Our viewpoint and even opinions form a very real world, accepted and guided by all that is.

For my part, one further expression has always been an artistic one.

As illustrated in my first book, *From Bear Rock Mountain*, starting from life in the high country I've always wanted to leave my mark, one way or another. Yet one of the things our Elders warn, is to always exercise caution and good judgment. Try to avoid jumping right into things.

Times of youth, on the other hand, are just for that.

Black Elk's high hill thus leads us to a more mental one, to American President Abraham Lincoln's Better Angels.

One's golden years thus become something of a stumbling block. Your toes, ankles and behind take a beating as never before as you kick yourself over the oft silly and downright stupid things you said and did so many years ago. You mentally wince, self-badgered, by all the times you went out and did them, standing before the judge to show some mercy to an otherwise hopeless case . . .

> Ending, utterly alone in the cell
> Of your own making,
> Whilst the World turns.

These times, if nothing else, are the best reason to now, especially now, look to the future, to lend a helping hand to the promise of tomorrow, the youth.

Of course, as it was with yourself, words of wisdom are bound to go unheeded in the rush to just *do*. Then again, the spoken word is a start.

If nothing else they can lead to a lasting record like this one. After all, if ol' Abe could foist forth such pearls of wisdom from the proverbial sow's ear so can we all harken, charge ourselves to the aid of others.

20/20 being what it is, the only real variable remaining is the lessons learned.

> Every mark we leave, then,
> like crude ancient cavemen markings,
> Are distant glimpses
> From lighthouse towers,
> Mere attempts
> To define, even guide
> The Human Spirit.

Our Infinite Wings

When old souls sit . . . in evening's reverie,

A kind of third Being
Softly alights.

The survivor, pinnacles-like.
Immobile, turtle-jawed.

Condemned beyond expression.

The other, chanced here, from the Real World.
Evidenced now, of only some massive chasm.
Yet heartfelt to bridge this unrecognized gap
Within abridged lives.

The moment somehow reminds
Of a long-forgotten need, once answered,
. . . and physically assuaged.

Yet the place, so obviously Here,
Even from deepest covenants of space,
Suspended, alien in its own way,

And forever timely . . . trapped,
In tissued memory.

For now, though,
The only release, and eventual healing,
The very breadth and expansive grandeur

To grow into
Such cathedrals and compassionate company
Impart.

. . . Just for the moment . . . Raven shudders . . .
from River, far below
And Light above

Alights on both
A warming blanket
of higher country,
Comforting wings,

. . . A sighed answer

Fluttering upon some distant echo

Distant eagles
Cry

A World!

There is one,
Of wonder and magic

This creation,
Just past your very best!

As you enter, straining,
Each twist and turn,
A torture

To stay within
And surely return

With the heaviest of trophies.

That end,
Comes all too soon,

But the crowning
of every challenge,

Your shining memories!

The Little Shadow

"What is life? It is the flash of a firefly in the night.
It is the breath of a buffalo in the wintertime.
It is the little shadow which runs across the grass and
loses itself in the sunset." —Chief Crowfoot, Blackfoot

IN MAY OF 1875, just two months before the famous Battle of the Little Bighorn, the Lakota Sioux leader Sitting Bull sent sacred tobacco north to Blackfoot Country, along with a request to fight the hated Wasichu, White soldiers, along with a promise to wipe out the fledgling Canadian Northwest Mounted Police. This offer of war was flatly rejected by Chief Crowfoot, who instead assured the Mounted Police that he would back them up should there be trouble, with two thousand warriors at the ready.

After General George Armstrong's command was terminally mauled, several thousand Lakota under Sitting Bull fled north and camped near the Blackfoot, between the Cypress Hills and Wood Mountain.

The astute Crowfoot was one of a handful who clearly realized that the formerly vast herds of sustaining buffalo in their millions were dwindling at an alarming rate and these southern intruders, though kindred First Nations, were also resented from past enmity.

Sitting Bull again sent tobacco for peace this time and was accepted on these terms. The potential for war on the western Canadian Plains, Grandmother's Country, for Queen Victoria, was great, with the tiny Northwest Mounted Police completely surrounded by Blackfoot, Lakota, Blood, Peigan, Sarcee, Stoney, and Cree Nations.

A treaty with representatives for the Crown was proposed and signed to dispel these very real dangers and to pave the way for a new transcontinental railway across a new Canada.

The end of the buffalo hunting days was indeed not far off, as the year following the treaty saw a prairie fire devastate the animal's prairie feed. In winter 1877–1878, the People began to starve, going so far as to boil down their parfleche leather bags and anything with hide for much-needed nourishment. One added twist to this story is that of mixed-blood leader Louis Riel, who sought to unite all of the warring Indian tribes and reclaim the entire west. He and Crowfoot met in the fall of 1879, with this prospect in the air between them for a spell.

The Métis leader's plan was for a grand meeting in the spring at the Tiger Hills, on Milk River, Montana.

The two were of an entirely different mind, though, with Crowfoot seeking more peaceful ways for the future of his Blackfoot People. After the police were warned, these actions were ceased.

Without Crowfoot's vision of a peaceable Grandmother's Country, the Canadian West would definitely have had a very different turn of events. Now, though, his other horror became real, the buffalo gone, never to return, fate was the only balance keeping everyone from simply starving. Crowfoot's Blackfoot now had no choice but to make the long journey north and home, back to their mountain homeland, casting a long shadow from their glorious past to one losing itself into the fragile Canadian sunset. Plans went ahead for a national railroad.

One nation's birth became a memory of a life now gone for another. For his part, though, in 1885, Métis leader Louis Riel proffered:

"My People will sleep for one hundred years, but when they awake, it will be the artists who give them their spirit back."

Right from the start, I've always realized myself as an artist, and to this day credit my Dene/Dineh spirituality with putting my life back together after some soul-rending traumas.

Enough, anyway, to have had a total of ten all-night ceremonials done for me in my beloved Navajo Nation in the American Southwest.

My own teepee yet *stands!*

Summoned, in DREAM!

She sat way across, unseen.

Like some other Peoples, we Dene hold our dreams in great esteem. So much so, in fact, that at one time, before Christian missionaries came to our land, individuals would make it a part of their burial dedication to spend an entire year out on the land alone, mainly to pay close attention to their dreams.

As opposed to modern 'progressive' thought of dreams as anything subconscious, we are somewhat removed from reality—we Dene believe them to be the very essence of life, if anything, a missing and necessary driving force. The burial rite was known as *Eht'sehch'i*, roughly translated to scourge or fast oneself on behalf of the deceased person for the People.

My mother had passed away almost a decade before, and it always made me a bit sad not to have made it to her funeral. The work I was doing, painting murals for the community of Tulita, was on a very tight schedule before I had to leave back south for school. Too, when I was told that there was only so much space on the chartered funeral flight to Radelie Koe, Fort Good Hope, I chose to let an Elder have my seat.

So, all of these years later, it certainly did me a world of good to actually have her appear in my dream.

I could not actually see her in the crowded log home of one of my very best friends, Johnny, "JC," Catholique, of Lutsel K'e. The event was a community feast, with so many people there that only a part of the crowd could sit at the large wooden table at a time.

I've always known the sound of her voice so was pleased to hear her say that she had made dry meat special for this event and that I should go and have some. Making my way to the place all sat at, I noticed my good friend Ron Desjarlais, already up there, eating. Finding a spot next to him, I noted with pleasure the entire table was piled with all the *Dene Bereh*, foods of the land. I quickly grabbed for a large bone with a good deal of meat on it and was joking with a young man on my other side about the different Dene words for "knife."

As our host JC came along to sit between us, I also noticed something very strange from out the big window along the side the long table was set at. First, an old man with ragged clothes came from up the hill a way, stopping just outside and looking longingly at his relatives, the Chipewyan Dene, busy eating inside. After he left, a group of three women came, too, slowly trudging downhill in the deep snow. They too stood out there, gazing in obvious hunger.

One of our ways has to do with getting in touch with people about these kinds of DREAMS, especially of past family members and close relatives. Those in them, like my good friends Ron and JC, hold a special place and could well better understand the real meaning.

... in Time ...

Well, Ron, a fine fellow, and especially to my late mom there. She was always that way, too, that you had to first take care of yourself before you could be of any use to the People. And, JC, too, apparent to me, being there in my darkest hour and never asking for anything in return.

As a part of the *Eht'sehch'i*, members of the burial detail, became to each other *Alet'seoneh*, meaning more than a regular relative, and would go out of their way to do things together not even extended to family!

For now, I awoke, very happy!

Why? Because from an artistic point of reference this combination of tradition, the arts, and the act of creation itself is the closest to divinity we are likely to achieve. Too, this is the reason for the resilience of the Indigenous Community.

> Beyond messianic zeal and human craze,
> Our little homes still sit,
> High above rivers of change,
> Each sandbar swept aside,
> In the coming years.

To a people who believe in reincarnation, the notion of death is, of course, very much present when you have to kill your food in order to survive. But to have continued flourishing even in the coldest place on earth demands something special; the feeling that we are never alone in life and that our footprints will never quite wash away but be sought by future generations.

Of the First Water

Peace and Quiet Within

A S FAR BACK as I can remember that ol' graveyard's always been a
refuge away from the town itself. It could be for the unknown ones
buried, there.

This original site for our Radelie Koe, Fort Good Hope Cemetery
was a joint Protestant/Roman Catholic burial ground, high up on the
banks of the Duhogah, Mackenzie River. At the time of the 1928–1929
Flu Epidemic that blew through the North, so many died that the chief
sent out the young men to bring back the bodies for this mass grave.

Three of the towns to the south (Hay River, Fort Simpson, and Jean-
Marie River) had already had much more of their share of ice and water.
We were next for whatever it was the Gods of flood and pain had in
store.

Over two decades ago, we had an onslaught like this one in the
spring of 2021. Like then, the entire ballfield in the old town became a
lake, the usually taciturn Ohndah Dek'ieh Leline, Jackfish Creek running along the east side of town, virtually overnight came down in
full force when the ice jammed upriver at the San Sault and Ramparts
Rapids stopped up again some twelve miles north, creating temporary
mayhem.

Our situation in Fort Good Hope is a little different, with two major
rapids just to the south. The 'first ice' is usually uneventful, passing
in a great gush, leaving little time before the 'big ice' comes through.
The town was prepared, though, with even a Cat, earth-moving heavy
equipment at the ready to stop the house-ramming ice from reaching
those on top.

Like everyone else, I was worried about my old place, very likely
one of the very oldest, back to the days of trapping and trading, even
the 1921 treaty itself. The man with the key, though, Enos Ellton, had
his share of fun putting me on about the damage: "All I have left of your
house is Your KEY!" says he. "You'll have to go all the way down to
Tuktoyaktuk, the Arctic Coast, to open up your house again!"

Truth be told, though, some of the houses got hit pretty hard. All of Ohndah Dek'ieh Leline pretty well shored up the hill to the airport. Uncle Peter Mountain's cabin had the gushing waters come right up to the windows, him hastily rummaging in the warehouse, making off with gas and fuel tanks and any sort of other gear.

In a small northern town plagued by shortages and high prices, anything missing is costly to find and replace.

Even innocent doghouses now floated around as the great circling waters decided what to do.

I was overjoyed to hear that my ol' house wasn't affected at all. Next door to my sister Betty's, with the flood coming right up to her building's elevated floor, mine was completely dry, spared for all of the precious art and supplies stored within.

For the place, I am always dependent on the mercies of yet another freezing winter, invariably closely followed by the spring thaw, and even onrushing waters like this.

I had done the previous summer with two large murals, to do with research for my Indigenous PhD Studies. This one, almost two hundred square feet in painted area. With the limited time for my summer stays to home I began to finish off the trims, painting them a bright red with good boat varnish over.

My next project, for the Sahtu Land and Water Board, already approved, was going to be a 7x14-footer, the connection between ourselves as Dene and our animal relatives.

Working with acrylics, I always need a steady supply of water to mix my paints and for cleaning up. I got some from the Kasho Got'ineh Self-Government building next door and placed it on a table for later use. Two days later, the container was totally empty, and my water was completely gone!

After checking it all around for any answer, I had only one possible: that the old graveyard just to the front and left had something to do with it. In return for having spared my place from the 2021 flood, the Dene relatives buried there yet needed their drink of water, they too, spared.

Alone and unbeknownst they all shared from my container, maybe even suggesting that next spring, too, my place would be fine.

I talked it over with one of the Elders, who said that we can communicate with these past relatives, asking them for various favours, leaving them things they need, matches and tobacco.

For They of
The First Water.

And the space, between our minds,
One lined
With Van Gogh's Vision, summer flowers
In Purples, Yellows and green, green-greens
of an efflorescent, eternal wind,

The other threadbare, downtrodden

The two joined
At Duhogah, BIG River

And somehow,
Always, Traversed
By Mother Water.

Kin to Fire, Kin to Bear!

. . . at the Naming . . .

A Traditional Naming Ceremony is not simply coming up with a pretty name for the newborn. An Elder is given tobacco, usually by the father of the child, to define and sustain them for a lifetime. The Elder must then consult closely with the spirits, to somehow find out where the child's soul's past might have been and what that purpose is here on Mother Earth.

. . . if directed right, this internal sojourn might meet.

Here, mother sits patiently cradling her infant in the womb of the relatives, in the fire. As the flames crackle deep into the night, the Elders see as we do, the elements at play.
An eagle cries forth, announcing, protecting the family's future.

"Kin to Fire, Kin to Bear"

Spirit of Sa, Bear, growls a warning to all near who threaten.

The flames envelope mother and child, warming a bright future.

One such, Nitsi Wereh, Before the Wind, I bestowed to my younger grandson, Gavin.

At a certain time of day, like at Morning Star, all movement stops on Mother Earth.

As if the Earth itself is taking to holding its breath, all stand still. A stirring of power deep from within the land. This long before we feel the power of wind, blowing all before it!

Visually as a work of art, you the viewer are being drawn through a tunnel, to sunlight, central Eagle cry stopping you to view! Knowing just at the rare moment . . .

Thus be a Spirit Reborn!

This Ephemeral World

*"As far as we can discern, the sole purpose of human existence
is to kindle a light of meaning in the darkness of mere being."*—Carl Jung

IN PAINTING, like life, it often takes much patience to fathom the right time for action. Even then, the how is yet another matter. For this particular work, *This Ephemeral World*, the idea was there for months, slowly germinating, for the right ray of light to strike.

When the time finally came for this work, it turned out to be the very basic foundation needed. Just the right shade of magenta put it all into focus . . . somewhat.

There are the five stages of grief we all go through.

At first, the sense of denial, that we simply don't want to know *this* is happening to us, me especially, at all. Then the anger, how could life choose this time, when I am so busy, or happily satisfied with what I worked so hard at, to happen?

Once vented of righteous rage, the bargaining.

We want God himself to know for a fact that we are somehow special, deserving for more time to do something over, to prove that the initial plan can do with some fine-tuning, which only we/I are capable of.

To emulate may be distance enough,
To warrant His goodwill.
But to e'en suggest replacing,
For this moment's whim,
A dream too far.

After a time of depression, once survived, an acceptance of simply going along with what our lot in life is all about ends up where we should have been from the very start.

Yet, in the Real World,
Of dreamed reality,
As reason dims, the spark was yours,
Wanders forth, to kindle in
Another.

The Past, Today

THE SAME WAY lessons from your parents, grandparents, and ancestors live on with you, so are their physical beings still here. I had to make a split-second decision to try to capture this image of a cousin, Angie Tobac, thirteen years old, of Radelie Koe, Fort Good Hope, at a wedding in the summer of 2017.

This is the way our old-timers used to stand, as if taking command, with true Dene Pride of Place, of what goes on around them!

Even the young ones do it . . .

You'd be asking questions of a seven-year-old, say, and the little guy will automatically lower his voice so you will take him seriously, like one of the hunters he wants to be someday.

Imprisoned

Between the notes,
Of Chopin's thought and sighs

A catch in heart.
. . . just Wanting more . . .

A meaning forever suspended.

We survivors,
Forever linked,
In chains of simple Being,

On guard,
Without
Ever changing.

What to say, what to do,

All just enjoined,
Like severed limbs,

With living memories,

of imprisoned pasts.

EPILOGUE

A PRAYER-SAVED

UNIVERSE

"There can be freedom, Only when no one owns it."
—Jackson Browne

THE MOMENT, now done with duty, always brought its own warmth, an ancient tradition carried on responsible shoulders, the unknowable hero! As the old Navajo man slowly makes his way back to the warm hogan in the back of his favourite place for the Morning Star Prayer, the early day's cold forms around all of the thought-out words he's spoken.

Hozho nashli, make It beautiful, repeated the four times, resounds off the winter-hardened sprigs of pale green sage, taking a step into the lightening blue beyond—

Becoming the Future

What makes all of this so true for me, at least, is that I had found myself in an impossible situation, almost three decades before, with a severe drinking problem and no way to support myself in an expensive and seemingly uncaring north.

From having gone south to visit with our southern Dineh relatives, the Navajo, prayers like that of the Child of Morning Star set me back on my human feet, had taken me all over the world as an artist to represent my Dene and Canada, assured me of an educational reality, and even on to this writing now.

This being about how art mirrors the health of community, there can be no better way to attest to the intent of the old man and his little bag of corn pollen than to say that even though I was born Dene right on the land, it has still taken me a lifetime of learning the hard way to appreciate that our traditions can only be carried on in the footsteps of our Elders.

Indeed, along the way, I have always equated the kind of ethics we need to practice any real art with the very ceremonials and traditions that carry forth our cultures.

As for the old man, just as he got done with his evening prayers, he could distinctly hear the sweet echoes of a lonesome train, far off in that clear high desert air.

Although the sound always did touch something deep in his Dineh soul, he'd never actually been on one nor knew if this one was freight or passenger. One thing he did suspect was that somehow, some kind of way as a true human being his spirit would be the last to board the Freedom Train, marking a step towards the Holy Ones.

As we go about our day, we unwittingly pass through
Them Gates of Dawn,
Opened in Prayer

Somewhere over the sacred Mountain, the plaintiff, lonesome, and long, drawn out wail, of our Freedom Train.

Far off, from its tired refrain, somehow emboldened, echoing,

... and Enclosed as the
First, Evening Star

Rises
To Greet our Dreams

Finished in Beauty ...
ALL finished in BEAUTY

ACKNOWLEDGEMENTS

Denendeh
NWT; Arts Council of NWT

Alberta
Dr. Lorene Shyba, Raymond Yakeleya, Durvile & UpRoute Books

Arizona
Gary & Mary Sandoval, Lawrence Curtis

Ontario
Mary Metcalfe, Andrew Hammond, Peter J & Pat McCann Smith,

Saskatchewan
Leora Harlington & Celeste Tootoosis,

SOURCES

Alighieri, Dante; *The Divine Comedy (Inferno, Pugatorio, Paradiso)*; Fall River Press; New York, NY; 2008

Arendt, Hanna; *Eichmann in Jerusalem; a Report on the Banality of Evil*; New York, NY; 1963

Bainton, Roland; *Here I Stand; The Life of Martin Luther*; Penguin; New York, NY; 1995

Bernstein, Carl and Woodward, Bob; *All The President's Men*; Simon & Schuster; New York, NY; 1974

Blondin, George; *When The World Was New*; Outcrop, The Northern Publishers; Yellowknife, NT; 1990

Brandes, Georg; *Michelangelo; His Life, His Times, His Era*; Frederick Ungar Publishing Co, Inc.; New York, NY; 1963

Bray, Kingsley M; *Crazy Horse, a Lakota Life*; U of Oklahoma Press; Norman, Okla; 2006

Brown, Dee; *Bury My Heart at Wounded Knee; An Indian History of the American West*; Henry Holt and Company; New York, NY; 1970

Brown, Vincent; *Crazy Horse; Hoka Hey!, (It's a Good Day to Die)*; Naturegraph Inc; Happy Camp, CA; 1971

Bugliosi, Vincent; *Helter Skelter; The True Story of the Manson Murders*; W. W. Norton & Co; 1994

Carroll, E. Jane; *Hunter; The Strange and Savage Life of Hunter S. Thompson*; A. Dutton Book; 1993

Chaat Smith, *Paul & Warrior, Robert Allen; Like a Hurricane; Indian Movement from Alcatraz to Wounded Knee,* The New Press 1997

Chicago, July; *Holocaust Project; From Darkness to Light;* The Penguin Group; New York, NY; 1993

Chomsky, Noam; *Understanding Power; The Indispensable Chomsky*; The New Press; New York, NY; 2002

Clark, Robert A, ed; *The Killing of Crazy Horse*; University of Nebraska Press; Lincoln, Neb; 1976

Cleaver, Eldridge; *Soul On Ice;* Delta; 1968

De Beauvoir, Simone; *The Ethics of Ambiguity*; Citadel Press; New York, NY; 1976

Deloria, Jr, Vine; *Custer Died for Your Sins;*

Dostoyevsky, Fyodor; *The House of the Dead*; Wordsworth Editions; Hertfordshire, UK; 2010

Fanon, Franz; *The Wretched of the Earth*; Grove Press; New York, NY; 1963

Frankl, Viktor E; *Man's Search for Meaning*; Beacon Press; Boston, Massachusetts; 1959

Freire, Paulo; *Pedagogy of the Oppressed;* Continuum International Publishing; New York, NY 1970

Fumoleau, Rene; *All Long as This Land Shall Last; A History of Treaty 8 and 11,* 1870-1939; McClelland and Stewart; Toronto, ON; 1973

Denendeh, A Celebration

Gabankova, Maria; *body broken, body redeemed;* Piquant Editions; Carlisle, UK, 2007

Gayford, Martin; *Michelangelo, His Epic Life*; The Penguin Group; London, England; 2013

Goodwill, Jean & Tootoosis, John; *John Tootoosis*; Pemmican Publications; Winnipeg, Man.; 1984

Guinn, Jeff; *Charles Manson; The Life and Times*; Simon & Shuster Paperbacks; New York, NY; 2013

Hagan, William T; *Quanah Parker, Comanche Chief*; University of Oklahoma Press; Norman, OK; 1993

Heller, Joseph; *Catch -22*; Simon & Shuster; 1961

Herman, Edward S. & Chomsky, Noam; *Manufacturing Consent; The Political Economy of the Mass Media*; Pantheon Books; New York, NY; 1988

Hibbard, Howard; *Michelangelo: Painter, Sculptor, Architect*; The Vendome Press; New York, NY; 1974

Hittman, Michael L; *Wovoka and the Ghost Dance*; U of Nebraska Press; Lincoln, Nebraska; 1990

Hogue, John; *Nostradamus, the Complete Prophecies*; Element Books; Rockport, MA; 1997

Holy Bible. "Book of Revelations; 7:1" (Angels to the Four Corners)

Jetsaa, Geir; Fyodor Dostoyevsky; *A Writer's Life*; Ballantine Book; New York, NY; 1987

Jonestown; Paradise Lost; DVD Documentary; 2007

Kendall, Richard, ed; *Degas by himself; Drawings, prints, paintings, writing*; Macdonald & Co; London, UK; 1987 ;

Kidd, Bruce; *Tom Longboat*; Fitzhenry & Whiteside; Markham, Ontario; 2004

King, David; *Six Days in August; The Story of the Stockholm Syndrome*; W.W. Norton & Co; New York, NY; 2020

Kingsley, Bray M; *Crazy Horse*; U of Oklahoma Press; Norman, Oklahoma; 2006

Kjetsar, Geir; Fyodor Dostoyevsky; *A Writer's Life*; Ballantine Book; New York, NY; 1987

SOURCES

Klein, Naomi; *The Shock Doctrine; The Rise of Disaster Democracy*; Vintage Canada; Toronto, ON; 2007

Kolson, Bren; *Myth of the Barrens*; Eschia Books, Inc.; 2009

Krystof, Doris; *Modigliani*; Taschen; Los Angeles, CA; 2006

Kulchyski, Peter, McCaskill, Don and Newhouse, David; *In the Words of Elders; Aboriginal Cultures in Transition*; University of Toronto Press; Toronto, ON; 1999

Lambert, Gilles; *Caravaggio (1517-1610), A Genius Beyond His Time*; Taschen; Germany; 2007

Lanzmann, Claude; *Shoah*; IFC Films; 1985

Legat, Alice; *Walking the Land, Feeding the Fire; Knowledge and Stewardship Among the Tlicho Dene*; University of Arizona Press; Tucson, Az;

Locke, Raymond Friday; *The Book of the Navajo*; Mankind Publishing Co.; Los Angeles, CA, 1976

Longhi, Roberto; *Caravaggio*; 1968

Lozan, Larrie; *The Weather Underground (film)*; Directed by Bill Siegel & Sam Green; New Video Group; 2003 DVD

Mails, Thomas E; *The Mystic Warriors of the Plains*; Double Day & Co; Garden City, New York, 1972

Marrus, Michael R; *Lessons of the Holocaust*; U of Toronto Press; Toronto, ON; 20164

Mathiessen, Peter; *In the Spirit of Crazy Horse*; The Penguin Group, New York, NY; 1983

McKeen, William; *Outlaw Journalist, the Life and Times of Hunter S. Thompson*; W. W. Norton & Co.; New York, NY; 2009

Metcalfe-Chenail, Danielle (ed); *In This Together; Fifteen Stories of Truth & Reconciliation*; Brindle & Glass Publishing; Victoria, BC; 2016

Miller, J.R.; *Shingwauk's Vision; A History of Native Residential Schools*; University of Toronto Press; Toronto, ON; 1997

Momaday, N. Scott; *House Made of Dawn*; Harper Perennial; New York, NY; 1968

The Man Made of Words; St. Martin's Press; New York, NY; 1997

Monti, Raffaele; *Michelangelo Buonarroti; Ministero per I Beni e le Attivia Culturali*; Firenze, Italia; 2000

Mountain, Antoine; *From Bear Rock Mountain; The Life and Times of a Dene Residential School Survivor*; Brindle & Glass; Victoria, BC; 2019

Naifen, Steven & White Smith, Gregory; *Van Gogh; the Life*; Random House; New York, NY; 2011

Nathan, Otto and Norden, Heinz; *Einstein on Peace*; Schocken Books; New York, NY; 1960

Neihardt, John; *Black Elk Speaks*; Simon and Schuster; Richmond Hill, ON; 197

North, Dick; *The Mad Trapper of Rat River*; Lyons Press; 2003

Obamsawin, Alanis; *Kanehsatake: 270 Years of Resistance (film)*

Oswald, Russell G; *Attica – My Story*; 1972

Rees, Laurence; *Auschwitz; A New History*; BBC Books; New York; 2005

Rudd, Mark; *My Life with the SDS and the Weathermen*: William Morris; 1973

Schutze, Sebastian; *Caravaggio; The Complete Works*; Taschen; 2021

Shakespeare, William; *Hamlet*; The University Society; New York, NY; 1901

Solzhenitsyn, Aleksandr; *In the First Circle*; Harper/Perennial; New York, NY; 2009

Stewart, Omer C; *The Peyote Religion*; U of Oklahoma Press; Norman, Oklahoma 1908

Stewart, Sarah and Raymond Yakeleya, Eds; *We Remember the Coming of the Whiteman*; Durvile & Uproute Books; Calgary, Alberta; 2020

Storm, Hyemeyohsts; *Seven Arrows*; Ballantyne Books; New York, NY; 1972

Usher, Peter; *Fur Trading Posts of the Northwest Territories, 1870-1970*; Northern Science Research Group; Dept of Northern Affairs & Northern Development

Waite, Robert, L; *The Psychopathic God*; Da Cappo Press; New York, NY; 1977

Well, Stanley & Taylor, Gary, eds; *The Oxford Shakespeare, the Complete Works*; Oxford U Press; Oxford, NY; 1988

Weltfish, Gene; *The Lost Universe*; Basic Books, Inc.; 1965

Yogananda, Paramahansa; *Autobiography of a Yogi*; The Philosophical Library; New York, NY; 1946

Zolbrod, Paul G; *Dine bahane; The Navajo Creation Story*; U of New Mexico Press; Albuquerque, NM; 1984

About the Author

A NTOINE MOUNTAIN is from the Radelie Koe/
Fort Good Hope area of the Dene Nation in
Northwest Territories, Canada. He is a Dene artist,
painter, and activist who focuses on depicting the
Dene way of life, his love for the land, and the spir-
itualism of his faith. He has attended the Ontario
College of Arts and Design for a Bachelor of Fine
Arts, holds a Master's in Environmental Studies
from York University, and is currently doing a
PhD in Indigenous Studies at Trent University.
Mountain uses his voice and art to ensure that
today's youth do not forget their Dene identity.

Seen above with his Epilogue painting
"A Reclaimed Universe"